Margaret Sutherland.

EDUCATION, WORK, AND PAY IN EAST AFRICA

EDUCATION, WORK, AND PAY IN EAST AFRICA

ARTHUR HAZLEWOOD

In collaboration with Jane Armitage, Albert Berry,
John Knight, and Richard Sabot

CLARENDON PRESS · OXFORD

1989

British Library Cataloguing in Publication Data
Hazlewood, Arthur 1921–
Education, work, and pay in East Africa.
1. East Africa. Labour market. Effects of secondary education
I. Title
ISBN 0–19–828685–6

Library of Congress Cataloging in Publication Data
Hazlewood, Arthur.
Education, work, and pay in East Africa/Arthur Hazlewood in collaboration with Jane Armitage . . . [et al.].
p. cm.
Bibliography: p. Includes index.
1. Labor market—Kenya—Statistics. 2. Labor market—Tanzania—Statistics. 3. Education—Economic aspects—Kenya—Statistics. 4. Education—Economic aspects—Tanzania—Statistics. 5. Manpower policy—Kenya. 6. Education and State—Kenya. 7. Education and State—Tanzania. 8. Economic development—Effect of education on. 9. Manpower policy—Tanzania. I. Title.
HD5840.5.A6H39 1989
331.11'423'096762021—dc20
ISBN 0–19–828685–6

Graphicraft Typesetters Ltd., Hong Kong

Printed and bound in
Great Britain by Bookcraft Ltd,
Midsomer Norton, Bath

Preface

Education is all things to all men, and all women: it is a human right; it is a source of personal success; it is essential for national cohesion. But of all the things it is seen to be, none is more widely acknowledged than that it is necessary for modern economic development. To learn more about this relationship was the aim of a research project, one product of which is this volume.

The companion volume, *Education, Productivity, and Inequality. The East African natural experiment*, by John Knight and Richard Sabot, provides a detailed expression of our gratitude and obligations to those who worked on and assisted the project, in East Africa and elsewhere, to which the reader is asked to refer. However, I must give my particular thanks to Denise Watt for her efficient typing and general assistance in producing the text of this volume, such as she has provided over a good many years and a good many projects, and to Maria Ameal for efficiently putting it on the World Bank's word-processor. I am also indebted to anonymous referees who made helpful suggestions for revisions.

Both volumes are based on data derived from surveys conducted in employing establishments in Dar es Salaam and Nairobi. The establishments to be sampled from both the private and public sectors were randomly selected and within the establishments the employees to be interviewed were also randomly selected. The samples can be regarded as representative of the wage-labour force in each city. Those interviewed were asked about their relevant personal characteristics, their family background, their education, their earnings, how long they had been with their present employer and with previous employers, the education of their children, and their links with the rural areas. The full questionnaire is reproduced in the Appendix.

John Knight and Richard Sabot have used the survey data for an econometric analysis of various important issues in the relationship between education and economic development, making comparisons between Kenya and Tanzania throughout. Their volume does not provide the reader with the data from the surveys, except in a highly processed form, but with conclusions derived from the data by complex analysis. In contrast, the present volume is designed principally as a statistical source-book. It provides the reader with detailed tabulations of the data produced by the surveys. The tables provide information on the relationship between education, on the one hand, and occupation and wages, on the other, on the relationship between an employee's education and his or her family background, and on the links maintained by urban workers of different educational levels and other characteristics with the rural areas. The set of tables in each chapter is accompanied by a text describing what seem to be the major relationships shown by the figures in each table. The chapters dealing with the survey results for each country are preceded by a chapter describing the economies and the educational systems of Kenya and Tanzania, to provide a context for the statistics. In the penultimate chapter, the survey results dealt with earlier for each country are summarized and compared. This chapter provides the reader with a brief comparative review of the results of the surveys together with a guide to the content of the tables. A concluding chapter draws attention to some implications of the surveys' results.

The volume is designed to present the data in sufficient detail for them to be usable by those with particular concerns, and will be of interest to policy-makers and educationalists and to social scientists generally. It is hoped that the introductory chapters will be helpful to readers, especially to those without particular knowledge or experience of East Africa.

Those who read the volume from the beginning will find the later chapters repetitive. The repetition is deliberate. The results of both surveys are described separately. And Chapters 8, 9, and 10 are designed to report in as closely similar a way as possible for Dar es Salaam the results described for Nairobi in Chapters 5, 6, and 7. It is expected that some users will be interested in one or the other country, more than in any comparisons between them. The volume could not properly serve such readers if those concerned with, for instance, Tanzania had constantly to refer back to the Kenya chapter to obtain a full explanation of the data, or if the relevant data had to be extracted from a comparative presentation. A certain repetitiveness in the text of the central chapters is therefore inevitable, and we ask those who are equally interested in the results of both surveys to bear with it. They may, indeed, find it a convenience in supplementing their reading of the concluding comparative chapter.

The strength of this volume lies in its presentation of information on matters of great public concern which can be obtained from no other source. The limitations of the data, which the user must always keep in mind, are that they refer only to the urban labour force in the major cities, not to employment in the rural areas, or possibly in other towns, to wage- and salary-earners, not to the self-employed, and to the labour force in employment, not to the unemployed. These limitations are not to be seen as inadequacies, but as the natural consequence of the subject-matter of the research. A study of the urban unemployed and of rural labour markets, important as that would be, is outside the scope of the surveys from which the data in this volume were derived. These surveys were concerned with the relationship between education and the urban labour market, with a particular focus on the labour force with post-primary education, a very high proportion of which is to be found in towns, and particularly in the major city. It is for this reason that data are of value which refer only to the urban wage-employed in Nairobi and Dar es Salaam. The reference of the data must be kept in mind if a reading of the tables and of the commentary on them is not to mislead; if it is kept in mind, it will be found that the data throw much light on important and sometimes hitherto unremarked, or at any rate unmeasured, character-istics of the educational process and the labour-market in Kenya and Tanzania.

Contents

List of Tables   xiii
Map 1. Kenya: Provinces with Population of Each (thousands)   xxxiii
Map 2. Tanzania: Regions with Population of Each (thousands)   xxxiv

1. Issues   1

2. The Economies, Education, and the Labour-Market   7
   A. The Economies   7
   B. Education   8
       1. Primary Education: The Move to UPE   10
       2. Educational Policy and Manpower Planning   15
       3. Contrasts in Policy and Practice in Secondary
           Education   19
       4. The Question of Quality   27
       5. Summary   32
   C. Labour   33
       1. The Kenyan Labour Force   34
       2. Industrial Relations in Kenya   35
       3. Incomes Policy in Kenya   36
       4. The Tanzanian Labour Force   39
       5. Labour Relations and Pay Policy in Tanzania   39
       6. Equality by Exhortation   41

3. Source and Presentation of the Data   42

4. Demographic and Educational Characteristics of Employees
   in Nairobi and Dar es Salaam   46

5. Educational Attainment and the Urban Labour-Market in
   Kenya   60
   A. The Relationship between Education, Occupation,
       Wages, and Inequality   61
   B. The Changing Relation between Education and
       Occupation: Filtering-Down   80
   C. Filtering Down and Wages   89
   D. Recruitment and the Role of Education: Actual and
       Perceived   93

E. Education and the Qualifications for Jobs: Employee
    Perceptions   97
F. Formal Training by Employers   98
G. Education and Labour Mobility   107
H. Summary   112

6. Who Gets Schooling in Kenya?   117
    A. Education of Employees: Variation with the Education
        of Their Parents   118
    B. Reasons for Discontinuing Education   125
    C. Education of Employees and Size and Location of Their
        Families   128
    D. Education of Employees' Children: Variation with the
        Education of Employees   130
    E. Attitudes to the Education of Children: Variation with
        Employees' Education and Income   132
    F. Expenditure on Children's Education: Variation with
        Employees' Education and Income   133
    G. The Independent Effect of Family Background on
        Occupation and Wages   137
    H. Summary   140

7. Education and Rural-Urban Links in Kenya   142
    A. Demographic Characteristics of Urban Migrant
        Employees   142
    B. Educational Characteristics of Migrants   143
    C. Migrants' Process of Adjustment on Arrival: The Role of
        Education   146
    D. Ties with Rural Areas: Variation by Level of Education 146
    E. Summary   161

8. Educational Attainment and the Urban Labour-Market in 162
    Tanzania
    A. The Relationship between Education, Occupation,   162
        Wages, and Inequality
    B. The Changing Relation between Education and
        Occupation: Filtering Down   183
    C. Filtering Down and Wages   190
    D. Recruitment and the Role of Education: Actual and
        Perceived   196
    E. Education and the Qualifications for Jobs: Employee
        Perceptions   200
    F. Formal Training by Employers   206

G. Education and Labour Mobility 211
H. Summary 218

9. Who Gets Schooling in Tanzania? 221
A. Education of Employees: Variation with the Education
    of Their Parents 222
B. Reasons for Discontinuing Education 228
C. Education of Employees and Size and Location of Their
    Families 230
D. Education of Employees' Children: Variation with the
    Education of Employees 232
E. Attitudes to the Education of Children: Variation with
    Employees' Education and Income 235
F. Expenditure on Children's Education: Variation with
    Employees' Education and Income 237
G. The Independent Effect of Family Background on
    Occupation and Wages 240
H. Summary 243

10. Education and Rural-Urban Links in Tanzania 246
A. Demographic Characteristics of Urban Migrant
    Employees 246
B. Educational Characteristics of Migrants 247
C. Migrants' Process of Adjustment on Arrival: The Role of
    Education 249
D. Ties with Rural Areas: Variation by Level of Education 253
E. Summary 266

11. Nairobi and Dar es Salaam: Similarities and Contrasts 267

12. Education, Employment, and Wages: The Major
     Relationships 279

Appendix. Employee Questionnaire 289

References 332

Index 335

List of Tables

2.1.	Characteristics of Kenya and Tanzania	9
4.1.	Kenyan Employees by Sex and Race: Distribution by Race and Sex	47
4.2.	Tanzanian Employees by Sex and Race: Distribution by Race and Sex	47
4.3.	Employees by Country, Race, and Sex: Distribution by Age; Mean Age	47
4.4.	Kenyan African Citizen Employees by Migrant Status, Sex, and Age: Distribution by Migrant Status, Age; Mean Age	49
4.5.	Tanzanian African Citizen Employees by Migrant Status, Sex, and Age: Distribution by Migrant Status, Age; Mean Age	50
4.6.	Employees by Country, Sex, and Marital Status: Percentage with Children; Mean Number of Children	51
4.7.	Employees by Country and Age: Mean Number of Wives and Children and of Persons Supported	51
4.8.	Employees, Their Fathers and Their Mothers by Country: Distribution by Education	52
4.9.	Kenyan Employees by Age and Sex: Distribution by Education; Mean Years of Education	53
4.10.	Tanzanian Employees by Age and Sex: Distribution by Education; Mean Years of Education	54
4.11.	Employees by Country and Ethnic Group: Mean Years of Education by Age and Sex; Distribution by Education	55
4.12.	African Employees by Country, Age, and Migrant Status: Distribution by Education	56

4.13.   African Migrant Educated Employees by Country, Age,   57
        and Education: Percentage Completing Education
        Before Migration

4.14.   Employees by Country, Age, and Type of School: 57
        Percentage who Attended Government School

4.15.   Employees by Country and Type of Secondary School   57
        Attended: Distribution by Highest Form Reached

4.16.   Employees by Country, Age, and Education: Mean   58
        Number of Wives and Children and of Persons
        Supported

5.1.   Kenyan Employees by Education: Distribution by   62
        Wage; Mean Wage by Sex

5.2.   Kenyan Employees by Occupation: Distribution by   64
        Education; Mean Years of Education

5.3.   Kenyan Employees by Occupation: Distribution by   65
        Wage; Mean Wage by Sex

5.4.   Kenyan Employees by Occupation, Education, and   66
        Years of Employment Experience: Mean Wage (Shs per
        month)

5.5.   Kenyan Employees by Occupation and Education: 67
        Mean Wage, Overtime, and Bonus (Shs per month)

5.6*a*.   Kenyan Employees by Education, All Occupations: 68
        Percentage Receiving Various Benefits from Employer

5.6*b*.   Kenyan Employees by Education, Particular   69
        Occupations: Percentage Receiving Various Benefits
        from Employer

5.6*c*.   Kenyan Employees by Occupation: Percentage   70
        Receiving Various Benefits from Employer

5.6*d*.   Kenyan Employees by Ownership of Firm: Percentage   71
        Receiving Various Benefits from Employer

5.7. Clerical and Secretarial Employees in Kenya by Years of Employment Experience, Education, and Sex: Mean Wage (Shs per month)   72

5.8. Kenyan Employees by Education and Sex: Distribution by Occupation   72

5.9. Kenyan Employees by Education, Occupation, and Sex: Mean Wage (Shs per month)   73

5.10. Kenyan Employees by Ethnic Group and Education: Mean Wage (Shs per month)   74

5.11. Male Kenyan Employees by Education, Occupation, and Ethnic Group: Mean Wage (Shs per month)   74

5.12. Kenyan Employees with Primary Education Only by Type of Primary School Attended: Distribution by Wage; Mean Wage (Shs per month) by Year Leaving School   75

5.13. Kenyan Employees with Secondary Education up to Form IV by Type of Secondary School First Attended: Distribution by Wage; Mean Wage (Shs per month)   75

5.14. Kenyan Employees with Complete Primary but No Further Education by Period in which Education Completed: Mean Wage of Those With as Percentage of Mean Wage of Those Without Primary Certificate   75

5.15. Kenyan Employees who Completed Education at Form IV by Result in Form IV Examination and Period in which Education Completed: Mean Wage (Shs per month)   76

5.16. Kenyan Employees who Completed Education at Form IV by Form IV Examination Result and Occupation: Mean Wage (Shs per month)   76

5.17. Kenyan Employees who Completed Education at Form IV by Grade of Form IV Examination Pass in Different Subjects: Mean Wage (Shs per month)   77

5.18.   Kenyan Employees With Complete Secondary but   77
         Without Post-Secondary Education by Result in Form
         VI Examination and Period in which Education
         Completed: Mean Wage (Shs per month)

5.19.   Kenyan Employees by Employment Status and   78
         Education: Mean Wage (Shs per month)

5.20.   Kenyan Employees by Occupation, Education, and   79
         Ownership of Firm: Mean Wage (Shs per month)

5.21.   Kenyan Employees by Size of Firm and Education: 80
         Mean Wage (Shs per month)

5.22.   Kenyan Employees by Wage: Average Number of Full   81
         and Part Dependants, Average Number of Full
         Dependants, and Average Wage (Shs per month) per
         Full Dependant

5.23.   Kenyan Employees by Education: Average Number of   82
         Full and Part Dependants, Average Number of Full
         Dependants, and Average Wage (Shs per month) per
         Full Dependant

5.24.   Kenyan Employees by Date of Joining Labour Force: 83
         Mean Years of Education

5.25.   Kenyan Employees by Education and Year of First   84
         Wage-Job: Distribution by Occupation

5.26.   Kenyan Employees by Occupation and Year of First   86
         Wage-Job: Distribution by Education

5.27.   Kenyan Employees by Particular Occupations and Years 88
         of Employment Experience: Distribution by Education

5.28.   Kenyan Employees by Education and Occupation: 90
         Mean Wage (Shs per month)

5.29.   Kenyan Employees by Occupation and Year Entering   91
         Labour Force: Mean Wage for Each Level of Education
         as Percentage of Mean Wage for All Levels; Mean
         Wage for All Levels of Education (Shs per month)

5.30. Kenyan Employees by Year Joined Labour Force: Mean Wage for Each Occupation as Percentage of Mean Wage for All; Mean Wage for All Occupations (Shs per month) 92

5.31. Kenyan Employees by Year Education Completed and by Education: Distribution by Months between End of Education and Start of Wage-Employment 93

5.32. Kenyan Employees by Occupation, Sector of Employment, and Years of Employment Experience: Percentage in Casual Employment 94

5.33. Kenyan Regular Employees by Occupation, Sector of Employment, Education, and Year Entered Wage-Employment: Percentage Starting as Casual Employees 95

5.34. Distribution of Kenyan Firms by Percentage of Employees in Regular Employment 96

5.35. Kenyan Employees by Employment Status and for Regular Employees by Employment Status at Time Employment Started: Distribution by Method of Job Application 96

5.36a. Kenyan Employees by Occupation: Distribution by Method of Job Application 98

5.36b. Kenyan Employees by Education: Distribution by Method of Job Application 99

5.37. Kenyan Employees who Started as Regular Employees by Education and Occupation: Percentage who Think They Would Not Have Been Employed if They Had Received Less Education 100

5.38. Kenyan Employees by Occupation and Education: Percentage who Believe They Are Qualified for a Better Job 101

5.39. Kenyan Employees by Occupation and Year of Entry into Wage-Employment: Average Years of Education of Those who Believe They Are Qualified for a Better Job as Percentage of Average Years of Education of All 102

5.40. Kenyan Employees Seeking Better Job by Occupation: 103
Percentage who Believe They Are Over-Qualified

5.41. Kenyan Employees who Believe They Are Over- 103
Qualified in Present Job by Occupation and Education:
Percentage who Are in Present Job because No Better
Available

5.42. Kenyan Employees who Believe They Are Over- 104
Qualified by Employment Status: Distribution by
Reason for Being in Present Job

5.43. Kenyan Employees by Occupation: Percentage Provided 104
with Training Course

5.44. Percentage of Total Trained Kenyan Employees with 105
Percentage of Establishments in which They Are
Employed and Percentage of All Employees Employed
in Those Establishments

5.45. Kenyan Establishments by Ownership and Economic 105
Activity: Percentage of Employees Trained

5.46. Kenyan Employees by Occupation and Education: 106
Percentage with Training Course

5.47. Kenyan Employees by Occupation and Whether 106
Provided with a Training Course: Mean Years of
Education

5.48. Kenyan Employees by Education, Occupation, and 107
Whether Have Had a Training Course: Mean Wage (Shs
per month)

5.49. Kenyan Skilled Manual Employees who Have and who 108
Have Not Taken Trade Test by Education: Mean Wage
(Shs per month)

5.50. Kenyan Skilled Manual Employees by Grade of Trade- 108
Test Pass: Mean Wage (Shs per month)

5.51. Kenyan Employees by Education: Distribution by Rate 108
of Job Mobility

5.52.   Kenyan Employees by Year Education Completed: 109
Distribution by Number of Previous Employers

5.53.   Kenyan Employees by Number of Previous Employers   109
and by Reason for Leaving Last Job: Distribution by
Number of Times Out of Wage-Employment

5.54.   Kenyan Employees by Years Since First Wage-Job: 110
Distribution by Total Months Out of Wage-Employment

5.55.   Kenyan Employees by Education: Percentage Leaving   110
Previous Job Voluntarily

5.56.   Kenyan Employees by Reason for Leaving Previous   111
Job: Percentage who Received Pay Rise after Changing
Job

5.57.   Kenyan Employees by Year Education Completed and   111
Occupation: Percentage Seeking Better Job

5.58.   Kenyan Employees who Have Been Out of Wage-   111
Employment by Education: Distribution by Main
Activity When Out of Employment

5.59a.   Kenyan Employees with Previous Job by Level of   113
Education: Mean Years in Last Job

5.59b.   Kenyan Employees with Previous Job by Size of Firm in   113
Last Job: Mean Years in Last Job

5.59c.   Kenyan Employees with Previous Job by Type of   113
Employer in Last Job: Mean Years in Last Job

5.59d.   Kenyan Employees with Previous Job by Sector of   113
Employment in Last Job: Mean Years in Last Job

5.60.   Kenyan Employees with Previous Job by Occupation in   114
Current Job: Distribution by Occupation in Last Job

6.1.   Kenyan Employees by Father's Education: Distribution   118
by Own Education

6.2.   Kenyan Employees by Own Education: Distribution by   119
Father's Education

6.3.   Kenyan Employees whose Fathers Had Primary   120
        Education by Mother's Education: Distribution by Own
        Education

6.4.   Kenyan Employees by Mother's Education and Father's   121
        Education: Mean Years of Education

6.5.   Kenyan Employees by Father's Education: Distribution   122
        by Mother's Education

6.6.   Kenyan Employees by Mother's Education: Distribution   122
        by Father's Education

6.7.   Kenyan Employees by Age and Father's Education: 124
        Distribution by Own Education

6.8.   Kenyan Employees by Age and Parents' Education: 125
        Mean Years of Education

6.9.   Kenyan Employees who Desired to Continue Their   126
        Education by Period at which Education Ceased:
        Distribution by Reason for Not Continuing

6.10.   Kenyan Employees by Form IV Examination Result: 127
        Percentage Reaching Form VI

6.11.   Kenyan Employees by Father's Education: Distribution   127
        by Form IV Examination Result

6.12.   Kenyan Employees with Passes in Form VI Examination   128
        by Father's Education: Distribution by Number of
        Passes

6.13.   Kenyan Employees by Sex and Education: Distribution   129
        by Education of Spouse

6.14.   Kenyan Employees by Own Level of Education, Age of   131
        First Child, and Whether Education of Child
        Continuing: Mean Years of Education of First Child

6.15.   Kenyan Employees and Spouses by Education and by   132
        Age of First Child: Mean Years of Education of First
        Child

6.16. Kenyan Employees with First Child Aged 15 or More 133
who Has Completed Education by Own Education:
Distribution by Education of First Child

6.17. Kenyan Employees by Education and by Wage: 134
Distribution by Action if Son Could Not Go to
Government Secondary School

6.18. Kenyan Employees by Number of Children in School: 134
Mean Expenditure on Education (Shs p.a.)

6.19. Kenyan Employees by Education and Wage: Mean 135
Expenditure (Shs p.a.) on Education of Children in
School, Total, per Child, as Percentage of Income

6.20. Kenyan Employees by Wage and Educational Level of 136
First Child in School: Mean Percentage of Employee's
Income Spent on Education of First Child

6.21. First Child of Kenyan Employees in School by Type of 136
School Attended: Mean Expenditure by Employees on
Education of First Child (Shs p.a.)

6.22. Kenyan Employees' First Child by Education and Sex: 136
Mean Cost of Education in Year (Shs)

6.23. Kenyan Employees by Education and Father's 138
Education: Distribution by Occupation

6.24. Kenyan Employees by Education, Years of Employment 139
Experience, and Father's Education: Mean Wage (Shs
per month)

6.25. Kenyan Employees by Education and Father's 139
Education: Distribution by Time between End of
Education and Start of Wage-Employment

6.26. Kenyan Employees with Previous Wage-Employment by 139
Education and Father's Education: Percentage
Continuously Employed

7.1. Kenyan African Migrant Employees by Sex: 143
Distribution by Age on Arrival in Nairobi; Mean Age

7.2.   Kenyan African Migrant Employees by Year of Arrival   144
        in Nairobi and Sex: Mean Years of Education

7.3.   Kenyan Educated African Migrant Employees by   144
        Education and Age on Arrival in Nairobi: Percentage
        who Completed Their Education before Migrating

7.4.   Kenyan African Migrant Employees by Education: 145
        Distribution by Age on Arrival in Nairobi; Mean Age
        on Arrival

7.5.   Kenyan African Migrant Employees who Completed   147
        Their Education before Migrating by Education,
        Age on Arrival, and Sex: Mean Time (months) to
        Find an Independent Source of Income after Arrival
        in Nairobi

7.6.   Kenyan African Migrant Employees who Completed   148
        Their Education before Migrating by Education:
        Distribution by First Independent Source of Income in
        Nairobi

7.7.   Kenyan African Employees by Education and Migrant   149
        Status: Percentage of Spouses in Nairobi and on the
        Shamba

7.8.   Kenyan African Employees by Age and Education: 150
        Percentage of Spouses in Nairobi and on the *Shamba*

7.9.   Kenyan African Employees by Education and Migrant   151
        Status: Percentage who Support Relatives Outside
        Nairobi and Percentage of Income Used in that Way

7.10.   Kenyan African Employees by Wage and Education: 152
        Percentage of Income Used to Support Relatives
        Outside Nairobi

7.11.   Kenyan African Employees by Wage, Education, and   154
        Migrant Status: Percentage of Cases where First Child
        Educated in the Rural Area

7.12.   Kenyan African Employees with Children in School Last   155
        Year by Wage and Place of Children's Education: Mean
        Cost of Education per Child (Shs per year)

7.13.   Kenyan African Employees by Education, Age, and   156
        Migrant Status: Percentage with *Shamba*

7.14.   Kenyan African Employees with *Shamba* by Wage and   157
        Education: Distribution by Method of *Shamba*
        Acquisition

7.15.   Kenyan African Employees with *Shamba* by Province   159
        of Birth: Distribution by Number of Visits to the
        Shamba during the Previous Year; Mean Number of
        Visits

7.16.   Kenyan African Employees by Education: Percentage   160
        with *Shamba*; Use of Employed Workers

7.17.   Kenyan African Migrant Employees by Education: 160
        Percentage who Plan to Return to the Rural Area

8.1.   Tanzanian Employees by Education: Distribution by   163
        Wage; Mean Wage by Sex

8.2.   Tanzanian Employees by Occupation: Distribution by   165
        Education; Mean Years of Education

8.3.   Tanzanian Employees by Occupation: Distribution by   166
        Wage; Mean Wage by Sex

8.4.   Tanzanian Employees by Occupation, Education, and   167
        Years of Employment Experience: Mean Wage (Shs per
        month)

8.5.   Tanzanian Employees by Occupation and Education: 168
        Mean Wage, Overtime, and Bonus (Shs per month)

8.6*a*.   Tanzanian Employees by Education, All Occupations: 170
        Percentage Receiving Various Benefits from Employer

8.6*b*.   Tanzanian Employees by Education, Particular   171
        Occupations: Percentage Receiving Various Benefits
        from Employer

8.6*c*.   Tanzanian Employees by Occupation: Percentage   172
        Receiving Various Benefits from Employer

8.6*d*.   Tanzanian Employees by Ownership of Firm: 173
           Percentage Receiving Various Benefits from Employer

8.7.   Clerical and Secretarial Employees in Tanzania by Years   174
           of Employment Experience, Education, and Sex: Mean
           Wage (Shs per month)

8.8.   Tanzanian Employees by Education and Sex: 174
           Distribution by Occupation

8.9.   Tanzanian Employees by Education, Occupation, and   175
           Sex: Mean Wage (Shs per month)

8.10.   Tanzanian Employees by Ethnic Group and Education: 175
           Mean Wage (Shs per month)

8.11.   Male Tanzanian Employees by Education, Occupation,   176
           and Ethnic Group: Mean Wage (Shs per month)

8.12.   Tanzanian Employees with Primary Education Only by   176
           Type of Primary School Attended: Distribution by
           Wage; Mean Wage (Shs per month) by Year Leaving
           School

8.13.   Tanzanian Employees with Secondary Education up to   177
           Form IV by Type of Secondary School First Attended:
           Distribution by Wage; Mean Wage (Shs per month)

8.14.   Tanzanian Employees with Complete Primary but No   177
           Further Education by Period in which Education
           Completed: Mean Wage of Those With as Percentage of
           Mean Wage of Those Without Primary Certificate

8.15.   Tanzanian Employees who Completed Education at   178
           Form IV by Result in Form IV Examination and Period
           in which Education Completed: Mean Wage (Shs per
           month)

8.16.   Tanzanian Employees who Completed Education at   178
           Form IV by Form IV Examination Result and
           Occupation: Mean Wage (Shs per month)

8.17.   Tanzanian Employees who Completed Education at   179

Form IV by Grade of Form IV Examination Pass in
Different Subjects: Mean Wage (Shs per month)

8.18.   Tanzanian Employees With Complete Secondary but   179
         Without Post-Secondary Education by Result in Form
         VI Examination and Period in which Education
         Completed: Mean Wage (Shs per month)

8.19.   Tanzanian Employees by Employment Status and   180
         Education: Mean Wage (Shs per month)

8.20.   Tanzanian Employees by Occupation, Education, and   180
         Ownership of Firm: Mean Wage (Shs per month)

8.21.   Tanzanian Employees by Size of Firm and Education: 183
         Mean Wage (Shs per month)

8.22.   Tanzanian Employees by Wage: Average Number of   184
         Full and Part Dependants, Average Number of Full
         Dependants, and Average Wage (Shs per month) per
         Full Dependant

8.23.   Tanzanian Employees by Education: Average Number   185
         of Full and Part Dependants, Average Number of Full
         Dependants, and Average Wage (Shs per month) per
         Full Dependant

8.24.   Tanzanian Employees by Date of Joining Labour Force: 186
         Mean Years of Education

8.25.   Tanzanian Employees by Education and Year of First   187
         Wage-Job: Distribution by Occupation

8.26.   Tanzanian Employees by Occupation and Year of First   189
         Wage-Job: Distribution by Education

8.27.   Tanzanian Employees by Particular Occupations and   191
         Years of Employment Experience: Distribution by
         Education

8.28.   Tanzanian Employees by Education and Occupation: 193
         Mean Wage (Shs per month)

8.29. Tanzanian Employees by Occupation and Year Entering   194
       Labour Force: Mean Wage for Each Level of Education
       as Percentage of Mean Wage for All Levels; Mean
       Wage for All Levels of Education (Shs per month)

8.30. Tanzanian Employees by Year Joined Labour Force: 195
       Mean Wage for Each Occupation as Percentage of Mean
       Wage for All; Mean Wage for All Occupations (Shs per
       month)

8.31. Tanzanian Employees by Year Education Completed   196
       and by Education: Distribution by Months between End
       of Education and Start of Wage-Employment

8.32. Tanzanian Employees by Occupation, Sector of   197
       Employment, and Years of Employment Experience:
       Percentage in Casual Employment

8.33. Tanzanian Regular Employees by Occupation, Sector of   199
       Employment, Education, and Year Entered Wage
       Employment: Percentage Starting as Casual Employees

8.34. Distribution of Tanzanian Firms by Percentage of   200
       Employees in Regular Employment

8.35. Tanzanian Employees by Employment Status and for   200
       Regular Employees Employment Status at Time
       Employment Started: Distribution by Method of Job
       Application

8.36a. Tanzanian Employees by Occupation: Distribution by   201
       Method of Job Application

8.36b. Tanzanian Employees by Education: Distribution by   202
       Method of Job Application

8.37a. Tanzanian Employees who Started as Regular   203
       Employees by Education and Occupation: Percentage
       who Think They Would Not Have Been Employed if
       They Had Received Less Education.

8.37b. Tanzanian Employees Allocated Job by Government by   203
       Education and Occupation: Percentage Allocated Job of
       First Choice

8.38.   Tanzanian Employees by Occupation and Education: 204
Percentage who Believe They Are Qualified for a Better
Job

8.39.   Tanzanian Employees by Occupation and Year of Entry 205
into Wage-Employment: Average Years of Education of
Those who Believe They Are Qualified for a Better Job
as Percentage of Average Years of Education of All

8.40.   Tanzanian Employees Seeking Better Job by 206
Occupation: Percentage who Believe They Are Over-
Qualified

8.41.   Tanzanian Employees who Believe They Are Over- 207
Qualified in Present Job by Occupation and Education:
Percentage who Are in Present Job because No Better
Available

8.42.   Tanzanian Employees who Believe They Are Over- 208
Qualified by Employment Status: Distribution by
Reason for Being in Present Job

8.43.   Tanzanian Employees by Occupation: Percentage 208
Provided with Training Course

8.44.   Percentage of Total Trained Tanzanian Employees with 208
Percentage of Establishments in which They Are
Employed and Percentage of All Employees Employed
in Those Establishments

8.45.   Tanzanian Establishments by Ownership and Economic 209
Activity: Percentage of Employees Trained

8.46.   Tanzanian Employees by Occupation and Education: 210
Percentage with Training Course

8.47.   Tanzanian Employees by Occupation and Whether 210
Provided with a Training Course: Mean Years of
Education

8.48.   Tanzanian Employees by Education, Occupation, and 211
Whether Have Had a Training Course: Mean Wage (Shs
per month)

8.49. Tanzanian Skilled Manual Employees who Have and who Have Not Taken Trade Test by Education: Mean Wage (Shs per month) — 212

8.50. Tanzanian Skilled Manual Employees by Grade of Trade-Test Pass: Mean Wage (Shs per month) — 212

8.51. Tanzanian Employees by Education: Distribution by Rate of Job Mobility — 212

8.52. Tanzanian Employees by Year Education Completed: Distribution by Number of Previous Employers — 213

8.53. Tanzanian Employees by Number of Previous Employers and by Reason for Leaving Last Job: Distribution by Number of Times Out of Wage-Employment — 213

8.54. Tanzanian Employees by Years Since First Wage-Job: Distribution by Total Months Out of Wage-Employment — 214

8.55. Tanzanian Employees by Education: Percentage Leaving Previous Job Voluntarily — 214

8.56. Tanzanian Employees by Reason for Leaving Previous Job: Percentage who Received Pay Rise after Changing Job — 215

8.57. Tanzanian Employees by Year Education Completed and Occupation: Percentage Seeking Better Job — 215

8.58. Tanzanian Employees who Have Been Out of Wage-Employment by Education: Distribution by Main Activity When Out of Employment — 216

8.59a. Tanzanian Employees with Previous Job by Level of Education: Mean Years in Last Job — 217

8.59b. Tanzanian Employees with Previous Job by Size of Firm in Last Job: Mean Years in Last Job — 217

8.59c. Tanzanian Employees with Previous Job by Type of Employer in Last Job: Mean Years in Last Job — 217

8.59*d*. Tanzanian Employees with Previous Job by Sector of Employment in Last Job: Mean Years in Last Job — 217

8.60 Tanzanian Employees with Previous Job by Occupation in Current Job: Distribution by Occupation in Last Job — 218

9.1. Tanzanian Employees by Father's Education: Distribution by Own Education — 222

9.2. Tanzanian Employees by Own Education: Distribution by Father's Education — 223

9.3. Tanzanian Employees whose Fathers Had Primary Education by Mother's Education: Distribution by Own Education — 223

9.4. Tanzanian Employees by Mother's Education and Father's Education: Mean Years of Education — 224

9.5. Tanzanian Employees by Father's Education: Distribution by Mother's Education — 225

9.6. Tanzanian Employees by Mother's Education: Distribution by Father's Education — 225

9.7. Tanzanian Employees by Age and Father's Education: Distribution by Own Education — 226

9.8. Tanzanian Employees by Age and Parents' Education: Mean Years of Education — 227

9.9. Tanzanian Employees who Desired to Continue Their Education by Period at which Education Ceased: Distribution by Reason for Not Continuing — 228

9.10. Tanzanian Employees by Form IV Examination Result: Percentage Reaching Form VI — 229

9.11. Tanzanian Employees by Father's Education: Distribution by Form IV Examination Result — 229

9.12. Tanzanian Employees with Passes in Form VI — 230

Examination by Father's Education: Distribution by
Number of Passes

9.13.   Tanzanian Employees by Sex and Education: 231
         Distribution by Education of Spouse

9.14.   Tanzanian Employees by Own Level of Education, Age   233
         of First Child, and Whether Education of Child
         Continuing: Mean Years of Education of First Child

9.15.   Tanzanian Employees and Spouses by Education and by   234
         Age of First Child: Mean Years of Education of First
         Child

9.16.   Tanzanian Employees with First Child Aged 15 or More   235
         who Has Completed Education by Own Education:
         Distribution by Education of First Child

9.17.   Tanzanian Employees by Education, by Wage, and by   236
         Number of Children: Distribution by Action if Son
         Could Not Go to Government Secondary School

9.18.   Tanzanian Employees by Number of Children in School: 238
         Mean Expenditure on Education (Shs per annum)

9.19.   Tanzanian Employees by Education and Wage: Mean   238
         Expenditure (Shs p.a.) on Education of Children in
         School, Total, per Child, as Percentage of Income

9.20.   Tanzanian Employees by Wage and Educational Level   239
         of First Child in School: Mean Percentage of
         Employee's Income Spent on Education of First Child

9.21.   First Child of Tanzanian Employees in School by Type   239
         of School Attended: Mean Expenditure by Employees
         on Education of First Child (Shs p.a.)

9.22.   Tanzanian Employees' First Child by Education and   240
         Sex: Mean Cost of Education in Year (Shs)

9.23.   Tanzanian Employees by Education, Period when   241
         Education Completed, and Father's Education:
         Distribution by Occupation

9.24.   Tanzanian Employees by Education, Years of   242
        Employment Experience, and Father's Education:
        Mean Wage (Shs per month)

9.25.   Tanzanian Employees by Education and Father's   243
        Education: Distribution by Time between End of
        Education and Start of Wage-Employment

9.26.   Tanzanian Employees with Previous Wage-Employment   243
        by Education and Father's Education: Percentage
        Continuously Employed

10.1.   Tanzanian African Migrant Employees by Sex: 247
        Distribution by Age on Arrival in Dar es Salaam; Mean
        Age

10.2.   Tanzanian African Migrant Employees by Year of   248
        Arrival in Dar es Salaam and Sex: Mean Years of
        Education

10.3.   Tanzanian Educated African Migrant Employees by   249
        Education and Age on Arrival in Dar es Salaam:
        Percentage who Completed Their Education before
        Migrating

10.4.   Tanzanian African Migrant Employees by Education: 250
        Distribution by Age on Arrival in Dar es Salaam; Mean
        Age on Arrival

10.5.   Tanzanian African Migrant Employees who Completed   251
        Their Education before Migrating by Education, Age on
        Arrival, and Sex: Mean Time (months) to Find an
        Independent Source of Income after Arrival in Dar es
        Salaam

10.6.   Tanzanian African Migrant Employees who Completed   252
        Their Education before Migrating by Education:
        Distribution by First Independent Source of Income in
        Dar es Salaam

10.7.   Tanzanian African Employees by Education and   253
        Migrant Status: Percentage of Spouses in Dar es Salaam
        and on the *Shamba*

10.8.   Tanzanian African Employees by Age and Education: 254
         Percentage of Spouses in Dar es Salaam and on the
         Shamba

10.9.   Tanzanian African Employees by Education and   256
         Migrant Status: Percentage who Support Relatives
         Outside Dar es Salaam and Percentage of Income Used
         in that Way

10.10.   Tanzanian African Employees by Wage and Education: 257
         Percentage of Income Used to Support Relatives
         Outside Dar es Salaam

10.11.   Tanzanian African Employees by Wage and Education: 259
         Percentage of Cases where First Child Educated in the
         Rural Area

10.12.   Tanzanian African Employees with Children in School   260
         Last Year by Wage and Place of Children's Education:
         Mean Cost of Education per Child (Shs per year)

10.13.   Tanzanian African Employees by Education, Age, and   261
         Migrant Status: Percentage with *Shamba*

10.14.   Tanzanian African Employees with *Shamba* by Wage   262
         and Education: Distribution by Method of *Shamba*
         Acquisition

10.15.   Tanzanian African Employees with *Shamba* by Region   264
         of Birth: Distribution by Number of Visits to the
         Shamba during the Previous Year; Mean Number of
         Visits

10.16.   Tanzanian African Employees by Education: Percentage   265
         with *Shamba*; Use of Employed Workers

10.17.   Tanzanian African Migrant Employees by Education: 265
         Percentage who Plan to Return to the Rural Area

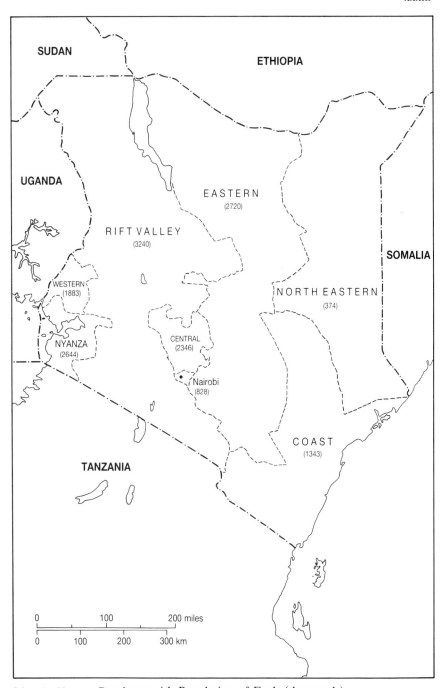

Map 1. Kenya: Provinces with Population of Each (thousands)

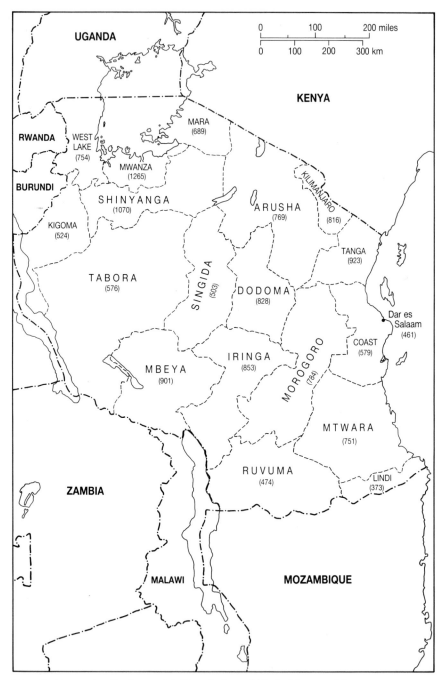

Map 2. Tanzania: Regions with Population of Each (thousands)

1

Issues

The importance of education in African countries is indicated by the increasing proportion of children in school, the rising educational level of the labour force, and the high claim of educational expenditures on government funds. Full enrolment of the relevant age-group in primary school is widely desired, and has been achieved or virtually achieved by some countries. Secondary school enrolments have also risen dramatically. The development of education is a major economic and political issue in the countries of Africa.

Decolonization and the Africanization of jobs occupied by expatriates evidently required a rapid expansion of education. In addition, populations have been growing rapidly, and school-age populations more rapidly still. Large expenditures on education have been required simply to prevent the educational provision for the school-age population from deteriorating. And there has been an immense popular demand for education which it has been politically necessary to satisfy. But a major reason that governments have had for wanting to raise the educational attainments of their populations is a belief in the connection between education and economic growth. Although an understanding of the role of educational attainment in economic growth is far from complete, it has been a widely held belief that the achievement of goals for economic development in Africa requires a great development of the educational system and in the supply of educated labour. In education lay the hope for progress.

The tightening of economic and fiscal constraints on the further development of education poses a severe dilemma. If long-run and sustained economic growth will require and cannot take place without an expansion of the education system, the long-run requirements conflict with the short-run constraints arising from the present level of economic development. Economic growth cannot take place without more education, but countries cannot afford more education until there is more economic growth. However, the reality of this dilemma depends on the realism of the hopes that have been pinned on the role of educational expansion in economic development. What if the resources that would be required to continue the rate of expansion of recent years would not be best used in that way? Attitudes have been changing. It would not nowadays be universally accepted that educational expansion is an essential prerequisite of economic development. There is more than a little disillusionment with education.

With the approach of universal primary education in some countries, the provision of secondary education becomes the major issue. Secondary education is expensive education, with higher-cost teachers, fewer pupils per teacher, and more equipment. The budgetary effects of a substantial expansion in secondary education are likely to be exceptionally severe. Would the resources be better used for some other purpose or does the productivity of education justify their use for education? That is the practical relevance of an answer to seemingly academic questions.

It is generally known that there is a positive relationship between education and pay in wage-employment: the more educated are paid more than the less educated. This relationship indicates the private productivity of education. Education is a good investment for those who acquire the education. Does the relationship between education and pay also indicate that education is a good investment for society? It may be taken to be so if the more educated are paid more because they are more productive, and their greater productivity is the result of their greater education. Education may then be viewed as investment in human capital. But is higher pay for more education simply 'credentialism', the application of a convention?

This volume does not attempt to choose between these alternative explanations, nor does it even provide all the data needed for making such a choice.[1] It does, however, take the first step. It is 'generally known' that the educated get higher pay than the uneducated, but more than this general knowledge is needed to go beyond the formulation of alternative explanations. A choice between explanations must be based on a detailed exposition of what is to be explained. Yet there are few data on the interrelationships between education and the labour-market. Detailed information is not to be found in the statistical handbooks; the relevant data must be specially collected.

A special collection of data is also needed to throw light on various forms of inequality in the labour-market and their relationship to education. One type of inequality is that in the wages of employees with different levels of education, that is, in the educational structure of earnings. How is that affected by an expansion of education? It might be

---

[1] The data in this volume, together with other, specially collected data, are used for econometric analysis in the companion volume to make a choice between the human capital and other explanations of the education-wage relationship.

expected that when persons with secondary and post-secondary education are scarce, they would command a substantial premium in their earnings, and that this premium would be reduced with an increase in the supply of such persons. What, in fact, is the responsiveness of relative wages to changes in the relative supply of employees of different educational levels?

If an increased supply of the educated compresses the educational distribution of earnings, by what means is this brought about? Under one mechanism the increased supply of persons with the appropriate education for a particular occupation would result in the wage for that occupation being bid down by competition between the job applicants. Another mechanism would involve the 'filtering down' of the educated into the lower-paying jobs that in the past have been performed by those with less education. This mechanism is likely to be the more powerful where institutional arrangements protect the wages of those already in employment, so that the adjustment is forced mainly on to new entrants into the labour-market.

The productivity of education in occupation-specific terms becomes the focus of attention with filtering down. Is a person's education 'wasted' if he is employed in a job for which he is 'over-qualified'? That way of looking at the matter implies a conventional idea of the 'proper' education–occupation matrix deriving from the practice of the past. But why should it be assumed that because in the past, when education was much scarcer than today, a particular job was performed by persons with a particular level of education, that is for ever the 'right' education for the job? Why should it be assumed, for instance, that an employee's secondary education is wasted if he is a skilled manual worker, simply because in the past the secondary-educated never took up such work?

The idea that there is no fixed education–occupation matrix is at variance with the concept behind the form of manpower planning introduced into Kenya and Tanzania at Independence. It began by predicting the number of jobs of each particular kind that would become available with the future growth of the economy—an awesome task in itself—and then went on to deduce the output required from the different levels of education to provide the right number of persons—not too few, and not too many—with the right education to take up those jobs. The aim was to produce just the right number of square pegs for the square holes, and of round pegs for the round holes. The educational requirements of particular jobs were taken to be so rigid that only a small change in the supply of the educated was needed to move from a situation of severe scarcity to one of substantial excess. No allowance was made for the possibility of large, and productive, upward shifts in the educational level of employees in particular occupations.

Other important labour-market issues include the effect of the educational level of job-seekers on the speed with which they obtain work, the extent to which education is supplemented, or substituted, by in-job training, and its effect on the inequality of earnings, and whether mobility between jobs differs with the level of education. Again, only special surveys can provide data for the study of these matters.

A further issue, one of equity, but also of efficiency, concerns the effect of educational expansion on the movement between occupations and income categories from one generation to another. To what extent do children enter the occupations of their fathers, unskilled manual workers, as it were, begetting unskilled manual workers; or to what extent do children of the unskilled become skilled workers, or clerical workers, or administrators? And to what extent do differences in educational policy or in the provision of education affect—and effect—these movements? In other words, to what extent is there movement, upward or downward, between the generations?

It is not an unrecognized issue. The folk wisdom of the north of England has an answer: clogs to clogs in three generations. The children may climb out of their class, but their children fall back into it. That is perhaps too jaundiced a view, but it acknowledges that there can be movement. How extensive is that movement, and what role is played by access to education?

Intergenerational movement in education is the first part of the issue. Do children achieve a higher educational level than their parents, and to what extent does such intergenerational movement depend on the scale on which education is provided? Does the expansion of education reduce the educational influence of family background? Or does the influence simply shift upwards, so that, while family background has less influence on entry to lower-secondary education, it counts even more for entry to higher-secondary and tertiary education?

And if the educational advantage of an educated family remains, does the advantage carry over into the jobs taken up after education is completed? It could be that an expansion in secondary education reduces the influence of family background on employment, so that school-leavers from an uneducated background are as likely as those from educated backgrounds to enter white-collar employment. Alternatively, the effect of 'filtering down' could be that the uneducated family background still leads disproportionately to manual employments. Upward mobility in education may not lead to upward mobility in the labour-market. There could be under way a process creating self-perpetuating, educated élites.

The possibility of upward movement is important, not only for equity, for the enlargement of opportunity, but also for efficiency. Resources will be inefficiently allocated if upward movement is denied or restricted, and if position in the economic hierarchy is not determined by merit. These various issues of equity and social mobility are other matters on which remarkably little information is available, and, if understanding is to be increased, information must be specially collected for the purpose.

Finally, important issues about urban populations in Africa, where the great mass of the people is rural, concern their relationship with the rural populations. How recently has the population of the towns been urbanized? How do the long-established residents and the recent migrants differ in their education? Did migrants tend to complete their education before migrating? How long did it take them to obtain employment on arrival in the town? How did this length of time depend on the level of their education? Do urban migrants constitute an élite that has cut its ties with its areas of origin? If not, what links do migrants retain? Do members of their close family remain in the rural areas? How often do migrants visit the rural areas? Where are their children educated? Do migrants retain an interest in farming? Are rural–urban income disparities diminished by transfers from urban employees? Are transfers to rural areas for farming an important form of saving for urban workers? Does the nature of the migrants' links with their areas of origin vary with their position on the educational and income ladders? Is migration permanent, or do migrants intend to return to the rural areas when they retire from employment? Again, such questions concerning the position of urban employees which are important for an understanding of migration and urbanization, and which are relevant to an understanding of such concepts as 'urban bias', can be answered only by collecting data from surveys designed for that specific purpose.

This volume makes available data on education and the labour-market in Kenya and Tanzania obtained from surveys of Nairobi and Dar es Salaam wage- and salary-earners. It is a unique source of information which has been entirely lacking in the past. No other statistical data are available to document in detail the matters dealt with. They include the educational history of the urban labour force, and the relationships between education and occupation, and between education and wages, including the changes in these relationships over time, as deduced from a comparison of age-cohorts. The monograph is not mainly concerned to draw conclusions about policy, or to make recommendations, though some suggestions are hazarded in the final chapter, but it provides information of great importance for those whose function it is to make policy. The information it contains is relevant to a wide range of policies: policies on manpower planning and employment, policies on wages, and policies for education and training among others.

The core of the volume consists of the tabular presentation of the data and of commentaries on them. But it begins with a more general discussion of the major relevant features of the two economies, and of their educational and labour-market policies to provide a context for the presentation of the survey data.

A reminder of terminology might be helpful: *primary school* and *primary education* refer to Standards 1 to 7 or 8; *secondary school* follows primary school, with *junior secondary* of Forms I to IV and *senior secondary* of Forms V and VI; *higher* or tertiary refers to education beyond Form VI of secondary school, and *graduate* to those who have obtained a university degree. *School-leavers* are pupils who finish their school education at any particular stage, including those who go through all the standards or forms of the school, and not 'drop-outs'. *Government* secondary schools are *aided* schools, some being *maintained* schools, for which the government meets most of the operating costs by means of grants and the supply of teachers, and a few *assisted* schools for which the government meets part of the salary costs of approved teaching staff and some other expenditures, the remaining costs being met by fees and other sources of income. *Private* schools are divided between institutions run on a commercial basis, some of very high quality, others not, and church schools; both kinds of private school are *unaided* by government. In Kenya there are also many *harambee* or 'self-help' schools, established by local initiatives, originally unaided, but increasingly receiving some assistance, particularly by the provision of a few teachers. *Migrant* is an employee who comes from another part of the country and neither was born in nor came to the city as a child. *Shamba* is a small farm.

When the present tense is used, the reference is normally to the year 1980, when the surveys were undertaken.

2

The Economies, Education, and the Labour-Market

A. The Economies

Major features of the two countries are set out in Table 2.1. The table shows both countries to be in terms of population in the size range 15 to 20 million, with Kenya at the bottom and Tanzania near the top of the range. Both populations are growing fast, with the World Bank predicting for Kenya an increase in the rate towards the feasible maximum. In both countries the population is young, no more than half being of working age. In terms of their general economic structure and characteristics, the table shows both to be poor countries, but with Tanzania at a much lower level then Kenya. The GNP per head is not only higher in Kenya, but growing faster. The GDP has also been growing faster in Kenya, particularly in the industrial sector. A significantly greater proportion of GDP derives from industry in Kenya than in Tanzania, where agriculture is a greater contributor than in Kenya. In both countries, however, more than three-quarters of the labour force is engaged in agriculture, including non-monetary production, mostly as self-employed farmers on small plots known as *shambas*. The exports of both countries are overwhelmingly composed of primary products.

The degree of urbanization is low—less than 15 per cent—in both countries, though growing fast. In each country there is only one large urban centre, which contains up to a half of the whole urban population. A small proportion of the labour force is in wage-employment—an extremely small proportion in Tanzania—and the importance of the major city as the location of wage-employment is great.

Central government expenditure on education per head is much higher in Kenya than in Tanzania. Both countries have effectively reached universal primary education, but there is a great difference between them in the extent of secondary education and in the expansion of its provision since 1960.

It is clear from the various characteristics of the two countries displayed in the table that they are broadly similar, but with some marked differences. In this characteristic of being sufficiently similar, but at the same time sufficiently dissimilar in some important features, they provide what may be called a 'natural experiment' from which important conclusions may be deduced. Some of the conclusions which emerge from a comparison of the two countries are taken up in the final chapter (and they are a central feature of the econometric study to which reference was made in the Preface). Although comparison is not the primary purpose of this volume, the differences between the two countries will become apparent to the reader. In the educational system, there is a striking difference in the provision of secondary education (see item 20 of the table). Secondary education is a major concern of the study of which this volume is one product. It is with secondary education that the debate about educational policy is now mainly concerned. There are few doubts about the desirability, or at least the political necessity, of Universal Primary Education (UPE). The extent to which resources should be devoted to secondary education is another matter. Both Kenya and Tanzania have now achieved UPE and the interest in the data presented on primary education to a large extent derives from the forward linkage of primary to secondary education: the extent to which primary school-leavers continue with their education at secondary schools. The data on education which are presented in subsequent chapters need to be read against the background of the educational system and its recent history, to the description of which we now turn.

B. Education

In both Kenya and Tanzania, at the time of the surveys the results of which are reported in this volume, the primary schools consisted of seven standards, a primary school-leaving examination, on the results of which selection for admission to secondary school was made, being taken at the end of Standard 7.[1] Secondary education was pursued through four forms to the East African Certificate of Education (EACE) at the end of Form IV, and, for the few, for a further two years of upper-secondary education to the end of Form VI and the East African Advanced Certificate of Education.

[1] Before it was abandoned between 1965 and 1973, an examination at the end of Standard 4 determined the transfer from junior to senior primary school. By 1968 all entry to secondary school was from Standard 7, Standard 8 classes having been discontinued.

Table 2.1. *Characteristics of Kenya and Tanzania*

	Kenya	Tanzania
(1) Population (m.) (mid-1980)	15.9	18.7
(2) Average annual growth of population (%) 1970–80	3.4	3.4
(3) Average annual growth of population (%) forecast 1980–2000	4.1	3.3
(4) Percentage of population aged 15–64 (1980)	48	51
(5) GNP per capita ($US) (1980)	420	280
(6) GNP per capita: average annual growth (%) 1960–80	2.7	1.9
(7) GDP: average annual growth, 1970–80, total (%)	6.5	4.9
(8) Industrial production: average annual growth, 1970–80 (%)	10.2	1.9
(9) Source of GDP: agriculture (%) (1979)	34	54
(10) Source of GDP: industry (%) (1979)	21	13
(11) Percentage of labour force in agriculture (1980)	78	83
(12) Primary products as a proportion of total exports (%) (1980)	84	84
(13) Proportion of labour force in wage-employment (%, late 1970s)	13	5
(14) Proportion of wage-employment in agriculture (%, late 1970s)	28	25
(15) Urban population as percentage of total (1980)	14	12
(16) Percentage of urban population in largest city (1980)	57	50
(17) Number of cities with population over 500 000 (1980)	1	1
(18) Urban population: average annual growth-rate (%) 1970–80	6.8	8.7
(19) Number in primary school as percentage of age-group 6–11		
1960	47	25
1980	108	104
(20) Number in secondary school as percentage of age-group 12–17		
1960	2	2
1980	18	4
(21) Number in higher education as percentage of age-group 20–24	1	0.5
(22) Central government expenditure per capita on education in 1979 (1975 $US)	13	7
(23) Percentage of central government expenditure on education in 1979	17.7	11.1

Source: World Bank, *World Development Reports*: *WDR* 1982, table 1 for items (1), (5), and (6), table 2 for items (7) and (8), table 3 for items (9) and (10), table 17 for items (2) and (3), table 19 for items (4) and (11), table 20 for items (15), (16), (17), and (18), table 24 for items (22) and (23); *WDR* 1983, table 10 for item (12), table 25 for items (19), (20), and (21). Items (13) and (14) calculated from data in *WDR* 1979, and *Economic Surveys* of Kenya and Tanzania, 1978.

The discussion of education in this chapter is focused on a number of important themes in the political economy of the development of education, broadly between 1960 and 1980. These themes provide a relevant context for the survey data which are presented in later chapters.

1. Primary Education: The Move to UPE

The Unesco conference on educational planning for Africa, held in Addis Ababa in 1961, adopted the aim of Universal Primary Education (UPE) by 1980. This was, at the time, a date in the remote future, and the objective cannot have been taken by some countries as more than a fanciful aspiration. Yet when the achievement of UPE came to be seriously tackled in Tanzania and Kenya, in the mid-1970s, it was virtually achieved by the end of the decade.

Tanzania. The expansion of primary education was not universally welcomed. Tanganyika's 1964 report on manpower planning contains a forceful exposition of the dangers in producing a supply of primary school-leavers, 'with their aspirations focused almost solely on wage-employment in the non-agricultural sector of the economy', greatly in excess of the number of wage-jobs available. The report strongly, if implicitly, criticized the Ministry of Education for permitting expansion of primary education 'beyond the magnitudes estimated in the Plan', whereas 'the Plan embodied an attempt to gear the primary output to some more reasonable relationship to the ability of the "modern" sector to create wage employment' (Smith 1966: 438–9).

At this time the provision of primary education was seen as a diversion of resources from the production of high-level manpower, and had to be restrained to the extent that was politically possible. The first Tanganyikan Five-Year Plan, 1964, declared that as 50 per cent of the school-age population was to be found in Standards 1–4 of primary school, there was 'a satisfactory percentage of young people benefiting from primary education' (i. 12), and 'in view of the limited funds available, it [was] not intended to embark upon a large scale primary school expansion' (ii. 112). The unwelcome implications of the policy of restraining the growth of primary education did not go unrecognized, but the policy was defended by saying, in effect, that a full stomach comes first.

In 1967 the President issued a statement on educational policy of major importance. It followed the *Arusha Declaration* (TANU 1967) of that year, which dealt with the whole range of social and economic issues in Tanzania. The impressive statement on *Education for Self-Reliance* reflecting sensibilities and motives which cannot but be admired, analysed the system of education and found it wanting. The statement proposed changes in the methods and ethos of education, and concluded with the call: 'Let our students be educated to be members and servants of the kind of just and egalitarian future to which this country aspires' (Nyerere 1967*a*). The answer to the education and employment problem was not to be more education for more people. Egalitarian ideals were best met by a proposed revolution in primary education which would make it an end in itself, rather than a preparation for further education, together with the introduction of 'working while learning' at all levels of education. With 'terminal primary education' for the vast majority, post-primary education need be provided only to the extent required to produce the bureaucrats, managers, and skilled workers necessary for 'the needs of an independent country and a developing country', to paraphrase the World Bank mission of 1959. This argument of *Education for Self-Reliance* may be seen partly as a response to the so-called 'primary school-leaver crisis' of 1966.

In 1965–6 the proportion of primary school-leavers who were able to obtain a place in secondary school fell dramatically from 30 per cent to 15 per cent. At the end of 1965 the entrance examination for secondary school was taken by 47 000 primary school pupils, of whom 7000 obtained a place. The proportion had fallen because of the accession to Standard 7 of the increased primary school entry of earlier years, and because in a number of regions, where conversion to the seven-year primary course was under way, there were examinees from both Standards 7 and 8. The shock to the expectations and aspirations of parents led to considerable discontent. The reply of political leaders that school-leavers should 'go back to the land' was not received kindly, because the whole purpose of education was generally seen as precisely to provide an escape from that. It was also pointed out that the size of the output from the primary schools was a sign of progress—so many children had received as much as seven years of education; they should compare their situation not adversely, with the few who were able to proceed to even more education, but favourably, with the many who had had much less or none. But it was not an appealing argument to those whose expectations had been formed in the days when primary education promised so much more than seemed now to be available to the Standard 7-leaver who would go no further.

Nor was it easy for the disgruntled to accept that a way out was to be found in the development of the primary school curriculum to give agricultural studies a larger role. There would have been many who remembered the campaign of TANU (Tanganyika African National Union) against just such a bias in 'colonial' education. Nevertheless, that was the direction of official thinking. In 1966 a Ministry of Education statement said that '96 per cent of children ... will become peasant farmers and, therefore, all teaching and all school activities should be directed to suit these children'. *Education for Self-Reliance* was the culmination of that line of thought. Only a radical change in the nature of primary education, turning it from a preparation for further education into a complete education in itself, could solve the school-leaver problem.

But the revolution in primary education was not to be accompanied by a rapid progress to UPE. *Education for Self-Reliance* had made no reference to a timetable for achieving UPE. The second Five-Year Plan of 1969 contented itself with the removal of the barrier between Standards 4 and 5 so that a child who did get a place could continue right through the school, and looked to a twenty-year transition. There were a further five years to wait until that policy was amended. Then the TANU National Executive Committee, meeting in Musoma in November 1974, called in what came to be known as the Musoma Resolution for the achievement of UPE in 1977.[2]

The Musoma Resolution did not come out of the blue, and the pressure for more primary education had been building up for a long time. Even before Independence politicians were attacking the restrictions on the growth of primary education, responding to 'unbridled mass enthusiam for education and its anticipated rewards' (Morrison 1976: 129). The Musoma Resolution called for 'mass mobilization and self-help, use of local resources for teaching and building materials, the use of older school pupils, school leavers and secondary school students, and local craftsmen, peasants and "elders" to teach' (Mbilinyi 1979*b*: 220). Such measures were largely effective, and Tanzania has virtually achieved universal entry to primary school.[3]

Kenya. In Kenya the move to UPE was accompanied by less ideological heart-searching than in Tanzania. The commitment to free primary education for all started as straight politics. The 1963 election manifesto of the Kenya African National Union said that it was the party's intention that 'every child in Kenya shall have a minimum of seven years' free education'. It was a popular policy, though nothing was said about when it would be implemented.

At the time of the Kenya Education Commission report (Ominde Commission)[4] it was estimated that 55 per cent of the 6–12-years age-

---

[2] More strictly, it called for Standard 1 places to be provided for all 7-year-olds by 1977, in other words, for universal primary *entry*.

[3] Although international comparisons cannot have had any effect on the demand for more education, it is of interest to note that Tanzania was lagging well behind other countries. In 1960 in Kenya 9.5% of the population was in primary school; in Tanzania (the age structure of the population was not significantly different) the percentage was 4.5.

[4] Part I, Dec. 1964; Part II, July 1965.

group was enrolled in school.[5] The Commission assumed that free primary education would become universal primary education, because it believed that 'the cost of school fees is the principal reason for the present shortfall in school enrolments' (para. 203). Subsequent events showed the substantial correctness of this view, thought the wide range of enrolment rates between different parts of the country indicated the operation of other factors.[6] Eight years after the Ominde Commission it was possible to point to parts of the country where schools were not fully utilized, even though tuition fees for those schools had been abolished, and to note the existence of 'fundamental social attitudes about formal education which can only slowly be eroded'. (Kenya 1973: 177).

The move towards free primary education began in 1971. In that year a Presidential Decree abolished tuition fees for districts where geographic conditions were unfavourable to school attendance. By 1973, when the first major move towards free primary education was instituted, the enrolment in Standard 1 had risen to 379 000 compared with 137 000 in 1963. In December 1973, in a gesture marking the tenth anniversary of Kenya's Independence, there was an unheralded Presidential Decree abolishing tuition fees over the whole country for Standards 1 to 4 of primary school. The enrolment in Standard 1 in the following year jumped to 959 000. This figure did not represent the regular annual intake under the new system, and the enrolment had dropped to 668 000 in 1975, and to 572 000 in 1976. The 1974 figure was a freak, but there can be no doubt that the abolition of tuition fees for the first four standards created a fundamental change in primary school enrolment.

This was so, even though the abolition of the formal tuition fee by no means ushered in an era of education at no direct cost to the parent. There remained an equipment levy, and further charges were imposed by local school committees, in particular a building fee, which in some areas, it is claimed, was bigger than the former tuition fee. There were also levies for uniforms and other purposes.

In 1975 the tuition fee was abolished for Standard 5, and then, in 1979, for Standard 6, and for Standard 7 in 1980. From the beginning of the 1979 school year there were other changes. The building fee and the

---

[5] The enrolment percentage is affected by enrolment of some children under 6 years and others, a substantial number, of more than 12. These enrolments make it possible for the percentage to be more than 100 in some areas. It was also discovered as the result of the 1977 National Demographic Survey that the size of the population was being underestimated. The quoted percentages, however, are sufficient to give an adequate, though imprecise, picture of the change during the years following independence.

[6] In 1972, for instance, primary school enrolment as a proportion of the estimated population aged 6–12 was 108% in Central Province and 10% in North-Eastern Province, to quote the extremes.

various supplementary fees and levies were eliminated, and the government began to distribute free milk to all schools.

With the abolition of the supplementary charges, Standard 1 enrolment increased from the 599 000 in 1978 to 906 000 in 1980. By 1980 the proportion of the primary school-aged population enrolled in all Standards was estimated to be 96 per cent. In 1978 the figure had been 80 per cent, in 1972 70 per cent, and in 1964, it will be recalled, only 55 per cent.

The plans and projections of the Ministry of Education became out of date with the unexpected Presidential Decree at the end of 1973. A great building programme was needed, there was a serious scarcity of school equipment, and a severe shortage of teachers. Nor was the expansion of enrolment after 1978 accompanied by a comparable increase in the number of classrooms and teachers. The proportion of qualified teachers in the primary school teaching staff was 70 per cent in 1980, whereas it had been 78 per cent in 1973.

The Ominde Commission, particularly in view of the rapid rise in the population of school age, had been perturbed about the expansion of enrolments beyond the supply of buildings and teachers, and about the effect of the abolition of fees on the public finances. In retrospect, the fears were less justified than might reasonably have been expected. It appears that school facilities, though overtaken by the sudden increases in enrolments, caught up fairly promptly. Fears of the fiscal burden have also sometimes been exaggerated. It has been suggested that 'demand for education might force the Government recurrent budget completely out of gear', that education 'has claimed an ever increasing proportion of the recurrent budget', and that it 'appears to absorb a disproportionate share of national resources' (World Bank 1975: 171)[7] In reality, in 1980/1 the recurrent and development account expenditure on education amounted to 18 per cent of the total, which was the same percentage as in 1970/1. In the years between it rose as high as 21 per cent (1974/5), but then declined to 16 per cent, and had begun to increase again only in 1979/80. Of course, these figures do not cover the total value of 'national resources'. There are large sums in the way of voluntary contributions (some of which must be thought of as 'voluntary'), but it would be difficult validly to argue that more resources are devoted to education than reflected the wishes of the population.[8]

The abolition of the building charges and other supplementary levies did not involve a directly corresponding increase in the fiscal burden. The

[7] In accepting the idea of a constantly increasing claim of education, the authors of the Bank study may have been misled by the effect on the figures of a transfer of responsibility for primary education from the County Councils.
[8] On this, and other matters, see Hazlewood 1979: 139–40 and 218.

shift was from the parents of specific pupils to the parents of primary school children in general and to the local community. Parent associations established for each primary school became responsible for raising the funds for the construction and maintenance of school buildings, and their furnishing and equipment, as well as for any extra-curricular activities. The main financial responsibility of the government was for the salaries of teachers.

The achievement by 1980 of primary school enrolment approaching UPE in both Kenya and Tanzania shifts the major interest to secondary education, in which the experience and achievement of the two countries have been radically different. The supply of the secondary-educated has been the primary focus of manpower planning.

2. Educational Policy and Manpower Planning

Tanzania. From the eve of Independence the provision of post-primary education in Tanzania has been related to the 'manpower needs' of the economy. A forthright statement of the case as it appeared at that time is to be found in the report of the World Bank mission of 1959, published as *The Economic Development of Tanganyika*. The report declared that 'A major and immediate call on the limited resources available to the Government of Tanganyika is for the expansion of secondary and higher education.' This was at a time when no more than 45 per cent of the school-age population was in primary school, even though enrolment in Standard 1 had more than doubled over the previous decade. The argument was that 'The needs of a country which is moving into independence and of a developing economy demand a major effort to increase the number of Africans receiving more than four or at most eight years of schooling' (International Bank for Reconstruction and Development 1961). The argument was accepted with conviction in the three-year *Development Plan for Tanganyika, 1961/62–1963/64* (Tanganyika 1961: 79).

The first Five-Year Plan, for the period 1964–9, continued the policy of providing post-primary education to meet manpower needs, with the intention that by 1980 the country would 'become self-sufficient in manpower in all economic fields and at all professional levels' (Tanganyika and Zanzibar 1964: i. 12–13). 'No problem facing this Government is more urgent than that of increasing the supply and improving the organization of highly qualified manpower needed for economic and social development.' Thus opened the government's statement on the report prepared by George Tobias between May and August 1962 on *High-Level Manpower Requirements and Resources in Tanganyika, 1962–1967* (Tanganyika 1963). The government was persuaded, 'consistent with the recommendations in the Tobias Report', to establish a Manpower Planning

Section within the Ministry of Development Planning, and this response to the Tobias report may be taken as the beginning of manpower planning in Tanzania. A concern about producing too many educated people was soon apparent, and the first Five-Year Plan stated:

The shift in educational programmes will be such as to match the number of school leavers at the various levels of formal and technical education to the needs for manpower within the economy without giving rise to a surplus of educated or semi-educated persons to aggravate the problem of unemployment. The latter problem can easily deteriorate into a serious moral and political one, highly prejudicial to social peace in the country (Tanganyika and Zanzibar 1964: i. 13).

The survey of manpower requirements for the Tobias report produced absurdly precise figures for future needs. For instance, it was deduced that in five years' time the requirement additional to present employment for engineers was 391, and for medical personnel 1252. The additional requirement for craftsmen in the various occupational groups was for 373 in electrical, 151 in transport and comunications, 9 in textiles, and so on (Tanganyika 1963: table 8). In a new survey in 1964 (Tanganyika 1965), the association between occupations and their educational requirement was set out, with high-level occupations being divided into three categories:

A. Occupations normally requiring a university degree
B. Occupations normally requiring up to three years of education or training after four years of secondary school
C. Occupations normally requiring a secondary school education, including skilled office workers and skilled manual workers

Again, very precise figures were estimated. Before Independence education had been a matter for educators. After Independence, 'often to the chagrin of educators, manpower planners began to play an increasingly important role in setting quantitative guidelines for development' (Morrison 1976: 311).

Kenya. African Socialism and its Application to Planning in Kenya (Sessional Paper No. 10 of 1965), the key policy document of the late 1960s, identified 'trained, educated and experienced manpower' as one of the three 'critical shortages in Kenya at the present time'. The extent of that shortage, with forecasts for later years was indicated by a survey of high-level manpower requirements and resources (Kenya 1965b).

In the early years of Independence, education was firmly established by the Ominde Commission's report as the servant of economic develoment; manpower planning was to be its controller. Primary education was seen, indeed, as an 'important social service [which] ought to be freely available to all children and to be supported out of the revenue' (Kenya 1964: para. 201, quoted Kenya 1965a: para. 532). But it was also seen to be of economic importance. The Ominde report argued against the view, said to be commonly held (para. 538) that only post-primary education made any direct contribution to economic development and that primary education contributed simply as a reservoir from which pupils capable of further education could be drawn. It emphasized the importance of on-the-job training and adult education as avenues to 'the activities of the modern world', all of which would be closed to those who did not have 'the fundamental education in respect of literacy, numeracy, manual dexterity and general knowledge of the world furnished by the primary school' The passage continues with the following powerful conclusion:

Thus, to use an economic metaphor, a primary education is the minimum basic educational requirement for take-off into the modern sector of our national life. Those that lack such advantages are liable to remain for the rest of their days largely outside the range of modern ways of living, unable to benefit from training or to share greatly in the rewards of a developed economy and becoming in the end an impoverished residue of a bygone age (para. 539).

Nevertheless, despite this poetic and persuasive argument for free and universal primary education, reality kept breaking through. Where were the resources to be found in the near future? The economic importance of primary education made a standstill in its provision unacceptable, and a steady advance towards universality was necessary—but 'what speed of development can the country afford'?

And then there was the question of priorities. The powerful argument for the economic benefits of primary education appears, significantly, in a section of the report headed 'The *Relative* Importance of Primary Education' (italics added), and the authors 'concede a prior claim to secondary, technical, commercial and higher education' (para. 541). And so, in the words of the summary of recommendations: 'Although primary education has economic importance, it is not so important in this respect as secondary, commercial, technical and higher education. Consequently, too great an emphasis on primary education must not be allowed to hinder adequate growth in these other sectors' (p. v). The claim of Africanization of high-level jobs was paramount. The expansion of effective primary education itself required an output of pupils from the secondary schools for training as teachers. The emphasis on secondary education was in line with that of earlier reports, such as that of the World Bank in 1963:

The shortage of well educated and trained Africans needs to be overcome if the future development of the economy is not to be impaired. The mission believes that in the period immediately ahead special emphasis will have to be placed on the secondary level of education, and our suggested program particularly concentrates on establishing more secondary schools, increasing teaching staff and so enrolling more pupils (International Bank for Reconstruction and Development 1963: 309).

By the time the Ominde Commission reported, they had available the survey of high-level manpower requirements during the period from 1964 to 1970, and the author of that survey had provided the Commission with projections of manpower demand up to 1980. The Ominde report's concluding chapter is in consequence entitled 'A Manpower Approach to Economic Development'. The manpower survey itself has the same fanciful and fatuous precision in its forecasts as the corresponding reports in Tanzania. It also has a classification of occupations by their educational requirements which is similar to the classification used in the Thomas survey in Tanzania. The Kenya (Davis) survey divides occupations into four categories:

A. Occupations requiring university or higher education
B. Professional occupations in which a university degree is not mandatory
C. Skilled technicians and workers needing secondary or trade school education
D. Qualified artisans

'Within each category, needs have been analysed by finely classified occupational groups', which is what leads to the production of such forecasts as the need by 1970 for 41 'Deck Officers and Pilots, Ship' and 498 'Telephone and Telegraph Oprs' (Kenya 1965c: 21).

Doubtless, the precise figures were not taken too seriously by the manpower planners themselves, who must have recognized them simply as the necessary result of the assumptions, rather than an expression of reality. Perhaps they were not taken too seriously by the policy-makers either. The danger was certainly recognized by the author of the Kenya report, who wrote that 'the Survey must be carefully studied, not casually interpreted' and that 'hasty interpretation could be misleading'. Of particular relevance is the point that 'the study attempts to define *minimum* needs' (italics added), and it is noted that the educational level of employees in most occupations tends to rise as the supply of educated people increases. That statement may be read as suggesting that additional education increases the productivity of labour in particular occupations. The emphasis on the need 'to watch very carefully the relation of supply and demand ... to avoid relative over provision' of Form I places (Kenya 1965a: p. ix), on the other hand, implies that the educational requirements of particular occupations are rather rigid—just so much is needed, but no more—and that was the view generally taken by the policy makers.

In this first post-Independence period, therefore, in both Kenya and Tanzania, the priority for the expansion of secondary education was clearly recognized. But it was also believed that it was easy to have too much of a good thing. Hence, secondary education was only to be expanded to the point at which it was producing enough, and not more than enough, secondary-educated people to fill the jobs requiring that level of education. It was the manpower planners who would say where that point was to be found. As it turned out, the experience of the two countries was to be very different.

3. Contrasts in Policy and Practice in Secondary Education

The statistics show the fundamental and remarkable difference in the educational development of the two countries. From roughly the same starting-point, and with roughly the same primary school output, between 1955 and 1980 the enrolment in secondary schools in Tanzania increased from 7000 to 65 000, whereas in Kenya it increased from 10 000 to 419 000. In both countries, 2 per cent of the relevant age-group were enrolled in secondary school in 1960; twenty years later it was 4 per cent in Tanzania and 18 per cent in Kenya. In the shorter period between 1965 and 1980, Form I enrolment increased by six times in Kenya, but by only three times in Tanzania, so that by 1980 in Kenya it was six times what it was in Tanzania. Over the same fifteen years, enrolments in Form I as a proportion of Standard 7-enrolments in the previous year were rising in Kenya, even though primary education was expanding. In Tanzania, with the expansion of primary education, the proportion was falling. By 1980 it was 40 per cent in Kenya; in Tanzania it was no more than 9 per cent.

Tanzania. Tanzania followed the path of manpower planning. The provision of post-primary education to meet manpower needs continued to be the policy pursued and expressed in successive Plans. It was pursued through surveys of manpower requirements and the work of a Manpower Planning Section originally set up in 1963 and becoming in 1966 the manpower planning unit of the Ministry of Economic Affairs and Development Planning.

The 1967 statement on *Education for Self-Reliance* showed that the expansion of secondary education was to be strictly limited. Tanzania could not afford to make access to education more egalitarian by providing more education. 'We cannot solve the "problem of primary school leavers" by increasing the number of secondary school places', and in fact the proportion of the national income spent on education 'ought to be decreased':

It is only a few who will have the chance of going on to secondary schools, and quite soon only a proportion of these who will have an opportunity of going on to University, even if they can benefit from doing so. These are the economic facts of life for our country. They are the practical meaning of our poverty (Nyerere 1967a).

The argument of *Education for Self-Reliance* may be seen as an application to education of the ideology of the Arusha Declaration and, as has already been suggested, as a response to the 'primary school-leaver crisis' of 1966. It may also be seen as a response to the dispute with the university students over national service.

The problem created by those who did acquire post-primary education, and particularly by those who went beyond secondary school, was seen as the social divisiveness that resulted when they adopted a fashion of life, and an ethos to go with it, which separated them from the mass of the people in ideas and in material satisfactions. The student demonstration of October 1966 was the culmination of a campaign against the decision to make national service compulsory for university graduates. Among the slogans of the demonstration was one that declared 'Colonialism was Better'. National service was not the only issue concerning students. There had been earlier disturbances, nominally over food and accommodation, issues which had within them, however, a desire to establish standards which the students thought appropriate to their social status. As one student put it: 'professionals demand certain standards of social etiquettes' (*Standard*, 14 January 1966).

The behaviour and attitude of the students laid them open to attack for their arrogance and élitism, and there can be no doubt that they failed properly to exhibit the social ethos that the President was concerned to develop. For 'true socialism', the President had written in 1962 in 'Ujamaa: The Basis of African Socialism', 'is an attitude of mind. It is therefore up to the people of Tanganyika ... to make sure that this socialist attitude of mind is not lost ... through the temptation to look on the good of the whole community as of secondary importance to the interests of our own particular group' (Nyerere 1968 *b*: 8). The evident failure of the students to satisfy this test and to develop the proper 'attitudes of mind' was taken to reflect on the nature of the education they had received. *Education for Self-Reliance* was a programme for putting things to rights.

Whatever the relative importance of manpower planning, ideology, and poverty in setting the constraints on the growth of education, they were certainly effective, as the statistics have shown. The authors of the 1977 World Bank *Basic Economic Report* saw the figures as a reason to congratulate the Tanzanians. The report declares:

In most developing countries vast resources are spent upon formal education systems which produce far more qualified labour than is required by the economy ... By the successful use of manpower planning, in particular the control in the growth in secondary education which in the period 1969–75 has expanded only at the rate of regular wage employment (40%), Tanzania has avoided repeating this costly experience ...

Tanzania has chosen instead to expand primary education ... This use of educational resources in both egalitarian and efficient (World Bank 1977*b*: 31).

The supply of the secondary-educated had evidently shifted from the gross undersupply of 1962 to what the authors of the report saw as a nice balance with demand. But had the policy to prevent the shift from going too far allowed it to go far enough? The restriction on the expansion of secondary education in Tanzania was so successful that by 1981 investigation revealed 'persisting and unexpected shortages of high and middle-level personnel' (Bowman 1981). Tanzania had certainly avoided the overexpansion of secondary education.

The operation of manpower planning came in for criticism by the International Labour Office (ILO), but on the grounds that it was not sufficiently constraining the growth of secondary education. The report listed a number of skilled jobs included among the 'Category C' occupations and questioned whether 'all these occupations do require secondary education' (International Labour Office 1978: 226). No consideration seems to have been given to whether a higher rather than a lower level of education helps to make these jobs better done. There was no questioning of the philosophy of manpower planning in the ILO report, only of its applications.

A more radical conclusion is reached in a 1981 Unesco report (Tanzania 1981): 'In light of the present scarcities of skilled manpower in so many fields, the record of past attempts to relate the overall development of education and training to manpower needs does not appear to have been successful' (5–6). This moderate statement, based on experience of manpower planning in Tanzania, is followed by a cogent paragraph on the deficiencies in the concept of determining educational policy by forecasts of manpower needs:

The economics of manpower planning is too uncertain a science on which to base the global development of a whole sub-sector of a national education system such as secondary education, which in any case in most countries is developed mainly on the basis of the demand for places and the funds available. Future manpower planning should adopt a more disaggregated approach: focusing on critical industries/economic sectors and on well-defined occupations such as accountants, teachers, engineers and particular categories of skilled manpower that require a specialized education or training. From an economic development standpoint, general secondary education has much the same status as primary education, in providing the basis both for future employment and future learning (in school or training institution, or on the job)(6).

The report continues by arguing that the development of education will in fact be governed by the willingness of government to devote resources to education as against competing claims, and argues that despite the great financial problems:

the evidence of a shortage of well-qualified Form IV leavers is strong and this argues in favour of a much bigger push to the expansion of secondary education in the next Five-Year Plan than in the current one. The same argument applies to technical and vocational education. These pragmatic empirical considerations should not be overshadowed by global theoretical questions which cannot be answered (6).

The effect of the restricted growth of secondary education is made very clear in the Unesco report. It is pointed out that the expansion of primary education towards UPE at the time of a slow expansion of secondary places 'will cause dramatic falls in the years ahead in the promotion rates from Standard VII to Form I' (18). By 1985 the effect of the 'UPE bulge' would reduce the promotion rate into government schools to a mere 1.4 per cent, which would rise to 2 per cent when the 'bulge' had passed on. Entry into private schools was expected to exceed that into government schools and to account for 1.8 per cent of Standard 7-leavers in 1985. The forecast for enrolment in government schools as a proportion of the relevant age group leads to the conclusion that the policy 'is likely to make Tanzania's the smallest public secondary school system in the world relative to population' (19).

The problem of the unemployed Form IV-leaver is also tackled by the Unesco report. It concludes, contrasting its view with that of the World Bank's *Basic Economic Report* of 1977, that there is no evidence that the problem exists (328). The identification of the problem and of its extent is based on the statistics of the 'placement' of Form IV-leavers in jobs in government and parastatals, which is an annual exercise for the Ministry of Manpower Development. They usually succeed in 'placing' some 70 per cent of Form IV-leavers, and the 'unplaced' 30 per cent are identified with the unemployed.

In reality, there is no information on what happens to those not placed by the Ministry. Nor is there evidence that the parastatals, in particular, recruit only through the annual placement. Although the unplaced are the least-qualified school leavers, who have generally failed their examinations, this does not demonstrate that they are unemployed, though it is likely that they are among the first to 'filter down' into jobs formerly the preserve of those with even less educational qualification. But 'filtering down' is not an indication of the over-expansion of secondary schooling. Again to quote the Unesco report: 'Indeed, this process by which jobs are filled over time by better educated persons is part of the overall process by which the potential productivity of the country's labour force is gradually improved. This positive view of the "unplaced" Form IV leavers has never been given enough attention in discussion of the prospective expansion of secondary education in Tanzania'(27). In other words, more education might make it possible not only to do a better job, but to do any job better.

Kenya. Secondary school enrolment in Kenya increased by 850 per cent between 1963 and 1974, from 20 553 to 195 674. In 1978 enrolment had risen to 362 025. The number of schools registered increased from 400 in 1966 to 1029 in 1974, and to 1486 in 1977.

Secondary schools can be classified in various ways. One distinction, to which reference has already been made, is between the government-aided (subdivided into 'maintained' and 'assisted') and the unaided schools. In 1966 half the total number of secondary schools were unaided; by 1977 the number of unaided schools had risen to 71 per cent of all schools. Unaided schools include church schools and private schools, frequently run for profit, but the great majority of them are *harambee* schools built and operated by local communities.

Secondary schools can also be divided into national schools, provincial schools and local schools. The national schools are 26 maintained schools, of which 15 are classified as academic and 11 as technical institutions. They draw their pupils from the whole country on the basis of geographic quotas. The provincial schools are those which draw their intake largely from within the province in which they are located, while the local schools are *harambee* institutions which take their pupils from their own narrow locality.

Despite their name, maintained schools are not fully financed by the government. Fees in maintained schools account for about one-quarter of total expenditure. In unaided schools fee income must meet all but a small part of the cost, and in consequence these schools have both higher fees and poorer facilities than the maintained schools.

Secondary school fees, even in the maintained schools, are high in relation to the fees that were charged for primary education. Maintained day schools in 1980 charged fees of between Shs 300 and Shs 600 a year, while fees for boarding schools ranged from Shs 690 to Shs 1800. Fees in the unaided *harambee* day schools ranged from Shs 450 to Shs 1200 and more.

The proportion of primary school-leavers proceeding to secondary school rose from 32 per cent in 1974 to 44 per cent in 1977 as the availability of Form I places increased. But ony 13 per cent of primary school-leavers went to government-aided schools. Over 70 per cent of secondary school enrolment in Form I was in unaided schools in 1977. 'Wastage' during secondary education for schools as a whole is low. In 1977 the enrolment in Form IV equalled 81 per cent of the Form I enrolment four years previously. But there is a marked difference in this statistic for different types of school: for unaided schools it was only 63 per cent, whereas for aided schools the figure was 109 per cent, the enrolment in Form IV in 1977 being larger than that in Form I in 1974, the cohort from which the 1977 Form IV-leavers would normally have been drawn, probably because of transfers from unaided schools.

Only a small proportion of secondary school pupils continue beyond Form IV. In 1977 Form V enrolment was only 11 per cent of the Form IV enrolment of the previous year. Here again, however, there is a marked difference between the aided and unaided schools. In the former, the figure was 18 per cent, whereas in the unaided schools the percentage was only 3.

The movement to establish self-help or *harambee* secondary schools began soon after Independence. Already by the time of the Ominde report, less than two years later, they were seen as creating a problem of uncontrolled and unplanned expansion of low-quality education. By 1977 the *harambee* schools accounted for 825 of the total 1042 unaided schools. In 1973 the unaided schools took 56 per cent of the pupils in Form I, while in 1977 they took as much as 71 per cent of the total. And this statistic in fact understates the importance of self-help efforts in the expansion of secondary education, because some *harambee* schools have been taken over by government and are now included in the figures for maintained schools. In reality, the majority of secondary schools established since Independence, both in the aided and the unaided sectors, began as *harambee* projects.

The Development Plan for 1974–8 proclaimed a policy of controlling the expansion of secondary and higher education. Government contribution to the running costs of additional *harambee* schools was to be curtailed, and the construction of new maintained secondary schools was to be restricted. Expansion within the aided sector was to be confined to the establishment of additional Form III streams for pupils transferring through competitive examination from unaided schools. The aim of the policy was to limit the growth in educational expenditure and to limit the increase in the number of unemployed secondary school-leavers, while making provision for higher and specialized levels of education to meet manpower needs.

The attitude of government to secondary education is worth elaboration. The Development Plan for 1974–8 had come a long way from the Ominde report's emphasis on the developmental importance of secondary education, and to its reflection in the government's intention to 'take steps to expand the output of secondary students as rapidly as capital and teacher limitations permit' (Kenya 1966: 305). The 1974–8 Plan expressed the government's concern with the objective of the educational system: 'Its objective is to produce a few individuals who are equipped for placement in the modern formal sector of the economy. Its highly selective nature and exclusive orientation towards the modern urban sector are in fundamental contradiction to the social and cultural values upheld by the Government' (Kenya 1974: 404). The reader might be excused for checking that he is not reading a Tanzanian document. But, of course, in

Tanzania the system was necessarily, with the slow development of secondary education, so much more 'highly selective'. The 'index of opportunity', to use the concept of the Ominde report, the number of Form I places in relation to the Standard 7 enrolment in the previous year, was 32 per cent in Kenya in 1974, compared with 13 per cent in Tanzania.[9]

This concern in Kenya about the results of the existing educational system was stimulated by the belief that 'the proportions of the "school-leaver" problem are growing: the number of jobless is increasing; the period required to obtain employment lengthens; and formal qualifications rise steadily and usually bear no functional relationship to the job concerned'. These considerations, as well as the increasing fiscal burden of the provision of education, caused the government to decide 'carefully [to] control the expansion of the educational system at the secondary and tertiary levels' (Kenya 1974: 407). However, the policy was effective only with respect to the maintained schools. The *harambee* movement continued with unabated effect, indeed with additional stimulus from the restrictions on the expansion of places in the maintained schools.

Between 1971 and 1974, the number enrolled in aided schools increased by 26 per cent, and in unaided, mostly *harambee*, schools by 57 per cent. For the period 1974 to 1977 the corresponding figures are 25 per cent and 105 per cent, and the proportion of total enrolments in unaided schools increased from 48 per cent to 60 per cent. Soon after that, however, the situation changed, with the adoption by government of what might be called an if-you-can't-beat-' em-join-' em strategy. The increasing predominance of the unaided schools was overcome by transferring them to the 'assisted' category, consisting mostly of *harambee* schools, which received a small amount of assistance, usually through the supply of one or two teachers.

But the provision of assistance to and the change in status of *harambee* schools was not the only change of importance in secondary education. The growth of the system had been slowed down. The lion of *harambee* had, after all, it seems, been tamed. The increase in Form I enrolment fell continuously from 29 per cent between 1975 and 1976 to under 3 per cent between 1979 and 1980. It looks as if secondary education had, at last, been 'brought under control'.

The Development Plan for 1979–83 stated that: 'The aims and programmes of secondary education will be primarily oriented to suit the pattern of employment opportunities. This requires the teaching of relevant practical skills among other subjects, so as to facilitate direct employment, self-employment and employment in the informal urban and rural sectors' (Kenya 1979*b*: 157). This is perhaps uncomfortably

---

[9] By 1980 the index in Tanzania was 9%; in Kenya 40%.

close to Lord Delamere's advocacy of the 'widespread teaching of the native in the skilled work of his hands'.[10]

Why was the experience of the two countries so different? Was it simply that the expansion of secondary education in Kenya was the result of the *harambee* self-help movement, which established and operated large numbers of low-grade secondary schools, whereas, in contrast, in Tanzania the expansion of secondary education was restricted because policy eschewed such popular initiatives?

In fact, private secondary education has not been unimportant relatively to public in Tanzania. In 1965 it was, indeed, of small importance, but in subsequent years the private sector rapidly increased its relative position so as to account for very nearly half of the enrolment in Form I and over 40 per cent in all forms.

The change began in 1966 when, in response to popular discontent resulting from what has already been referred to as 'the school-leaver crisis', the Tanzanian government changed its former policy of opposition to private education and announced that it would permit more private schools to be opened. The number of private secondary schools increased rapidly. By the end of 1966, 27 unaided schools were registered, compared with seven in 1965 (Min. of Ed. statistics, mimeo). Several more opened in 1967 (Morrison 1976: 205), and by 1974 there were 53 private and 83 public schools in operation.

The expansion in private enrolments occurred particularly in the lower forms. In 1979, when enrolment in Form I was virtually the same in public and private schools, the number enrolled in Form IV in private schools was only half that in public schools. The proportion of Forms V and VI pupils in private schools was even lower, and amounted to only 11 per cent of the total. This difference in numbers in the different forms in the private schools could simply have been the result of the rapid expansion in private enrolments, making enrolments in the lower forms large relative to those in the upper forms until the new entrants had worked their way through the schools. It could reflect different drop-out rates from private and public schools. Doubtless, these together are part of the explanation, but only part. There is good reason to think that transfers from private to public schools after Form I also had an effect: the absolute numbers enrolled in 1979 decline through Forms I–IV in the private schools and increase in the public schools (Tanzania 1980). There is said to be a back-door access to the higher forms in public secondary schools. Large numbers transfer from private schools after Forms I, II, and III, creating serious overcrowding in the public schools (Mbilinyi

---

[10] Quoted in Huxley 1935, p. 84. Lord Delamere was a leader of the Settler community. The remark dates from 1920.

1979*b*: 224): 'up to one third of total Form III enrolments consisting of such students. These are mainly children of "big people" ... Headmasters and Headmistresses are obliged to "receive" such students' (Mbilinyi 1979*a*: 110).

Despite the statistical obscurity created by the shifts in the classification of schools, and the absence of figures for enrolment in *harambee* schools, there can be no doubt that the *harambee* movement contributed enormously to the expansion of secondary education in Kenya. The modest increases in enrolments in the private schools in Tanzania came nowhere near to matching it. Nevertheless, it would be quite wrong to attribute the difference between the two countries solely to Tanzania's policy of avoiding the establishment of schools on the lines of the *harambee* schools in Kenya. That is not the whole story, by any means. In 1965 enrolment in government maintained schools in Kenya was merely one and a half times greater than in Tanzania; by 1980 it was more than seven times greater.

A very substantial part of the difference in educational provision is, therefore, due to the more generous provision of funds by government in Kenya than in Tanzania. It is true, of course, that Tanzania is the poorer of the two countries, but it is not only a question of poverty. Again, that is not the whole story. It is also a question of priorities.

The central government in Tanzania allocated 12.5 per cent of its expenditure to education; in Kenya the percentage was 18.7 (World Bank 1981).[11] Education was evidently given a smaller proportion of a smaller budget, that is, a lower priority in Tanzania than in Kenya. In 1979 central government expenditure per head of population in 1975 US dollars amounted to $7 in Tanzania compared with $13 in Kenya (World Bank 1982: table 24).

4. The Question of Quality

Quantity is not the only consideration in secondary education: quality also counts, though it is so much more difficult to count. Has the expansion of secondary places in Kenya been entirely at the expense of quality, so that the contrast with Tanzania is between a large, low-quality system, and a small, high-quality one? There is no doubt that one of the objections to *harambee* development is the fear of producing a large number of uneducated school-leavers with nominally a secondary school education. And there is no doubt a wide range of quality among secondary schools in Kenya.

---

[11] We assume the authors of this report have done their homework, and have avoided the deep statistical traps which litter the path of such tricky statistical comparisons.

Kenya. Various criteria of quality indicate that it is lower in unaided than in maintained schools in Kenya. There is strong competition for entry to maintained schools, which is dependent on examination results, whereas there is generally no such test for entry into unaided schools. All other criteria point to the wide disparity between aided and unaided schools. Classes are larger in unaided schools. In aided schools in 1977, 88 per cent of the teachers were trained, as compared with 26 per cent in unaided schools. In a grading based on the facilities provided by the school, 57 per cent of maintained schools were graded A and B compared with 1 per cent for unaided schools (i.e. in this case *harambee* schools), and as this grading was applied only to schools offering candidates for the EACE examination it excluded the worst-equipped *harambee* schools. Unaided schools are particularly ill equipped to provide teaching in science, lacking laboratories and equipment needed if pupils are to take science subjects in EACE examination. It should be mentioned, however, that the private schools, though often of poor quality (25 per cent graded A and B), and sometimes of very poor quality, include a few very high-quality schools. The unaided schools, despite their number, provide few opportunities for Form V and Form VI pupils. In 1977 they contributed only 18 per cent of Form V enrolment in arts subjects and only 3 per cent in science subjects. The maintained schools present more candidates than other schools for EACE, offer a greater variety of subjects, and have a lower failure rate.

The Ominde Commission saw a number of dangers associated with the unplanned growth of secondary education. In the first place, the Commission was concerned with the legality of the new schools. There was a legal requirement for schools to be registered, and most *harambee* schools were established without benefit of registration. The major worry of the Commission, a reading of the report suggests, was about the quality of education in *harambee* schools: 'we were much disturbed by the probability that *many of the children in these schools would not in fact receive an education that would justify the description of secondary*' (Kenya 1964: paras 209–12, quoted Kenya 1965a: para. 600, original italics). The Commission took the view that the establishment by means of 'self-help' of secondary schools of an acceptable standard was simply beyond the capacity of most communities to organize. Failure was highly probable: disastrously poor examination results were inevitable, and schools might not be able to continue because of lack of funds and teachers. 'The resentment and political unrest that could flow from such a catastrophe are obvious' (1965a: para. 601). The uncontrolled establishment of *harambee* schools was also to be condemned as the antithesis of planning.

Yet at the same time as the uncontrolled expansion of *harambee* schools was worrying the Commission, they were also greatly concerned at the contraction in 'educational opportunity', in the sense of the decline in the chance of a primary school-leaver gaining access to a public secondary school, caused by the rapid expansion of primary education.

The solution was to plan the development of education in terms of an agreed 'index of opportunity'. Provincial plans for education should show what development of secondary education was needed to achieve the agreed value of the index. *Harambee* schools should be permitted only if they fitted in with the plan—and with the availability of teachers (para 624). These arrangements would, the Commissioners believed, allow proper scope for community initiative, but only to the extent of providing schools that were needed, and for which government assistance could properly be foreseen in the future.

The expansion of *harambee* education that in fact took place in the years after the Ominde report was on a scale that cannot have been dreamt of in the Commissioners' philosophy. And yet their expectations of future government aid to *harambee* schools was fulfilled with the increasing transfer of such schools from the unaided to the assisted class that has been described above.

The Commissioners' expectations about the low quality of *harambee* schools were also borne out. It can most easily be judged in relation to that of the aided schools. In 1976 in aided secondary schools, 92 per cent of the teachers were trained; in unaided schools the figure was 28 per cent. The EACE failure rate in aided schools in 1975 averaged 33 per cent; in *harambee* schools it averaged 62 per cent. Poor results are hardly surprising given the lack of equipment and the difficulty of recruiting highly qualified teachers. Teachers were a particular difficulty, and 'it was the lesser-qualified teachers, with little more than a basic secondary education themselves, and experience only in primary schools, who took on the brunt of the initial challenge of *harambee* secondary school development' (Anderson 1975: 384).

Harambee schools were undoubtedly a 'second-best' for those desperate for education. The high wastage rate is an indication of this as well as of other characteristics of *harambee* education: 'only about 63 per cent ... who registered in Form I in unaided schools in 1974 survived to enroll in Form IV in 1977. Aided schools have the advantage of being able to fill vacancies and replace dropouts by recruiting students from the unaided sector'. (Kenya 1979*a*: 57).

Yet, despite all this, one observer came to the conclusion that 'judged in context a number of schools made a sufficiently worthwhile contribution to education to suggest that the dynamics of localised self-help education should be studied very much more carefully' (Anderson 1975: 389). It is also relevant to speculate on what the political situation in Kenya would have been without the safety valve of the *harambee* schools.

And what would the economic effect have been if their contribution to education had been denied?

Tanzania. The 'quality' of education in Tanzania has changed in a number of ways, and the term is subject to a number of meanings. One way in which the effectiveness of education was undoubtedly improved was by the increase in the years of primary education given to those who were in school. The primary school career of many pupils was cut short at Standard 4 by their failure to proceed further. There would, of course, always be drop-outs from education (primary education not being compulsory), and it would be expected that the size of an entry cohort would diminish as it passed through the school. But until the system was changed after 1973, the educational system was designed to remove a substantial proportion of pupils from the schools at the end of Standard 4. The effect of this system was to leave many with so few years of schooling that they retained little of their education and the expenditure on them was largely wasted. The policy adopted was to extend the years of education of those who started school, instead of providing a few years of schooling for a higher proportion of the school-age population. It was a decision to increase the depth of education rather than its breadth. Those who entered primary school were to be better educated by the time they left school than many school-leavers in the past, simply because they would have had a long enough education for it to 'stick'.

An attempt to achieve a major change in the quality of education arose from a concern for 'relevance'. The relevance of education is an issue in many countries with widely different economic, social, and educational systems. In Tanzania it was relevance to the life which would be led by the great majority of school-leavers and to the society which it was the intention of the country's socialist policies to develop. It was a criticism of the content of primary education, as well as of the ethos of the educational system, that it was directed at preparing pupils for the secondary and further education that all but a tiny minority would never experience: it was preparation for examinations rather than a preparation for life. Under the policies expressed in *Education for Self-Reliance* in 1967, all this was to change. Primary education was to be an end in itself, and its content was to be changed to make it so. The emphasis on relevance to the life of the masses was to be accompanied and reinforced by policies to prevent a separation in feelings and experience between the more and the less educated. 'Education and work were to be united in all educational institutions, not only to cover costs of schooling, but also to ensure that youth developed the correct attitude to manual labour as future peasants and workers, and to break down the petty bourgeois arrogance of students in higher educational institutions who would become the future bureaucrats and experts' (Mbilinyi 1979*b*: 220). And the entry age into primary education was raised to seven years, so that primary school-leavers, at the end of the seven-year course, would not be too young to undertake productive labour (Mbilinyi 1979*b*: 219; Nyerere 1968*b*: 60).

In a report to the TANU Executive Committee ten years later, the President of Tanzania stated that in the period:

our teaching at all levels has become increasingly appropriate to the needs of our people and of Tanzanian society taken as a whole. In the primary schools ... there has been new emphasis given to technical and agricultural training, and the pupils no longer spend most of their time preparing for secondary school educa-tion which the majority of them will never receive ... The Secondary schools are also giving increased emphasis to technical and scientific subjects, with most schools now specialising in either agriculture, science or technology (Nyerere 1979: 49).

In this report reference was also made to the 'economic activities in our schools', though it was to the financial rather than the moral benefits resulting. These activities, it was remarked, 'include the growing of differ-ent crops—mostly food which was consumed by the schools—and the raising of chickens and livestock ... In addition, many schools made bricks, furniture or clothes, either for their own use or for sale. These self-reliance activities are still small and often ill-organised, but they are being accepted as part of the normal educational system'(49).

It has been argued that the response in the schools to the changes adumbrated at a high political level has been limited because 'the teaching methods and organisation of school and classroom ... are di-ametrically opposed to the objectives of developing creativity, critical thinking, self-confidence and cooperation' (Mbilinyi 1979*b*: 222). Be that as it may, it would not be surprising if the redirection of educational policy towards relevance and self-reliance, to the extent that it has had an effect on what the schools do, as well as the large increase in the number of pupils and consequent pressure on teaching resources, has had an adverse effect on the quality of education as measured by the tests of basic cognitive skills.

Secondary education has been subjected to many changes which might be expected in the short run adversely to affect academic standards, at any rate as conventionally measured. The teaching staff has been local-ized, and although some 40 per cent are university graduates the propor-tion is declining. On top of the addition of new subjects of study, as already mentioned, such as agriculture, commerce, domestic science, and crafts, the syllabus for particular subjects has been changed to give emphasis to matters conceived to be of Tanzanian relevance, and new textbooks and teaching materials have been produced. Examinations have been set by the National Examinations Council since 1971, when Tanzania withdrew from what had been common arrangements for the East African countries, and since 1974 continuous assessment has been used to reduce the weight of the final examination. The schools have remained predominantly residential, however, to the extent of over 80 per cent of pupils in Forms I–IV and of 90 per cent or more of pupils in Forms V–VI.

In the period 1977–9 there were failure rates of between 40 and 60 per cent in the Form IV and Form VI examinations in mathematics and physical sciences. The 1980 Unesco team concluded that the results of tests they administered 'tend to give credibility to much of the recent concern over a fall in academic standards in secondary schools'. The Unesco report concludes with a comparison which, whether or not it is an entirely appropriate one, is certainly striking: 'In mathematics overall, after three years of very selective secondary education, available to 2.2 per cent of the age cohort, Tanzanians 17 years and older are performing at the same level as 13-year-olds in developed countries who are about to complete their basic cycle of education' (Tanzania 1981: 20).

The official medium of instruction in secondary schools in Tanzania continues to be English, but it is reported that teachers are increasingly using Swahili because of the failure of pupils by the time they enter secondary school to have achieved a sufficient command of English (23).[12] The quality of the primary education is, of course, an important element in the success of secondary education.[13] It may be that the rush to UPE, as well as the changes in the nature of education envisaged in *Education for Self-Reliance*, took its toll in terms of the quality, by conventional criteria, of the input into secondary schools.

It is obviously not a simple contrast between Tanzania, small and good, and Kenya, large and bad. In both countries the range of quality is wide, and it is evident that small does not necessarily mean beautiful.

5. *Summary*

Three stages in the post-Independence histories of education policy may be identified in Kenya and Tanzania. At first, both put emphasis on the

---

[12] 'teachers have increasingly begun to use Swahili ... to make themselves better understood by students *whose exposure to English in primary school is increasingly infrequent*' (italics added).
[13] With the move to UPE the number of pupils per class and per teacher increased, but not dramatically in Kenya. The available Tanzania figures are not recent enough to show this effect. What they do show, for the period for which they are available, is a very much larger number of pupils per class than in Kenya—much larger even than for Kenya after the great influx of pupils. On this test, the quality of primary education is substantially lower in Tanzania than in Kenya.

need to expand secondary education to meet the deficiencies in the availability of a skilled labour force. In both the expansion was under the influence of manpower planning which, while expansion was the obvious and accepted need, stressed at the same time the dangers of overproduction of the educated. Then there was a switch in emphasis and, under the pressure of the masses, or of the politicians, which was the same thing at one remove, there was a rapid expansion of primary education and the effective achievement of UPE. But before the move to UPE, a second stage in the development of secondary education was ushered in, during which events in the two countries radically diverged. Tanzania continued its constraints on the expansion of secondary education, holding to a belief in and maintaining a mechanism for manpower planning, while believing the country was too poor to do more. Kenya, in contrast, though formally committed to the precepts of the dangers of overproduction of the more educated, did not withstand the popular pressure for the provision of secondary education. In consequence, in 1980 Kenya had a secondary school entry of 40 per cent of primary school-leavers, while Tanzania had only 9 per cent, and would have no more than 4 per cent when that year's entry into Standard 1 of primary school reached Standard 7. It was then likely to have, to quote again the Unesco report, 'the smallest public secondary school system in the world, relative to population'.

There is a further divergence between the two countries in that, in Kenya, with its less ideological approach, there has been less official educational theorizing. It is difficult to imagine *Education for Self-Reliance* as an official publication in Kenya. The declarations on fundamental matters in Tanzania led to radical changes in education, and the effect of these ideological upheavals on the quality of education may not have been entirely beneficial to the production of cognitive skills.

C Labour

People like me live in a permanent state of frustration. My education is just enough to give me a mediocre job, a job that is dull and dreary. But I have no choice. I am suspended somewhere in the middle. I am neither a manager nor a sweeper, neither rich nor poor, neither happy nor sad. My pay packet is neither fat nor thin, and debts can never disappear (Ruheni 1972).

That might seem to argue for increased provision for education, to give those like the speaker more education than the little they have, and to give at least some education to those who have none. In reality educational policy in both Kenya and Tanzania has been dogged by the fear of producing too much education. This concern with the danger of overproduction is not new, and it is thought-provoking to realize that 'probably the greatest pitfall is over-production' was the opinion of the Tanganyika Director of Education in 1926 (Cameron and Dodd 1970: 209). In 1926!

As was shown above, the fear of overproduction of the educated maintained its hold over policy in Tanzania, and the growth of secondary education has been slow. In Kenya, the King Canutes of manpower planning did not hold back the tide of popular demand and there has been a very large increase in the supply of the secondary-educated. In this respect the forces operating on the labour-market in the two countries have been radically different. But the supply of labour of different levels of education is not the only influence on the labour-market. Another is the policy adopted, and its effectiveness, towards industrial relations and incomes. Both countries have such policies and elaborate mechanisms for implementing them. In this section these policies are outlined, following a brief description of some characteristics of the labour force.

1. The Kenyan Labour Force

Only a small proportion of the Kenyan labour force participates directly in the wage-labour market. The great majority of Kenya's workers are small farmers. A rural survey in 1974–5 estimated the small-farm population to be 10.3m., when the total population was estimated at 13m. In addition to small-scale farming and wage- and self-employment in the formal sector, a number estimated to total 123 000 in 1980 are economically active in the so-called 'urban informal sector'.

In the census year 1979, wage and salary employees numbered 972 000 and amounted to nearly 14 per cent of the population of working age (15–59). In the previous census year, 1969, employees numbered only 627 000, but they nevertheless accounted for more than 12 per cent of the working-age group.[14] As a proportion of the population, therefore, there does not seem to have been any significant expansion in wage-employment.

Whatever the relative size of the wage-labour force, the number in employment, at more than a million, is large enough to be of importance. It is also likely to contain a high proportion of the Kenyans who have secondary education, which makes it the group of particular relevance for this study. There are no official data describing the educational structure of wage-employees, and one purpose of this study is to draw such information from the sample survey.

Although there was a decline in employment in agriculture, except for

[14] In the census year 1962, the proportion would appear to have been very nearly 14%, though there have been changes in coverage of the statistics since then.

a set-back in 1975, there has been a consistent rise in other sectors, and they have increased their share of total employment. Manufacturing has increased its share more than most, but in 1980 it still accounted for no more than 14 per cent of the total, well behind agriculture (private and public), still with 23 per cent, and the largest sector of all, 'Community, social and personal services', with 39 per cent. Within this category of services, education was the most important, having increased its share of total wage-employment from just under 11 per cent in 1973 to just under 15 per cent in 1980. The impact of educational expansion is highlighted by other statistics: between 1972 and 1977 the increase in the employment of teachers, by about 40 000, accounted for more than 20 per cent of the total increase in wage-employment and 46 per cent of the increase in public-sector employment.

About 16 per cent of those in formal sector wage- or salary-employment in 1980 were women. Total employment, estimated at 1 006 000, was very roughly equally divided between private and public establishments: 534 000 private; 472 000 public, of which 215 000 were in central government. A little less than one-quarter was employed in agriculture (including forestry); a little more than half was in urban areas. Employment in Nairobi amounted to 274 000.

2. Industrial Relations in Kenya

For all practical purposes, strikes are outlawed while the unions themselves do not have the necessary financial resources to engage in a protracted strike (Rempel and House 1978: 106).

The first half of the 1960s was a period of inter-union rivalry and industrial strife. In 1965 the government established a single central organization, COTU (Central Organization of Trade Unions), to which all unions are affiliated except for the teachers' and civil servants' organizations. The general-secretary of COTU is appointed by the government, and the government is represented on the executive committee. There is in principle government control over the unions, though it is said that in practice there is little government intervention in the administration of COTU and of individual unions. The Trade Disputes Act of 1965 requires disputes to be referred to the Ministry of Labour, and enables stoppages to be declared illegal if negotiating procedures have not been fully used.

The Federation of Kenya Employers represents most associations of employers, and in addition has a membership of individual firms. It plays an important part in industrial relations.

The Industrial Relations Charter, drawn up in 1962 and agreed by the government, employees, and trade unions, sets out agreed principles of negotiation. It provides a model 'recognition agreement', which has tended to standardize procedures for negotiations on wages and conditions.

The troubles of the early 1960s have not recurred, and the established procedures, together with the iron hand of government, have led to relative industrial peace. When the procedures for conciliation have failed to lead to a settlement, the parties involved may refer the dispute to the Industrial Court, which has powers to adjudicate over a wide range of issues of pay and conditions of service. The Court became of increased importance from 1973 when the government took a larger role in the fixing of wages. All negotiated agreements were to be submitted to the Ministry of Labour which, if it had no objections to make, would forward them to the Court for registration. If the Ministry objected to the agreement, it was to be referred back to the parties involved for revision to make it conform to the official guidelines. If the agreement was not revised to the satisfaction of the Ministry it was to be forwarded to the Court with an accompanying objection. The Court was then required to make an award which did not violate the guidelines; it became an instrument of the government's incomes policy.

3. Incomes Policy in Kenya

Arguments in favour of an incomes policy had been in circulation for some years. The aim, it was argued, should be to reduce the gap in incomes between small farmers and the urban employed, and between the educated and the uneducated, and to increase employment. The need for an incomes policy was recognized in the *Development Plan, 1970–74*, where a section was devoted to it (Kenya 1969: 130–40). In the first place, the Plan declared that the government would take firmer control of salaries throughout the public sector (including local authorities and statutory authorities) and would reduce the existing salary differentials. In the private sector the control would be exercised through the Industrial Court, which would operate on the basis of guidelines issued by the government,[15] and would be concerned in its decisions to narrow the gap between the lowest- and the higher-paid workers.

The guidelines for the control of wages as first issued to the Court were tightened up or relaxed from time to time in response to the changing economic situation. They were also affected by political considerations. At the beginning of 1975, with a worsening economic situation, directives

---

[15] The labour legislation had been amended in August 1971 to provide for this form of intervention, but the powers were not utilized before 1973.

were issued to the Court for a more restrictive interpretation of the guidelines.

However, in one of those well-timed populist interventions for which the Kenyatta Era was noted, in May of 1975 the President announced salary increases for workers all over Kenya. He also emphasized that while 'union members are free to negotiate salary increases with the employers without any hindrance ... the Government ban on strikes still stands'. The statement was reported to have been received with jubilation by trade unionists, and COTU at once called off the national strike that had been threatened (*Daily Nation*, 2 May 1975).

The latest instruction to the Court during the period with which we are concerned was issued in February 1979 in the context of a new 'decision' to increases employment. In December 1978 there had been a Presidential announcement that employment would be increased by 10 per cent in 1979. There had been two earlier tripartite agreements, between government, employers, and unions, to increase employment, and during the period of those agreements no wage increases had been allowed. It was recognized that a total wage freeze was now impossible (during the earlier agreements there had not been a rapid rate of price inflation) and the instruction to the Court was that wage increases on average should amount to no more than one-half of the rise in the cost of living (compared with two-thirds in the preceding instruction of 1977), though higher increases should be allowed for the lower paid.

The *Development Plan, 1979–1983* reiterated that it was a major policy of the government to reduce differentials between high and low earned incomes. High differentials were alleged to be the main reason why school-leavers clung to unrealistic employment aspirations and were unwilling to accept the lower-paid jobs. The trade unions were seen as the main protection for the workers, and the lowest-paid would in addition be protected by minimum-wages legislation. These guidelines were to be applied to wages in both the public and private sectors.

At this point it is as well to recall the fact that these arrangements for the implementation of incomes policy are not the only force operating on the wage structure. 'The lot of the trade unionist in Kenya ... is not a happy one,' it has been said (Muir and Brown 1978: 140). The unions are weak, the employers strong, and there is the government to face. 'There is also the problem of unemployment, with a large number of people prepared to fill any vacancies.' With respect to the educational wage structure, the very large increase in the supply of job applicants with secondary education must provide support for the effectiveness of pay policy.

Inequalities of various kinds among urban employees are examined in this study, drawing upon the sample data. For non-urban, non-formal sector, non-wage incomes, the available information is meagre. One analysis of the evidence concludes that: 'between 1971 and 1977 the rural–urban income differential may have fallen by one-third, as real wages declined because of government policy limiting wage settlements and while rural incomes rose because of the coffee boom' (World Bank 1983*b*: 1. para. 121).

Nevertheless, wide differences remain even within the wage sector between urban and rural occupations. In 1980 average wage earnings in agriculture were £215 p.a., in manufacturing they were £742, and in finance and insurance £1488. It might have been expected that the wide gap between rural and urban earnings would cause the urban labour-market to be dominated by an inflow of migrants from the rural areas. Even though there was already unemployment in the towns, potential migrants might think the gap between their incomes and the high urban wage was big enough to make it worth taking the risk of not getting a job. If potential migrants behaved like that, the inflow would exceed the expansion of job opportunities, and urban population and unemployment would be likely to increase rapidly.

The Kenya labour-market does not appear to have worked in that way. The scale of urban unemployment and the informal sector have not been expanding, and Nairobi's population has not been growing explosively.[16] Doubtless, part of the explanation is the narrowing of the rural–urban real-income differential, in relation to the risk aversion of potential migrants, through the government wage controls. But there is another influence on the differential through a mechanism that effectively reduces the urban wage: the 'filtering down' of the educated into lower-paid jobs. As the supply of job applicants with a particular level of education increases relative to the jobs available, applicants accept lower-paid jobs than it was customary in the past for persons with that level of education to occupy—a Form IV secondary school-leaver will be employed in a job which in the past, when there were fewer Form IV-leavers seeking work, was usually performed by a primary school-leaver. This 'filtering down' of the educated into lower-level jobs results in the effective reduction of the wage available to migrants with a particular level of education, and further narrows the urban–rural income differential. This is a process on which a good deal of evidence is presented in subsequent chapters. It will be seen that unrealistic aspirations are not so firmly held as is sometimes suggested.

---

[16] The population of Nairobi has been said to have been growing at perhaps 5% p.a. during the 1970s (World Bank 1983*b*: i. para. 120).

4. The Tanzanian Labour Force

As in Kenya, only a small part of the total labour force of Tanzania is in wage- and salary-employment. The labour force in 1980 numbered around 9.5m. out of a population of 18.7m (World Bank 1982);[17] wage-employment totalled less than 0.5m.[18] A high proportion of those in wage-employment worked in the towns, as in 1977 agriculture and related activities and mining and quarrying accounted for only 26 per cent of the workers employed (Tanzania 1978). A substantial proportion of urban employees were in Dar es Salaam. In 1977 it accounted for 30 per cent of employment outside agriculture and mining (Tanzania 1978). The proportion located in Dar es Salaam had been slowly increasing.[19] and by 1980 it was likely to have been between a third and a half, a large enough proportion to make a survey of the Dar es Salaam labour force of interest in its own right, even if it was not representative of the urban wage-labour force as a whole. It is certain that a high proportion of employees with secondary education is in the towns, and they are probably disproportionately represented in the labour force of Dar es Salaam.

5. Labour Relations and Pay Policy in Tanzania

Trade unions catering for the small wage-labour force in Tanzania existed at the time of Independence. At that time there were some dozen different unions with less than 150 000 members, and an 'umbrella' organization, the Tanganyika Federation of Labour. In 1964, following an army mutiny in which there appeared to be some trade-union implication, the government decided on a drastic reorganization. A single union, the National Union of Tanganyika Workers (NUTA), was established by statute; all existing unions were dissolved and their assets transferred to the new body. The year after its establishment, NUTA affiliated to TANU, the political party of government, and became increasingly subjugated to official party policy.

The Permanent Labour Tribunal was established by the Act of that name in 1967, and was issued with 'guidelines' for its decisions. The

---

[17] The population of working age, defined as 16–64 years, is reported as 51 per cent of total population. In the largely rural economy of Tanzania, the population of working age is likely to be roughly the same as the labour force, though the Bank's definition of working age should not perhaps be taken too literally and is different from that of the Kenyan census (see above). Urban population in 1980 was only 12 per cent of the total.

[18] In 1977 the figure was 474 000 (Tanzania 1978). The total had fluctuated, but there was no strong upward trend; in 1973 it was 473 000. It is to be noted that the survey procedure which produces these figures has been criticized as totally inadequate. See Weinstein 1978.

[19] It had been 20 per cent in 1974.

Tribunal was to be concerned 'to maintain a fair relation between the incomes of different sectors of the community' (Jackson 1979: 233, quoting Act) and 'to establish and maintain reasonable differentials in rewards between different categories of skills and levels of responsibility' (Jackson 1978: 35, quoting Act).

The introduction in 1967 of the machinery of pay policy followed recommendations of an ILO report. This drew attention to the widening rural–urban differential in income and the 'exploitation' of the countryside by the town and to the considerable inequalities among wage employees themselves (International Labour Office 1967: paras 12–19).

Voluntary agreements had to be registered with the Tribunal if they were to be effective. Disputes had to be referred to the Tribunal and its decisions were binding. In effect, strikes and lock-outs were prohibited by these provisions of the Act, replacing in this respect the Trades Disputes (Settlement) Act 1962, which, even before the curbing of unions by the establishment of NUTA, effectively banned strikes.

The Arusha Declaration of 1967, announcing that Tanzania was to take the road to socialism, was followed by the nationalization of companies which became part of the 'parastatal sector'. The nationalization policy was directed particularly at multinational companies, where wage levels were generally a great deal higher than in the rest of the economy. This was one reason why the parastatals were subjected to a stricter incomes policy than the rest of the economy. Also in 1967 the Standing Committee on Parastatal Organizations (SCOPO) was set up with, among other functions, the responsibility to examine the salaries and conditions of service of parastatal employees. One of the early directives of SCOPO severely restricted the fringe benefits provided for employees. They had been generous, being mainly provided for expatriate staff. Most expatriates were to be replaced by locals, and the restrictions were designed to prevent Tanzanians from inheriting the benefits of their predecessors. In another directive, SCOPO laid down incremental scales modelled on those of the Civil Service, for all grades of staff, which interestingly included manual workers. The incremental increases in pay under the scales provided some relief from the strictness of the pay policy. These scales remained unrevised for six years, from 1968 until 1974.

Parastatal wage scales were amended, however, to take account of changes in the legal minimum wage. The existence of this legal minimum has been of importance; it is relatively high. Increases in the minimum have been used to 'take the heat off' the constraints of pay policy in the face of rising prices, in addition to the safety valve of the incremental scales. The constraints of pay policy were further eased by in-service promotions and the reclassification of jobs (World Bank 1977a: 15; Jackson 1979: 247–51).

The potential importance of SCOPO as an instrument of pay policy is shown by the rise in the importance of parastatals. There were 64 in 1967 and by 1975 the number had increased to 142. Employment in parastatals increased by 222 per cent between 1967 and 1977, and the proportion of the total wage bill for which parastatals were responsible increased over that period from 13 per cent to 24 per cent (Jackson 1979: 247–51).

6. *Equality by Exhortation*

In Tanzania, however, in contrast with Kenya, the machinery of pay policy was not assisted in its effectiveness by greatly increased supplies of the educated. The educated and the skilled were scarce, and the effect of this scarcity on the disparity of incomes was well recognized: 'the wage differentials in Tanzania are now out of proportion to any conceivable concept of human equality ... yet we cannot at present greatly reduce this gap because of our shortage of skilled and qualified people'. (Nyerere 1967*b*: 16).

Could nothing be done to resolve this conflict between the claims of equity and the reward for skill and education? One approach was to change the attitudes of the educated to prevent them from seeing themselves as a class apart. Changes in the educational system were a contribution to this approach. In the secondary schools, the system under which it could be said of the pupils, 'they do not learn as they work, they simply learn' (Nyerere 1968*a*: 279) was to be changed. Changes in access to post-secondary education were also to be introduced to diminish the élitist attitude of the students. There was to be a struggle against such attitudes. The effects of incomes policy were backed by an exhortation: 'Let no one base a claim for increased income on the fact that his position has been worsened relative to those below him—for it is our intention that it should be' (Nyerere 1968*a*: 211).

Even though the scarcity of the educated was recognized as responsible for inequality, there was to be no rapid increase in the supply of the educated. Incomes policy was adopted as the road to greater equality, assisted perhaps by political exhortation, but not by large increases in the supply of the educated.

3

Source and Presentation of the Data

The next seven chapters present tables of the data obtained from sample surveys of the educational and labour-market characteristics of wage- and salary-earners in Nairobi and Dar es Salaam. The present chapter provides a brief review of their subject-matter and explanations of how the surveys were conducted and how the data are presented.

The data were obtained from surveys of the wage-labour force in Dar es Salaam and Nairobi at places of employment. First, a sample of establishments (sometimes for brevity called 'Firms' in the tables) stratified by size (number of employees) and sector of productive activity, was randomly drawn from frames maintained by the central statistical bureaus of the two countries. Then within each establishment a random sample of employees was drawn from a complete list of employees provided by the employers. In each country the sample had to be large enough in total for inferences to satisfy tests of statistical significance, and to ensure that when the sample was divided into subgroups by several variables simultaneously the size of the cells would be adequate. It was concluded that a sample size of between 1500 and 2000 would satisfy these requirements. It seemed reasonable to interview more people from larger establishments, but unreasonable to interview more than 60 employees in any single establishment. These considerations, as well as those of time and manpower, indicated the selection of 70 establishments with 2000 employees in total in each city. The employees were interviewed in 1980 at their place of work by university students, trained and led in the field by the research economists conducting the study. The interviewers worked with enthusiasm, and the interviewees were forthcoming in their answers.

The Employee Questionnaire (see Appendix) was printed in both English and Swahili, and the interview was conducted in one or the other language, according to the preference of the interviewee. No difficulty in comprehension arose. The questionnaire ran to 30 pages, with a hundred or so questions and subquestions. The questions were grouped under the following headings:

Personal characteristics
Family background
Education
Earnings
Employment experience in the firm
Previous employment experience
Rural–urban links
Education of children

The questions were pre-coded, in other words all expected answers to each question were listed on the questionnaire form and each assigned a number. The interviewer had simply to tick the relevant number, or write the answer in an 'other' space when it was not one of those specified. The pre-coding greatly facilitated the preparation of the data, reduced the danger of errors in coding, and helped avoid vague and imprecise answers. In addition to the questions asked of all employees in the sample, tests of reasoning ability, literacy and numeracy were administered to a subsample. The results of those tests are embodied in the econometric work reported in a companion book. They are not dealt with in this volume.[1]

Establishments with fewer than five employees were excluded for a purely practical reason: the lists from which a sample of establishments could be drawn did not include them. An establishment-based survey was employed for a number of cogent reasons. In the first place, since the main focus of the research was to be on educated workers, the great majority of whom would be in wage-employment, employing establishments appeared as the natural source of data. Secondly, data on wages and occupations are likely to be more accurate when collected in the employing establishment than when collected in the household. Thirdly, the employer in the establishment can also be a source of data, both as a check on that provided by employees and to supply additional relevant information. Finally, of course, for a given expenditure on the survey, a much larger sample of educated workers could be obtained from establishments than from households. It follows from the fact that the data are obtained from urban estblishments that they refer to those in employment at the time of the surveys. The experience of the unemployed is not reflected in the data, nor that of rural workers or the self-employed.

---

[1] The numbers are generally too small for the relationships to be presented usefully in the form of cross-tabulations. A fuller description of the survey procedures is given in an Appendix of the companion volume, *Education, Productivity, and Inequality*.

The major cities may be said to be important rather than typical with respect to the matters studied.[2] A high proportion of the employed urban labour force is employed in them (more than half the total in Nairobi and about a third in Dar es Salaam); it is probable that they contain a higher proportion of the more highly paid, a higher proportion of migrants from the rest of the country, including the more distant areas, and a higher proportion of the more highly educated than other urban areas. All these characteristics make them of particular importance for the subject of the research.

Chapter 4 gives information on the demographic characteristics and educational attainments of the urban employees who were included in the sample. The unbiased nature of the sampling procedures suggests that the sample characteristics can be accepted as being similar to those of employees in the two cities as a whole. Chapter 4 provides an introduction to the information on education and the labour-market, on the educational and employment relationships between generations, and on education and the links urban employees retain with the rural areas, which is presented in the succeeding chapters. Chapter 4 deals with both countries together, but in the subsequent chapters the data are presented separately, first, in Chapters 5, 6, and 7, for Kenya, and then, in Chapters 8, 9, and 10, for Tanzania.

The tables in Chapters 5 and 8 show the relationships between education, occupation, wages, and inequality, the changes over time in the educational level of those in particular employments, and the accompanying changes in the occupational and educational structure of wages. These topics constitute the central subject-matter of the chapters, which also deal with a number of associated matters, such as the effect on the wage of the type of school attended, the examination results achieved, the size and ownership of the employing firm, and the effect of differences in the number of dependants on the inequality of pay.

In Chapters 6 and 9 the relationships between the education of the employees and that of their parents, on the one hand, and that of their children, on the other, are presented. The purpose of this intergenerational analysis is to determine the relationship between the educational level achieved by one generation and that of the next, so as to throw light on the extent of upward mobility from one generation to another. These chapters also examine the reasons why the employees' education finished when it did, the relationship between the employees' education and their spouses' education, and the employees' expenditure on the education of their children, as depending on their own education and other variables.

---

[2] Though there is evidence from earlier work in Tanzania that Dar es Salaam is acceptably representative of urban areas in respect of relevant wage-employment characteristics (Sabot 1979).

Nairobi and Dar es Salaam are cities whose residents were almost all born elsewhere. Unlike the situation in some developing countries, migration to an urban area does not by any means end migrants' ties to their rural area of origin. The relationships between education, the act of migration, and the results of that migration for the individual and his/her family constitute an important set of issues pertinent to educational policy. How successful are migrants in the Nairobi and Dar es Salaam labour-markets, and how important is their level of education in such success as they have? Do they bring their families with them? What is the nature of post-migration rural–urban links? What part of their earnings do migrants remit to the rural areas? How are such remittances used? Which members of the urban labour force plan to return to the country at a later date? These are among the questions studied in Chapters 7 and 10.

The data in the following chapters are presented in the form of tabulations of the values of variables. Sometimes the tables show percentage distributions of the values, as in Table 4.1, sometimes percentages of particular characteristics, as in Table 4.6, and sometimes means or averages, as in the bottom row of each section of Table 4.3. A number in parentheses below the value shows the size of the sample from which the value derives. Where the results are presented as a distribution the sample size is that of the total distributed; where a percentage is quoted the number in parentheses refers to the number of instances equal to 100 per cent; where the result is presented as a mean, the sample size is that of the number of individual values from which the mean is calculated. The sample size is intended to indicate the reliability of the value derived from the sample as a measure of the true value. No result is presented where the number of observations is five or less. The sign '. .' indicates that a value is not available for this or some other reason. For each table in a chapter on one of the surveys, a table in the corresponding chapter on the other survey is designed to provide the same information. Where it does not, it is generally because one of the surveys provides too few instances. An example is Table 5.20 in which only 30 unskilled and semi-skilled manual workers are employed in public corporations, compared with 223 in Table 8.20. The heading of a table attempts to describe its content as fully as possible. Many headings are complex and need to be read with great care if the meaning of the table is to be fully appreciated. Although the names of the countries are frequently used in the text and in the table headings when the reference is to survey data, they are simply shorthand for 'the sample of wage-labour in the major city of Kenya/Tanzania'.

4

Demographic and Educational Characteristics of Employees in Nairobi and Dar es Salaam

This is the first of the chapters which present the results of the two surveys. It consists, as do the others, of a commentary followed by tables. In this chapter, as distinct from the following six chapters, each of which deals with one of the countries alone, there is a general review of the characteristics of both sample populations as a background to the data in the subsequent chapters.

Table 4.1 shows that the Kenya sample is composed of Africans to the extent of 95 per cent. Asians account for only 4 per cent and Europeans for 1 per cent. Table 4.2 shows a very similar pattern for Tanzania, the corresponding figures being 97 per cent, 3 per cent and less than 1 per cent. Men constitute 87 per cent of the sample of Africans and 75 per cent of Asians in Kenya, and 86 per cent of both Africans and Asians in Tanzania. The predominance of Africans means that in most tabulations non-Africans are too few in number for it to be either statistically legitimate or necessary to make a racial distinction. Similarly, in most tabulations there are too few women for it to be statistically legitimate to show them separately from the males.

The samples indicate (Table 4.3) that in both countries the labour force is young: fewer than half are over the age of 30; the mean age for Kenyan Africans is barely 32 years, with African women being about $3\frac{1}{2}$ years younger, and Asians $1\frac{1}{2}$ years older. Tanzanians in the sample are marginally younger than the Kenyans.

In each country, only 1 per cent of African employees are not citizens. But 29 per cent of those of other races are not citizens in Kenya, whereas the corresponding figure in Tanzania is only 5 per cent. Of the citizens 97 per cent are Africans in both countries, and of the non-citizens 45 per cent are Africans in Kenya and 81 per cent in Tanzania. African citizen

Table 4.1. *Kenyan Employees by Sex and Race: Distribution by Race and Sex*

	Male	Female	All
Distribution by race			
African	96	91	95
Asian	4	7	4
European	<1	2	1
	(1528)	(250)	(1778)
Distribution by sex			
African	87	13	(1697)
Asian	75	25	(72)

Table 4.2. *Tanzanian Employees by Sex and Race: Distribution by Race and Sex*

	Male	Female	All
Distribution by race			
African	97	97	97
Asian	3	3	3
European	<1	<1	<1
	(1505)	(248)	(1753)
Distribution by sex			
African	86	14	(1692)
Asian	86	14	(59)

Table 4.3. *Employees by Country, Race, and Sex: Distribution by Age; Mean Age*

Age (years)	African			Asian All	All
	Male	Female	All		
Kenya					
15–20	4	8	4 ⎤		4
21–25	22	28	22 ⎜		22
26–30	26	39	28 ⎬ 61		28
31–35	19	14	19 ⎦		18
36 and over	29	11	27	39	28
Mean age	32.4	28.2	31.9	33.5	31.9
	(1450)	(227)	(1676)	(71)	(1764)
Tanzania					
15–20	4	10	5	2	5
21–25	21	32	23	29	23
26–30	26	31	27	22	27
31–35	21	17	20	13	20
36 and over	28	10	25	34	25
Mean age	31.9	27.7	31.3	33.1	31.3
	(1433)	(237)	(1670)	(59)	

employees are overwhelmingly, to the extent of 90 per cent in Kenya and 82 per cent in Tanzania, migrants from outside the city. Women are rather less predominantly migrants than males, but even so more than 80 per cent of them in Kenya and more than three-quarters in Tanzania are migrants. In Kenya the migrants are older than the non-migrants. Whereas half of the migrant men and three-quarters of the migrant women are aged 30 or less, for non-migrants the proportions are, respectively, 73 per cent and 80 per cent (Table 4.4). In contrast, in Tanzania the age distribution of migrants to the city is not significantly different from that of other employees (Table 4.5).

In both Kenya and Tanzania, more than 90 per cent of married employees have children. The average number of children for men is nearly 4 in Kenya and more than 3 in Tanzania, and in both countries it is a little under 3 for women. Of those never married, 6 per cent of the men and 54 per cent of the women have children in Kenya, the corresponding figures for Tanzania being 15 and 40 per cent (Table 4.6).

For all age-groups taken together, the members of the sample have in Kenya an average of 4.2 and in Tanzania 3.2 wives and children dependent on them. For employees older then 50 the number supported is more than 6 in Tanzania and nearly $8\frac{1}{2}$ in Kenya. However, the number of persons supported by an employee, including the other dependants, is on average considerably greater than the number of wives and children supported. For all ages it is nearly 6 in Tanzania and more than 7 in Kenya. For those aged 41–50 the number supported is over 8 in Tanzania and over 10 in Kenya (Table 4.7).

In summary, the tables show that in each country urban employees are to an overwhelming extent composed of young, male Africans who are migrants to the city. There are hardly any African employees who are not citizens but approaching a third of the non-African employees are not citizens in Kenya whereas in Tanzania very few are not citizens. Very few married employees do not have children while a substantial proportion of those who have never been married, particularly among the women, do have children. Employees with no children are predominantly in the younger age-groups. The number of wives and children supported is quite large—more than 6 for the over-40s—and the number of persons supported is even larger. The picture of the educational attainment of the labour force which it is possible to draw from the results of the surveys is displayed in the tables which follow.

Table 4.8 reflects the increase in education over time and shows striking differences between the level of education of the employees in the samples and that of their parents. The difference is particularly notable in the proportion with no education and with secondary education. There is an important difference between Nairobi and Dar es Salaam shown in

Table 4.4. *Kenyan African Citizen Employees by Migrant Status, Sex, and Age: Distribution by Migrant Status, Age; Mean Age*

Age (years)	Migrant			Non-migrant			All
	Male	Female	Total	Male	Female	Total	
Distribution by migrant status							
15–20	76	84	78	24	16	22	(65)
21–25	87	74	85	13	26	15	(369)
26–30	89	86	89	11	14	12	(454)
31–35	94	83	93	6	17	7	(304)
36–40	95	93	95	5	7	5	(165)
41–45	96	..	96	4	..	5	(115)
46–50	96	..	96	4	..	4	(94)
51 and over	96	..	94	4	..	6	(60)
All	91	82	90	9	18	10	(1626)
Distribution by age							
15–20	3	8	4	9	7	9	9
21–25	21	25	21	32	42	34	34
26–30	26	41	28	32	31	32	32
31–35	20	15	19	13	14	13	13
36–40	11	6	11	6	2	5	5
41–45	8	3	8	4	0	3	3
46–50	7	0	6	2	0	2	2
51 and over	4	2	4	2	4	2	2
Mean age	32.78	28.48	32.25	28.40	27.79	28.25	31.84
	(1279)	(181)	(1461)	(126)	(39)	(165)	(1626)

Table 4.5. *Tanzanian African Citizen Employees by Migrant Status, Sex, and Age: Distribution by Migrant Status, Age; Mean Age*

Age (years)	Migrant			Non-migrant			All	(F)	(M)
	Male	Female	Total	Male	Female	Total			
Distribution by migrant status									
15–20	72	40	63	28	60	37		(58)	(24)
21–25	81	72	79	19	28	21		(297)	(75)
26–30	87	84	87	13	16	13		(361)	(71)
31–35	82	85	82	18	15	18		(295)	(40)
36–40	85	92	85	15	8	15		(175)	(13)
41–45	81	..	83	19	..	17		(79)	
46–50	81	..	80	19	..	20		(71)	
51 and over	77	..	77	23	..	23		(49)	
All	83	76	82	17	24	18		(1385)	(232)
Distribution by age									
15–20	4	5	4	7	26	10	5		
21–25	21	30	22	23	38	26	23		
26–30	27	34	28	19	21	20	27		
31–35	21	20	21	22	10	20	21		
36–40	13	7	12	11	2	10	12		
41–45	5	3	5	6	0	5	5		
46–50	5	1	5	6	3	5	4		
51 and over	3	0	3	5	0	4	3		
Mean age	31.88 (1148)	28.34 (175)	31.41 (1324)	31.97 (237)	25.62 (56)	30.76 (294)	31.29 (1618)		

Table 4.6. *Employees by Country, Sex, and Marital Status: Percentage with Children; Mean Number of Children*

	Males		Females	
	Never married	Married	Never married	Married
Kenya				
% with children	6	92	54	91
Mean number of children	0.22	3.95	1.18	2.93
	(305)	(1188)	(108)	(130)
Tanzania				
% with children	15	91	40	91
Mean number of children	0.34	3.33	0.88	2.74
	(445)	(1032)	(111)	(119)

Note: Married includes widowed, divorced, separated.

Table 4.7. *Employees by Country and Age: Mean Number of Wives and Children and of Persons Supported*

Age	Kenya		Tanzania	
	Wives and children supported	Persons supported	Wives and children supported	Persons supported
15–20	0.64	3.77	0.27	2.75
	(74)		(81)	(79)
21–30	2.44		1.80	4.65
	(873)	(866)	(851)	(840)
31–40	5.46	8.37	4.39	6.83
	(499)	(493)	(536)	(533)
41–50	8.16	10.23	6.28	8.39
	(225)	(221)	(176)	(174)
51+	8.39	9.68	6.08	7.21
	(69)	(69)	(55)	(55)
All	4.20	7.21	3.15	5.72
	(1740)	(1723)	(1699)	(1681)

Table 4.8. *Employees, Their Fathers and Their Mothers by Country: Distribution by Education*

Country and education	Employees			Employees' fathers	Employees' mothers
	All	Males	Females		
Kenya	7	7	4	58	76
None	43	45	26	33	21
Primary	39	37	56	7	2
Secondary, I–IV	11	11	14	2	1
Post-Form IV	(1765)	(1513)	(251)	(1765)	(1770)
Tanzania	10	11	5	45	71
None	52	54	39	47	28
Primary	27	24	47	7	1
Secondary, I–IV	11	11	9	1	0
Post-Form IV	(1760)	(1506)	(254)	(1715)	(1733)

Table 4.8: the Nairobi parents were less educated than those in Dar es Salaam—58 per cent uneducated fathers compared with 45 per cent, and 33 per cent primary-educated compared with 47 per cent—whereas the Nairobi employees are more educated than those in Dar es Salaam—39 per cent Forms I–IV compared with 27 per cent.

The proportion of employees in Kenya with no education, it can be seen from Table 4.9, rises with age from the 15–20 age-group, where it is zero, to the 41-and-over group, where it is 21 per cent. The proportion with post-primary education falls with age: it is 72 per cent for the 15–20s and only 18 per cent for those aged over 40.

In Tanzania (Table 4.10) only 2 per cent of employees in the 21–5 age-group, but 31 per cent in the 41-and-over group have no education. In fact, among the over-50s the proportion with no education is as high as 45 per cent. The proportion completing primary education declines with age, from 61 per cent in the youngest group to only 10 per cent among the over-40s. The proportion with post-primary education is 46 per cent for the 21–5s and only 22 per cent for the over-40s. It is also relatively low for the youngest age-group, which includes employees who are too young to have received education beyond primary school. The proportion with no education is slightly higher in this 15–20 group than in the older group.

Although these general conclusions apply both to men and women (the small numbers in the sample of women aged over 35 makes a full comparison impossible), in both countries there is a notably higher proportion of women with post-primary education than of men in every

Table 4.9. *Kenyan Employees by Age and Sex: Distribution by Education; Mean Years of Education*

Sex and education	Age						All
	15–20	21–5	26–30	31–5	36–40	41 and over	
All employees							
None	0	3	3	3	8	21	7
Primary	28	28	35	46	66	60	42
[Primary 7–8]	[24]	[20]	[25]	[32]	[43]	[20]	[26]
Post-primary	72			51	26	18	51
Mean years	9.7	9.3	9.2	9.0	7.4	5.1	8.3
	(75)	(389)	(495)	(324)	(182)	(296)	(1765)
Males							
None	0	4	4	2	8	21	7
Primary	25	30	37	49	67	61	45
[Primary 7–8]	[21]	[22]	[27]	[34]	[43]	[20]	[28]
Post-primary	75	66	59	49	25	17	48
Mean years	10.0	9.1	9.1	8.9	7.3	5.2	8.1
	(52)	(319)	(394)	(287)	(170)	(283)	(1513)
Females							
None	0	0	0	14	19		4
Primary	34	17	28	21	43		26
[Primary 7–8]	[34]	[10]	[20]	[16]	[24]		[18]
Post-primary	66	83	72	65	38		70
Mean years	8.8	10.5	9.6	9.1	6.2		9.4
	(19)	(70)	(101)	(37)	(21)		(251)

Note: [Primary 7–8] included in primary.

age-group (except the youngest in Kenya). For female employees of all ages, those with post-primary education constitute as much as 70 per cent of the total in Kenya, compared with 48 per cent for men. In Tanzania the corresponding figures are 55 per cent and 35 per cent.

The higher educational attainments of female than of male employees is in remarkable contrast with the lower education of women in the population as a whole. In Kenya, for instance, although by 1980 girls had almost achieved parity with boys in most primary school standards, in secondary school they remained well behind, with only 40 per cent of the enrolment. And this enrolment in both kinds of school was a great increase from the very small representation of girls in the past. The limited extent of female education until recently is indicated by the fact that, in 1976, 35 per cent of the male population was illiterate, and 69 per cent of the female.

Demographic, Educational Characteristics

Table 4.10. *Tanzanian Employees by Age and Sex: Distribution by Education; Mean Years of Education*

Sex and education	Age						All
	15–20	21–5	26–30	31–5	36–40	41 and over	
All employees							
None	5	2	6	9	16	31	10
Primary	68	52	55	46	56	47	52
[Primary 7–8]	[61]	[40]	[42]	[25]	[18]	[10]	[32]
Post-primary	27	46	39	45	28	22	38
Mean years	7.5	8.4	8.2	8.7	6.5	5.0	7.7
	(86)	(403)	(466)	(347)	(199)	(234)	(1737)
Males							
None	7	3	7	9	16	31	11
Primary	73	56	57	47	56	49	54
[Primary 7–8]	[65]	[42]	[43]	[24]	[18]	[11]	[32]
Post-primary	20	41	36	44	28	20	35
Mean years	6.9	8.2	8.1	8.5	6.5	4.9	7.5
	(62)	(317)	(391)	(308)	(186)	(224)	(1487)
Female							
None	0	0	3	7	25		5
Primary	56	37	43	40	20		40
[Primary 7–8]	[49]	[32]	[35]	[32]	[8]		[33]
Post-primary	44	63	54	53	55		55
Mean years	9.0	9.3	9.0	9.6	7.1		9.0
	(24)	(86)	(75)	(40)	(24)		(250)

In both Kenya and Tanzania the period of education is longer for the younger than for the older employees, but in both age-groups Asians on average have had substantially longer education than Africans. This is also true for both sexes. Moreover, for both Africans and Asians, women have more years of education than men. The same relationships are shown in the distribution by level of education. Asians have more education than Africans: they have a lower percentage with no education and a much higher percentage with post-primary education (Table 4.11).

Table 4.12 shows that African employees who are migrants to Nairobi, in total and in each age-group except 31–5, are less educated than those born in the city: a higher proportion have no more than Standard 6 primary school education. In Dar es Salaam it is the other way round, migrants being more educated than employees native to the city. The differential in favour of migrants is particularly wide in the oldest age-

Table 4.11. *Employees by Country and Ethnic Group: Mean Years of Education by Age and Sex; Distribution by Education*

	Kenya		Tanzania	
	African	Asian	African	Asian
Mean years of education by age and sex				
15–30 years	9.2	13.1	8.1	11.4
31 years and over	7.0	10.6	6.9	9.5
Males	8.2	11.7	7.4	10.5
Females	9.2	12.2	8.9	10.7
All	8.2	11.9	7.6	10.5
Distribution by level of education				
None	7	0	10	3
Primary	44	17	54	22
Secondary Forms I–IV	40	28	31	55
Post-Form IV	9	55	5	20
	(1697)	(72)	(1686)	(59)

group. In both countries, the majority of migrants had completed their education before migrating, though the percentage declines through the educational hierarchy (Table 4.13).

The proportion of employees who attended a government primary school is much higher for the younger than for the older age-groups: 87 per cent for the 15–20s compared with 55 per cent for the over-40s in Kenya; 96 per cent for the 15–20s compared with 51 per cent for those over 35 in Tanzania (Table 4.14). Almost all (90 per cent) of those whose primary school was not a government school attended a mission school. The proportion attending a government secondary school is smaller than that attending a government primary school; it shows no particular variation with age in Kenya but declines with age in Tanzania. Non-government secondary schools are predominantly *private* schools, run as businesses not charitable institutions, though *harambee* or self-help schools are important for Africans in Kenya.

A very high proportion of those who had been to private and *harambee* schools in Kenya 'dropped out' before reaching Form IV, and a very small proportion reached Form VI. The pattern is the same for the Tanzanian sample, the drop-out rate being much higher from private than from government schools, though not as high as from private and *harambee* schools in Kenya. By this test the government schools performed better than the others, though the high cost of private schools may well

Table 4.12. *African Employees by Country, Age, and Migrant Status: Distribution by Education*

Country, education and migrant status	Age				All
	15–25	26–30	31–5	36 and over	
Kenya					
None					
Migrant	4	4	4	16	7
Non-migrant	0	0	0	15	3
Primary 1–6					
Migrant	9	11	13	35	18
Non-migrant	0	7	24	25	8
Primary 7–8					
Migrant	23	27	33	30	28
Non-migrant	8	27	28	45	22
Post-primary					
Migrant	64	58	50	19	47
Non-migrant	92	66	48	15	67
	(362)	(413)	(286)	(418)	(1484)
	(69)	(54)	(21)	(20)	(167)
Tanzania					
None					
Migrant	3	5	8	23	10
Non-migrant	4	7	13	41	14
Primary 1–6					
Migrant	12	14	19	36	20
Non-migrant	11	11	31	43	23
Primary 7–8					
Migrant	45	43	26	13	33
Non-migrant	43	50	23	10	33
Post-primary					
Migrant	40	38	47	28	37
Non-migrant	42	32	33	6	30
	(348)	(378)	(280)	(326)	(1337)
	(110)	(56)	(59)	(69)	(299)

have been the explanation for the departure of their pupils before they had completed the course (Table 4.15).

In most age-groups the number of dependants, both of wives and children and of all dependants, increases with education up to Standards 5–8 and then declines (Table 4.16).

In summary, the tables show the following in both countries: the young

Table 4.13. *African Migrant Educated Employees by Country, Age, and Education: Percentage Completing Education Before Migration*

Country and education	Age				All
	15–25	26–30	31–5	36 and over	
Kenya					
Primary 1–6	91	91	95	94	93
Primary 7–8	86	84	87	90	87
Post-primary	77	68	59	87	71
Tanzania					
Primary 1–6	83	81	75	65	88
Primary 7–8	69	69	73	68	69
Post-primary	60	64	62	64	63

Table 4.14. *Employees by Country, Age, and Type of School: Percentage who Attended Government School*

Country and type of school	Age					
	15–20	21–25	26–30	31–5	36–40	41 and over
Kenya						
Primary	87	88	90	84	67	55
	(74)	(369)	(463)	(311)	(156)	(260)
Secondary	62	60	64	59	68	71
	(52)	(259)	(297)	(160)	(37)	(37)
Tanzania						
Primary	96	89	68	53	51	51
	(80)	(381)	(433)	(306)	(149)	(147)
Secondary	72	69	68	68	60	51
	(21)	(181)	(175)	(153)	(53)	(45)

Table 4.15. *Employees by Country and Type of Secondary School Attended: Distribution by Highest Form Reached*

Highest form reached	Kenya			Tanzania	
	Government	*Harambee*	Private	Government	Private
Below Form IV	14	53	43	11	32
Form IV	61	44	50	59	53
Form VI	25	3	7	30	15
	(499)	(141)	(180)	(402)	(184)

Table 4.16. Employees by Country, Age, and Education: Mean Number of Wives and Children and of Persons Supported

Education	Age					
	21–30		31–40		41–50	
	Wives and children	Persons	Wives and children	Persons	Wives and children	Persons
Kenya						
None	2.43	4.78 (29)	7.16	9.12 (23)	8.46	10.16 (31)
Standards 1–4	2.59	5.45 (29)	6.16	8.33 (42)	8.53	10.33 (57)
Standards 5–6	3.22	6.42 (49)	5.69	7.89 (44)	10.00	11.96 (34)
Standards 7–8	3.14	6.52 (200)	6.00	8.73 (179)	8.40	10.64 (55)
Forms I–IV	2.30	5.91 (443)	4.88	8.62 (171)	6.88	9.56 (38)
Post-Form IV	1.45	4.80 (123)	3.56	5.84 (40)	2.67	4.31 (10)
All	2.44	5.87 (873)	5.46	8.37 (499)	8.16	10.23 (225)
Tanzania						
None	2.38	4.86 (36)	4.32	5.71 (60)	5.67	7.51 (49)
Standards 1–4	2.39	5.10 (70)	4.44	6.44 (99)	5.60	8.39 (37)
Standards 5–6	2.60	7.08 (34)	5.19	7.28 (47)	7.05	10.17 (26)
Standards 7–8	2.10	5.01 (351)	4.54	7.26 (120)	7.56	9.01 (19)
Forms I–IV	1.35	4.31 (261)	4.34	7.07 (134)	7.19	8.67 (34)
Post-Form IV	0.94	2.84 (87)	3.75	6.82 (73)	3.65	5.50 (8)
All	1.80	4.65 (841)	4.39	6.82 (533)	6.29	8.40 (174)

are more educated than the old, the women than the men, Asians than Africans, and employees than their parents. A much higher proportion of the young than of the old were educated at government schools. The major difference in the two samples is the higher educational level of employees in Nairobi compared with those in Dar es Salaam.

Educational Attainment and the Urban Labour-Market in Kenya

Chapter 4 documented the rise in the educational level of the urban wage-labour force in Nairobi. In effect, it provided information on the changing supply of educated labour. The present chapter turns to the demand side of the equation, bringing the demand for educated labour into relation with that supply. It may be read as describing the result of supply increasing to a greater extent than demand.

This chapter answers a range of questions about the effect of the greater expansion in the supply of, than in the demand for, educated labour. What is the educational level of the labour force in relation to its occupational structure? What does a survey at a particular time of cohorts who entered employment at different dates show about changes that have occurred over time? For instance, has 'filtering down', the process observed in other countries by which over time persons with a given level of education take up jobs lower in the hierarchy of occupations, occurred in Nairobi? Putting it the other way around, has the educational level of those in any given occupation risen over time? How has the relationship between education and wages altered? Has the inequality in the educational structure of wages changed? It is possible that the increased supply of educated labour has reduced the reward for education, narrowing the gap between the pay of the educated and the uneducated, and between that of the more and the less educated. Such narrowing may have occurred either as a result of the operation of competitive forces in the labour-market or as a result of the more educated filtering down into lower-paid jobs, if the labour-market is characterized by occupational wage rigidity. Whatever the mechanism, has there been a reduction in the educational inequality of the pay of the wage-labour force in Nairobi? These are some of the many questions about the relationship between education and the labour-market which can be asked of the data presented in this chapter. And in the course of considering such questions a number of other issues are examined.

Section A presents evidence on the existing relationship between the educational level of employees and the size of their wage, as it is affected by seniority in the firm and in the labour force. It also deals with such related matters as the effect of the type of school attended, examination results, and the ownership of the employing firm on the wage, as well as the extent to which wage inequality is altered by overtime and bonus payments, non-monetary remuneration, and the number of dependants. It is a cross-section analysis providing a picture of the situation at the time of the survey.

Changes over time are introduced by means of the analysis of different entry-cohorts. Section B is concerned with filtering down over time in the relationship between level of education and occupation, a hierarchy of occupations having been defined for this purpose. The order is from unskilled manual work at the bottom to professional employment at the top. The ordering conforms broadly to accepted ideas of 'higher' and 'lower' occupations, and serves its purpose, though with such wide categories there is room for argument about the place of some particular jobs. Section C looks at the effect of filtering down on the relative wages paid in different occupations.

The role of education in recruitment is dealt with in section D, including the relationship between level of education, on the one hand, and length of job-search and method of recruitment, on the other. The employees' own perceptions of their qualifications for employment are examined in section E. Section F is concerned with the training provided by employers to recruits and during the course of employment, and looks at training in relation to education, occupation, and wage.

In section G, data are given on job mobility, relating it to education and to other characteristics of the employee and employer. Finally, the results of the analysis are summarized with comments in section H.

A. The Relationship between Education, Occupation, Wages, and Inequality

Table 5.1 deals with the educational structure of wages. It sets the scene for analysis of the relationship between education and the labour-market. It shows, first of all, the close relationship between the level of education of an employee and his or her wage, and the resulting highly unequal educational distribution of wages. A monthly wage of Shs 750 or less is received by as many as 83 per cent of uneducated employees. A smaller proportion of employees at successively higher levels of education falls into this wage-group. The proportion drops sharply to 65 per cent for those with education in the first four classes of primary school, and again

Table 5.1. Kenyan Employees by Education: Distribution by Wage; Mean Wage by Sex

Wage (Shs per month)	Education					
	None	Standards 1–4	Standards 5–6	Standards 7–8	Forms I–IV	Post-Form IV
0–750	83	65	65	50	30	1
751–1000	11	18	17	22	18	9
1001–1500	5	10	12	15	21	17
1501 and over	1	7	6	13	31	73
Mean	649	801	746	985	1422	3238
Mean (males)	664	816	780	978	1386	3404
Mean (females)	483	578	360	1056	1571	2549
(All)	(118)	(154)	(133)	(459)	(688)	(186)
(Females)	(10)	(10)	(11)	(45)	(136)	(36)

sharply from 50 per cent for employees with complete primary education to 30 per cent for those with Forms I–IV of secondary education, and to a mere 1 per cent for those with education beyond that. At the upper end of the wage distribution, the proportion receiving more than Shs 1500 jumps from 13 per cent to 31 per cent and 73 per cent for increases in education from Standards 7–8 to Forms I–IV and beyond that. The same story is told by the figures for the average wage of each educational group. Standards 7–8 education brings a marked increase over the wage of those with less education, but there are even sharper increases for secondary education, particularly for education beyond Form IV, for which group the mean wage is more than three times that received by employees who did not go beyond primary school.

The relation between education and occupation is clearly evident in Table 5.2. the average years of education of the employees in the different occupations increases consistently through the order in which the occupations are listed. Although unskilled manual workers have on average, perhaps surprisingly, nearly $5\frac{1}{2}$ years of education, professional employees have two and a half times that. Only in manual occupations are there workers who are entirely without education, and a significant number only in unskilled manual jobs.

A rather high proportion (24 per cent) of unskilled workers have secondary education. Rising through the hierarchy of occupations there is a sharp increase in the proportion of employees with more than primary education, from 30 per cent for skilled manual workers to just short of 80 per cent for clerical and secretarial employees.

Table 5.3 provides a justification for the occupational classification: the distribution of wages shifts upwards through the hierarchy of occupations. The proportion receiving a monthly wage of not more than Shs 750 declines through the hierarchy from 86 per cent for unskilled manual employees to 68 per cent, 42 per cent, 14 per cent, and so on. Correspondingly the proportion receiving more than Shs 1500 rises through the hierarchy, though professional employees do less well than managers and administrators.

The longer the time spent in employment, the higher the wage (Table 5.4). Much the same is true for long service with the current employer. The average wage for employees with no more than four years of education, but with between 8 and 14 years of employment, is greater than that of employees with Standards 7–8 education and less than 4 years of employment experience. Employees with no more than 4 years of education but 15 or more years of wage-employment average a higher wage than recent recruits with Forms I–IV secondary education. The premium paid for experience increases with education and through the hierarchy of occupations. Length of employment experience is evidently a very important influence on the employee's wage.

Table 5.2. *Kenyan Employees by Occupation: Distribution by Education; Mean Years of Education*

Occupation	Mean years of education	Education					
		None	Standards 1–4	Standards 5–6	Standards 7–8	Forms I–IV	Post-Form IV
Manual							
Unskilled	5.43	24	14	12	26	24	0 (321)
Semi-skilled	6.17	9	23	13	30	25	0 (290)
Skilled	7.27	4	11	12	43	28	2 (410)
Clerical and secretarial	10.37	0	1	1	19	67	12 (564)
Technical and semi-professional	11.23	0	1	5	14	44	36 (52)
Managerial and administrative	12.16	0	0	0	13	44	43 (49)
Professional	13.56	0	0	0	2	11	87 (93)
All	8.31	7	9	8	26	39	11 (1780)

Table 5.3. *Kenyan Employees by Occupation: Distribution by Wage; Mean Wage by Sex*

Wage (Shs per month)	Occupation							All
	Manual, unskilled	Manual, semi-skilled	Manual, skilled	Clerical and secretarial	Technical and semi-professional	Managerial and administrative	Professional	
0–750	86	68	42	14	15	0	0	41
751–1000	10	16	27	19	6	3	12	18
1001–1500	3	13	18	27	3	1	10	16
Over 1500	1	3	13	40	76	96	78	25
Mean	598	698	1301	1622	2229	3918	3890	1399
Mean (males)	604	731	1309	1570	2220	3965	4229	1384
Mean (females)	545	447	..	1758	..	..	2617	1486
(All)	(312)	(286)	(403)	(559)	(48)	(45)	(85)	(1728)
(Females)	(31)	(40)	..	(154)	..	..	(18)	(246)

Table 5.4. *Kenyan Employees by Occupation, Education, and Years of Employ-ment Experience: Mean Wage (Shs per month)*

Occupation and education	Years of employment experience				All
	0–3	4–7	8–14	15 and over	
All manual					
None	510	643	624	630	609
	(16)	(10)	(11)	(53)	(90)
Standards 1–6	513	530	635	905	753
	(30)	(33)	(55)	(141)	(261)
Standards 7–8	582	697	789	998	783
	(69)	(66)	(112)	(87)	(334)
Forms I–IV	660	787	899	1637	808
	(111)	(71)	(57)	(15)	(254)
All	610	705	782	940	776
	(228)	(182)	(237)	(300)	(948)
Clerical and secretarial					
Standards 7–8	734	1258	1063	1964	1424
	(11)	(19)	(33)	(42)	(105)
Forms I–IV	997	1265	1765	2371	1606
	(78)	(94)	(147)	(56)	(374)
Post-Form IV	2213	1829	2694	..	2116
	(29)	(27)	(9)		(66)
All	1271	1360	1673	2134	1620
	(118)	(141)	(192)	(106)	(558)
Other non-manual					
Forms I–IV	..	2294	2893	4182	3185
		(11)	(24)	(17)	(53)
Post-Form IV	2560	3685	4634	5004	3707
	(33)	(37)	(23)	(13)	(107)
All	2523	3349	3393	4377	3415
	(35)	(49)	(54)	(37)	(175)
All					
None	510	643	624	630	609
	(16)	(10)	(11)	(53)	(90)
Standards 1–4	502	489	646	912	786
	(13)	(14)	(27)	(93)	(147)
Standards 5–6	530	545	610	973	746
	(19)	(21)	(34)	(57)	(132)
Standards 7–8	634	825	865	1411	979
	(81)	(85)	(149)	(134)	(450)
Forms I–IV	799	1152	1671	2745	1432
	(190)	(179)	(228)	(88)	(685)
Post-Form IV	2368	2866	3924	6093	3222
	(64)	(66)	(34)	(19)	(183)
All	990	1306	1428	1621	1352
	(384)	(375)	(483)	(445)	(1688)

Table 5.5. *Kenyan Employees by Occupation and Education: Mean Wage, Overtime, and Bonus (Shs per month)*

	Wage	Overtime	Bonus	Total
Occupation				
Manual	598	41	6	645
Unskilled	(310)	(287)	(312)	
	698	64	9	771
Semi-skilled	(286)	(263)	(283)	
	1301	86	3	1390
Skilled	(401)	(373)	(407)	
	1622	55	18	1695
Clerical and secretarial	(553)	(514)	(540)	
	2229	30	31	2290
Technical and semi-professional	(48)	(45)	(47)	
	3918	148	4	4070
Managerial and administrative	(45)	(43)	(47)	
	3890	68	47	4005
Professional	(85)	(85)	(78)	
Education				
None	649	26	6	681
Standards 1–4	801	90	9	900
Standards 5–6	746	79	6	831
Standards 7–8	985	55	11	1051
Forms I–IV	1422	63	12	1497
Post-Form IV	3238	77	25	3340

Table 5.4 also shows a consistent, increasing relationship between the wage and the occupation for each level of education, and between the wage and the level of education in a particular occupation.

Payments for overtime and annual bonus widen the earnings differential within the manual grades, and somewhat narrow it between the manual and non-manual and within the non-manual grades, but the effect is small. These payments do nothing to narrow the differential paid for education (Table 5.5).

Direct monetary payments are not the only form of employee compensation. Other benefits are provided by employers which may be neutral with respect to the education level of the employee, or they may reinforce or offset the association between wages and education. Table 5.6 shows the extent to which the employer provides free or subsidized benefits in addition to the wage. There is a fairly clear tendency for the percentage of employees receiving most of these various benefits to rise with the level of education. They tend to add to, rather than offset, the positive relation between education and the wage.

Table 5.6a. *Kenyan Employees by Education, All Occupations: Percentage Receiving Various Benefits from Employer*

Benefit	Education						All
	1	2	3	4	5	6	
Annual bonus	22	26	20	16	16	18	18
	(115)	(153)	(127)	(440)	(667)	(172)	(1678)
Paid annual leave	63	73	71	78	88	95	81
	(119)	(152)	(133)	(456)	(685)	(184)	(1734)
Rations	6	8	10	6	6	8	7
	(119)	(158)	(133)	(463)	(696)	(187)	(1761)
Medical treatment	40	42	46	55	68	70	59
	(117)	(157)	(132)	(464)	(692)	(186)	(1754)
Transport	18	12	21	11	9	12	11
	(117)	(154)	(127)	(453)	(689)	(188)	(1734)
NSSF	64	71	69	69	74	78	72
	(113)	(153)	(131)	(453)	(681)	(184)	(1720)
Pension, other	18	17	21	29	38	48	32
	(113)	(150)	(129)	(449)	(670)	(181)	(1698)
Loans	56	52	47	45	53	65	52
	(114)	(154)	(125)	(444)	(635)	(159)	(1635)

Note: 1: None; 2: Standards 1–4; 3: Standards 5–6; 4: Standards 7–8; 5: Forms I–IV; 6: Post-Form IV

There is also a tendency for the proportion receiving these benefits to rise through the hierarchy of occupations, just as it rises with the wage. There is a general tendency for the provision of benefits to skilled manual workers to rise with the level of education, but the relationship is less strong with clerical employees. In fact, the wide extent to which benefits are provided is a more striking feature of this table than the extent to which they are provided differentially to the higher paid and better educated.

The provision of some benefits in addition to the wage varies substantially in extent with the type of ownership of the firm. For instance, the payment of an annual bonus is virtually confined to the private sector, whereas medical treatment is provided to a much smaller extent by private than by other employers.

Table 5.1 is informative about the relative wages of men and women. Although for most levels of education men are paid substantially more than women, that relationship is reversed for those with education at the level of Standards 7–8 and Forms I–IV.

Table 5.8 provides some explanation of the higher wage for women by

Table 5.6b. *Kenyan Employees by Education, Particular Occupations: Percentage Receiving Various Benefits from Employer*

Benefit	Education						All
	1	2	3	4	5	6	
Skilled manual							
Annual bonus	26	20	19	6	6	0	10
Paid annual leave	61	75	89	78	88	86	81
Rations	0	4	5	3	2	5	3
Medical treatment	63	35	70	63	78	100	66
Transport	10	1	9	7	3	0	5
NSSF	50	54	75	59	69	24	62
Pension, other	33	18	25	28	28	80	28
Loans	50	41	49	37	39	66	40
	(17–18)	(40–43)	(43–47)	(168–176)	(105–115)	(9)	(386–409)
Clerical/Secretarial							
Annual Bonus	..	..	..	24	15	15	17
Paid annual leave	..	..	95	90	93	100	93
Rations	..	..	5	5	5	13	6
Medical treatment	..	..	16	61	72	85	70
Transport	..	..	5	11	9	8	9
NSSF	..	..	100	75	78	88	78
Pension, other	..	..	17	44	49	64	49
Loans	..	..	53	62	60	66	61
			(7–8)	(95–105)	(345–379)	(51–66)	(502–562)

Note: 1: None; 2: Standards 1–4; 3: Standards 5–6; 4: Standards 7–8; 5: Forms I–IV; 6: Post-Form IV

Table 5.6c. *Kenyan Employees by Occupation: Percentage Receiving Various Benefits from Employer*

Benefit	Occupation							All
	1	2	3	4	5	6	7	
Annual bonus	20	26	10	17	21	5	27	18
Paid annual leave	62	76	81	93	84	94	93	81
Rations	7	15	3	6	6	6	5	7
Medical treatment	35	51	66	70	73	86	48	59
Transport	19	14	5	9	10	32	12	11
NSSF	68	78	62	78	60	66	80	72
Pension, other	13	19	28	49	52	72	20	32
Loans	47	50	40	61	44	67	69	52
	(305–320)	(270–290)	(386–409)	(502–562)	(43–50)	(44–49)	(75–85)	(1635–1761)

Note: 1: Manual, unskilled; 2: Manual, semi-skilled; 3: Manual, skilled; 4: Clerical and secretarial; 5: Technical and semi-professional; 6: Managerial and administrative; 7: Professional

Table 5.6d. *Kenyan Employees by Ownership of Firm: Percentage Receiving Various Benefits from Employer*

Benefit	Private	Public corporation	Local government	Government	All
Annual bonus	27	3	2	1	18
Paid annual leave	74	95	100	93	82
Rations	10	2	4	0	7
Medical treatment	41	85	86	93	59
Transport	15	7	0	5	11
NSSF	78	61	44	68	72
Pension, other	20	54	88	41	32
Loans	56	54	58	28	52
	(1033–1106)	(269–296)	(66–73)	(259–286)	(1636–1763)

Table 5.7. *Clerical and Secretarial Employees in Kenya by Years of Employment Experience, Education, and Sex: Mean Wage (Shs per month)*

Education and employment experience (years)	Male	Female
Standards 7–8	674	..
0–3	(9)	
	747	..
4–7	(11)	
	1017	1147
8–14	(21)	(12)
Forms I–IV	979	1013
0–3	(54)	(22)
	1150	1467
4–7	(60)	(34)
	1729	1836
8–14	(98)	(49)

Table 5.8. *Kenyan Employees by Education and Sex: Distribution by Occupation*

Occupation	Education					
	Standards 7–8		Forms I–IV		Post-Form IV	
	Male	Female	Male	Female	Male	Female
Manual	77	50	44	15	7	0
Clerical	19	50	47	83	31	45
Other	4	0	9	2	62	55
	(421)	(45)	(559)	(139)	(162)	(36)

showing that in the relevant education groups they are employed dispro-portionately in clerical relatively to manual occupations—83 per cent of women with Forms I–IV education are in clerical, and only 15 per cent in manual jobs, compared with 47 and 44 per cent respectively for men. However, it is not simply the concentration of women with higher-primary and lower-secondary education in a relatively highly paid occupa-tion that accounts for their being paid more than men. Within that occupation itself they are paid more than men at every relevant educa-tional level (Table 5.9), and Table 5.7 shows that the advantage to women in these educational levels holds for the various lengths of em-ployment experience.

Table 5.9. *Kenyan Employees by Education, Occupation, and Sex: Mean Wage (Shs per month)*

Occupation and education	Male		Female		All
Manual, unskilled					
None	570	(69)	589	(6)	572
Standards 1–8	585	(146)	511	(15)	578
Forms I–IV	565	(61)	568	(10)	566
Manual, semi-skilled					
Standards 7–8	744	(76)	586	(10)	725
Clerical and secretarial					
Standards 7–8	1391	(82)	1543	(23)	1424
Forms I–IV	1566	(259)	1581	(115)	1571
Post-Form IV	1993	(50)	2494	(16)	2116

Although the number of Asians in the sample is small, Table 5.10 provides pretty clear evidence that the average wage of Asian employees is substantially larger than that of Africans with the same level of education. The differential persists after standardization for occupation and education (Table 5.11).

The type of primary school attended is related to the wage of employees with only primary school education. Those from mission schools do substantially better than those educated at government schools, if no distinction is made according to the date at which education ceased. But the experience of different cohorts is different. For those who left school before 1960, the wage of mission-school pupils is a good deal higher than that of government pupils. But for those who left school in later years the relationship is the reverse of that (Table 5.12). Those with education up to Form IV who attended a government secondary school have done rather better than those who attended a private school. A wage of Shs 1000 or less is received by 54 per cent of those who attended a private school, by 62 per cent of those who were at a *harambee* school, and by only 39 per cent of those who had been to a government school. The figures for the mean wage tell the same story (Table 5.13).

Employees who completed only the full course of primary education and obtained a Primary School Certificate are paid more than their peers who did not receive a certificate. The difference has been increasing over time, and is large for the decade 1970–9 and negligible for the period back from 1959 (Table 5.14).

The relationship between examination results and earnings is remarkably strong for secondary school Form IV-leavers. Table 5.15 shows that each Division or grade of Pass in the examination commands a premium

Table 5.10. *Kenyan Employees by Ethnic Group and Education: Mean Wage (Shs per month)*

Education	African	Asian
Standard 8 and below	847	2620
	(847)	(10)
Forms I–IV	1368	3458
	(670)	(17)
Post-Form IV	2522	4507
	(141)	(37)
All	1199	3907
	(1658)	(64)

Table 5.11. *Male Kenyan Employees by Education, Occupation, and Ethnic Group: Mean Wage (Shs per month)*

Occupation and education	African	Asian
Clerical and secretarial		
Forms I–IV	1569	2742
	(362)	(9)
Post-Form IV	1947	3137
	(56)	(8)
Professional		
Post-Form IV	2866	4697
	(43)	(25)

over that below it, for the sample as a whole and for each period identified. The pattern also holds within occupations (Table 5.16) and for results in particular subjects (Table 5.17).

These impressive results on the relationship between quality of examination performance and wage are open to more than one interpretation. On the one hand, it is possible that the cognitive skills acquired in school possess an economic value: that is the 'human capital' interpretation of the results. On the other hand, it is possible that the qualities which cause some candidates to shine in examinations—qualities such as intelligence, drive, and determination—also help them to earn more at work.

Whatever the basic reason for the observed correlation, it may come about in practice because employers use examination results as the criterion for recruitment to the more-demanding (and better-paying) jobs. However, the somewhat limited data in Table 5.16 suggest that a higher

Table 5.12. *Kenyan Employees with Primary Education Only by Type of Primary School Attended: Distribution by Wage; Mean Wage (Shs per month) by Year Leaving School*

Wage (Shs per month)	Primary school type	
	Government	Mission
500 and under	26	19
501–750	41	32
751–1000	16	24
1001–1500	11	17
Over 1500	6	8
Mean		
All periods	751	842
	(408)	(135)
Before 1960	858	936
	(108)	(84)
1960–69	782	764
	(166)	(27)
After 1969	636	581
	(131)	(22)

Table 5.13. *Kenyan Employees with Secondary Education up to Form IV by Type of Secondary School First Attended: Distribution by Wage; Mean Wage (Shs per month)*

Wage (Shs per month)	Secondary school type			All
	Government	*Harambee*	Private	
0–1000	39	62	54	46
1001–1500	22	22	19	22
Over 1500	39	16	27	32
Mean	1626	1049	1299	1425
	(366)	(132)	(161)	(712)

Table 5.14. *Kenyan Employees with Complete Primary but No Further Education by Period in which Education Completed: Mean Wage of Those With as Percentage of Mean Wage of Those Without Primary Certificate*

Period education completed			
1959 or earlier	1960–9	1970–9	All
103	110	134	105
(47/17)	(106/36)	(86/14)	(245/69)

Table 5.15. *Kenyan Employees who Completed Education at Form IV by Result in Form IV Examination and Period in which Education Completed: Mean Wage (Shs per month)*

Examination result	Period education completed		All
	1960–9	1970–9	
Div. 1	..	2527	2672
		(17)	(21)
Div. 2	2745	1443	1989
	(40)	(64)	(105)
Div. 3	2012	1399	1614
	(49)	(128)	(185)
Div. 4	1530	921	1054
	(22)	(80)	(103)

Table 5.16. *Kenyan Employees who Completed Education at Form IV by Form IV Examination Result and Occupation: Mean Wage (Shs per month)*

Occupation	Examination result			
	Div. 1	Div. 2	Div. 3	Div. 4
Manual				
Unskilled	..	..	..	625
				(15)
Semi-skilled	..	..	815	746
			(8)	(13)
Skilled	..	1045	1308	718
		(7)	(20)	(19)
Clerical and secretarial	2218	1840	1609	1344
	(13)	(75)	(130)	(55)
Technical and semi-professional	..	2369	2905	..
		(7)	(10)	

grade of pass commands a higher wage even in particular occupations. The numbers are too small to make it possible to standardize for employment experience. However, it is likely that the relationship would be even stronger if the effect of that were removed, as examination-grade requirements for each occupation have probably risen over time. Even as it is, the relationship for clerical and secretarial employees is impressive.

The pattern for results in the Form VI examination, however, is less clear, particularly for those who took the examination in the more recent period. It is possible that there has not been time for the quality of the

Table 5.17. *Kenyan Employees who Completed Education at Form IV by Grade of Form IV Examination Pass in Different Subjects: Mean Wage (Shs per month)*

Examination grade	Mathematics		English		Best science subject	
1	4858	(7)		..	3835	(6)
2	2678	(10)	2389	(19)	2821	(9)
3	2324	(23)	2615	(34)	2633	(39)
4	1981	(28)	1726	(23)	1457	(26)
5	1986	(17)	1688	(44)	1701	(41)
6	1935	(64)	1527	(102)	1507	(80)
Pass	1447	(135)	1426	(147)	1292	(135)
Fail	956	(115)	798	(45)	1104	(36)
All	1589	(399)	1582	(416)	1597	(372)

Table 5.18. *Kenyan Employees With Complete Secondary but Without Post-Secondary Education by Result in Form VI Examination and Period in which Education Completed: Mean Wage (Shs per month)*

Result in examination	Period education completed	
	1972 or earlier	1973 or later
1 pass	3769 (11)	2745 (12)
2 passes	..	2378 (35)
3 passes	4044 (12)	3404 (40)
4 or more passes	..	2759 (7)

more highly qualified to emerge and to be reflected in their wage, or that those with four or more passes at A level who did not continue their education were in some way unusual (Table 5.18).

Casual employees—those paid by the day—are paid substantially less than the regulars (except for the uneducated) and the advantage of the regulars increases with the level of education—for those with Forms I–IV education regulars receive a wage more than twice that paid to casuals. The lower wage of the casual worker may in part be a reflection of the 'seniority effect'. Many regulars start as casuals, being taken on to the regular payroll only after some time (see section D). The low pay of the casual workers would then reflect their being the most junior employees, as well as their casual status as such (Table 5.19).

There are wide differences in the wages paid to employees with the

Table 5.19. *Kenyan Employees by Employment Status and Education: Mean Wage (Shs per month)*

Education	Employment Status	
	Regular	Casual
None	589	865
	(86)	(27)
Standards 1–4	808	756
	(123)	(27)
Standards 5–6	786	622
	(102)	(28)
Standards 7–8	1047	667
	(377)	(79)
Forms I–IV	1499	723
	(622)	(62)
Post-Form IV	3267	..
	(177)	

same education in establishments in different ownership, (Table 5.20),[1] though the pattern of difference is not simple.

Public corporations pay substantially more than either the private sector or the government to manual employees. For clerical employees they pay more than the private sector for the lower levels of education and less for the higher. Clerical workers are paid very much less by government than by other employers. For employees as a whole, public corporations pay more than private industry for all levels of education except the highest, and the excess is particularly large for the lower educational levels. Wages in government are roughly similar to those of the private sector, and except for the highest education level, below those in public corporations.

There is no discernible pattern in the relationship between the size of the firm and the wage paid to employees with a given level of education. But the consistent relationship between the level of education and the wage is quite well maintained within each size-group (Table 5.21).

The association between educational attainment and inequality of income from employment is an important matter upon which the data from the survey throw light. The degree of inequality associated with different wage and educational attainments may be affected by the number of dependants an employee supports. Table 5.22 shows that, in fact, this

---

[1] The differences in the provision of benefits in addition to the wage have already been discussed.

Table 5.20. *Kenyan Employees by Occupation, Education, and Ownership of Firm: Mean Wage (Shs per month)*

Occupation and education	Ownership of firm		
	Private	Public corporation	Government
Manual, unskilled and semi-skilled			
All	621	930	597
	(527)	(30)	(27)
Manual, skilled			
None	623	..	885
	(12)		(6)
Standards 1–4	708	1194	..
	(24)	(16)	
Standards 5–6	905	1268	722
	(22)	(14)	(9)
Standards 7–8	873	935	987
	(63)	(78)	(32)
Forms I–IV	841	1288	892
	(37)	(36)	(42)
All	831	1128	925
	(159)	(149)	(93)
Clerical and secretarial			
Standards 7–8	1429	1639	838
	(56)	(23)	(10)
Forms I–IV	1756	1743	1063
	(190)	(71)	(82)
Post-Form IV	2782	2201	1039
	(29)	(11)	(15)
All	1786	1767	1039
	(286)	(105)	(107)
Other non-manual			
Post-Form IV	3826	..	2447
	(70)		(20)
All	3518	3935	3607
	(110)	(9)	(33)
All occupations			
None	638	..	787
	(104)		(8)
Standards 1–4	701	1223	..
	(116)	(28)	
Standards 5–6	697	1102	695
	(102)	(17)	(10)
Standards 7–8	921	1102	983
	(286)	(103)	(52)
Forms I–IV	1427	1631	1153
	(376)	(120)	(157)
Post-Form IV	3443	2573	3369
	(103)	(20)	(52)
All	1263	1422	1502
	(1087)	(293)	(283)

Table 5.21. *Kenyan Employees by Size of Firm and Education: Mean Wage (Shs per month)*

Education	Size of firm (no. of employees)			
	1–99	100–199	200–499	500 and over
None	496	568	604	782
	(53)	(23)	(22)	(21)
Standards 1–4	564	814	640	1096
	(59)	(40)	(11)	(43)
Standards 5–6	623	701	603	951
	(40)	(28)	(20)	(45)
Standards 7–8	941	1009	737	1056
	(115)	(102)	(42)	(201)
Forms I–IV	1237	1626	1689	1334
	(157)	(140)	(80)	(313)
Post-Form IV	3335	3856	..	2972
	(80)	(31)		(71)
All	1299	1418	1135	1366

effect is small. The number of dependants is highest for employees with wages between Shs 1500 and 2000 a month, so that dependants have some equalizing effect up to that wage, but the number of dependants of those with a higher wage than that declines quite sharply. For the higher levels of wages, therefore, the number of dependants compounds the inequality.

In relation to education, the number of dependants certainly does not fall into an equalizing pattern: the more educated have fewer than the less educated, even allowing for the fact that they are on average younger and are likely to accumulate more of them over time, because within the same age-group they have fewer (Table 4.16). There is, therefore, greater inequality in the wage per dependant than in the wage itself. The mean wage of employees with post-Form IV education is 5 times that of the uneducated (Table 5.1). It may be calculated from Table 5.23 that for the wage per full dependant the corresponding figure is 15.

B. The Changing Relation between Education and Occupation: Filtering Down

The next step in the analysis of the links between education and the labour-market is to set out the data on the relationship between the education and the occupations of employees. In addition to the relationship between the two at any one time, the change in the relationship

Table 5.22. *Kenyan Employees by Wage: Average Number of Full and Part Dependants, Average Number of Full Dependants, and Average Wage (Shs per month) per Full Dependant*

Wage (Shs per month)	Wives and children			Persons		
	Av. no. of full and part dependants	Full dependants		Av. no. of full and part dependants	Full dependants	
		Av. no.	Av. wage		Av. no.	Av. wage
0–500	4.25 (279)	4.00	143	7.11	5.33	108
501–750	4.49 (425)	4.07	220	7.42	5.38	168
751–1000	4.21 (304)	3.70	342	7.63	5.20	264
1001–1500	4.16 (279)	3.70	493	7.20	5.19	366
1501–2000	4.76 (127)	4.26	550	8.20	5.47	438
2001–3000	4.08 (154)	3.47	1197	7.31	5.17	856
Over 3000	3.51 (137)	3.13	2187	5.70	4.17	1914
All	4.25 (1705)	3.81	546	7.28	5.20	431

Table 5.23. *Kenyan Employees by Education: Average Number of Full and Part Dependants, Average Number of Full Dependants, and Average Wage (Shs per month) per Full Dependant*

Education	Wives and children			Persons		
	Av. no. of full and part dependants	Full dependants		Av. no. of full and part dependants	Full dependants	
		Av. no.	Av. wage		Av. no.	Av. wage
None	6.47 (115)	6.12	100	8.25	7.26	84
Standards 1–4	6.87 (153)	6.59	119	9.00	7.48	105
Standards 5–6	6.01 (132)	5.57	134	8.51	6.74	111
Standards 7–8	4.85 (455)	4.34	226	7.83	5.76	170
Forms I–IV	3.11 (691)	2.69	532	6.69	4.35	329
Post-Form IV	1.88 (194)	1.48	2177	4.66	2.48	1299
All	4.20 (1740)	3.78	358	7.21	5.16	262

Table 5.24. *Kenyan Employees by Date of Joining Labour Force: Mean Years of Education*

Date of joining labour force		
Before 1951	5.91	(105)
1951–60	7.06	(174)
1961–70	8.98	(464)
After 1970	9.59	(909)

over time is of great interest. An often-observed feature of this change, particularly in countries where education is expanding rapidly, is the so-called 'filtering down' process. In this process, as the supply of educated labour increases over time, so persons with a given level of education enter 'lower' occupations. The other way to describe the process is to say that the level of education attained by employees in a particular occupation rises over time, so that, for instance, an occupation filled in times past by those with no more than primary education is manned increasingly by those with secondary education.

Table 5.24 shows that the length of education of recruits to the labour force has risen over time. Consistently with that, Table 5.25 shows a clear change over time in the occupational distribution of employees with each particular level of education. For every level of education, jobs lower in the hierarchy of occupations are more important for more recent entrants to the labour-market than for earlier entrants. For those in the three lowest educational categories distinguished in the table, a higher proportion of more recent than of earlier recruits are in unskilled employment.

For employees who completed primary school but received no further education (Standards 7–8-leavers), there is a rise over time in the proportion in unskilled manual occupations, but the change appears most strikingly as a consistent decline in the proportion engaged in non-manual occupations: the figure is 44 per cent in clerical and other non-manual occupations for those who entered the labour-market before 1959 and only 15 per cent for the most recent recruits. Fewer than a quarter of Forms I–IV-leavers who entered wage-employment before 1959 were in manual work, to be contrasted with 60 per cent for the most recent cohort, with no fewer than a quarter being in unskilled jobs. There has been a striking increase in the proportion of employees with post-Form IV education who are in clerical and secretarial jobs, from which they have increasingly displaced Forms I–IV-leavers. This pattern of change is seen in Table 5.25 as a lower position in the hierarchy of occupations for more recent entrants to the labour-market with a given level of education.

Table 5.25. *Kenyan Employees by Education and Year of First Wage-Job: Distribution by Occupation*

Education and occupation	Year of first wage-job				
	Before 1959	1959–65	1966–72	1973–6	1977–80
None					
Manual, unskilled	44	37	66	96	78
Manual, semi-skilled	37	40	4	4	20
Manual, skilled	19	23	30	0	2
	(41)	(12)	(11)	(10)	(16)
Standards 1–4					
Manual, unskilled	24	23	14	44	48
Manual, semi-skilled	43	47	41	39	34
Manual, skilled	30	24	43	3	18
Clerical and secretarial	3	6	2	14	0
	(65)	(28)	(27)	(14)	(15)
Standards 5–6					
Manual, unskilled	5	13	36	57	55
Manual, semi-skilled	28	23	26	33	31
Manual, skilled	60	49	25	10	10
Clerical and secretarial	7	15	5	0	4
Technical and semi-professional	0	0	8	0	0
	(42)	(18)	(34)	(21)	(18)
Standards 7–8					
Manual, unskilled	9	10	16	16	35
Manual, semi-skilled	8	10	21	28	20
Manual, skilled	39	50	38	33	30
Clerical and secretarial	36	26	22	22	12
Technical and semi-professional	1	2	2	0	1
Managerial and administrative	7	1	1	1	0
Professional	0	1	0	0	2
	(57)	(81)	(150)	(85)	(84)
Forms I–IV					
Manual, unskilled	9	1	4	9	25
Manual, semi-skilled	1	2	8	13	14
Manual, skilled	13	12	13	18	21
Clerical and secretarial	58	66	64	54	40
Technical and semi-professional	5	0	6	3	0
Managerial and administrative	14	17	3	1	0
Professional	0	2	2	2	0
	(32)	(56)	(229)	(178)	(195)

Table 5.25. *(Continued):*

Education and occupation	Year of first wage-job				
	Before 1959	1959–65	1966–72	1973–6	1977–80
Post-Form IV					
Manual, skilled	25	17	6	3	2
Clerical and secretarial	0	0	27	41	39
Technical and semi-professional	27	20	12	8	6
Managerial and administrative	26	0	35	4	5
Professional	22	63	20	44	48
	(7)	(13)	(34)	(67)	(74)
All					
Manual, unskilled	18	10	11	16	27
Manual, semi-skilled	24	15	15	16	14
Manual, skilled	33	33	23	17	18
Clerical and secretarial	18	30	40	38	30
Technical and semi-professional	2	2	5	3	1
Managerial and administrative	4	5	4	1	1
Professional	1	5	2	9	9
	(246)	(208)	(485)	(377)	(402)

In Table 5.26 the same pattern of change appears as a rise in the level of education of employees in a particular occupation. Only 18 per cent of unskilled manual workers who entered wage-employment before 1959 have more than Standard 6 education, compared with 72 per cent of the most recent cohort. It is the same with the other manual occupations. Only 9 per cent of the semi-skilled workers who entered employment before 1959 have complete primary education, whereas for the most recent recruits that figure is 75 per cent. The proportion of skilled workers with complete primary education or more is 35 per cent for the earliest, and 94 per cent for the latest cohort.

The change is as striking with clerical/secretarial employees. Ninety per cent of those who most recently entered wage-employment have at least secondary education, compared with 43 per cent who had their first job before 1959. In the higher occupations, the change takes the form of a shift in the distribution between the first stage of secondary school and post-Form IV education. Only 38 per cent of employees in these higher occupations who entered employment before 1959 have post-Form IV education, whereas 96 per cent of the most recent cohort have that education.

Table 5.26. *Kenyan Employees by Occupation and Year of First Wage-Job: Distribution by Education*

Occupation and education	Year of first wage-job				
	Before 1959	1959–65	1966–72	1973–6	1977–80
Manual, unskilled					
None	42	21	13	16	12
Standards 1–4	35	30	7	11	7
Standards 5–6	5	11	22	22	9
Standards 7–8	12	36	43	24	27
Forms I–IV	6	2	15	27	45
	(45)	(21)	(55)	(54)	(108)
Manual, semi-skilled					
None	25	15	0	0	6
Standards 1–4	46	42	16	9	9
Standards 5–6	20	13	12	12	10
Standards 7–8	8	27	45	40	29
Forms I–IV	1	3	27	39	46
	(60)	(31)	(71)	(60)	(57)
Manual, skilled					
None	10	4	3	0	0
Standards 1–4	24	10	10	1	4
Standards 5–6	31	13	8	3	2
Standards 7–8	28	60	51	44	35
Forms I–IV	5	10	26	49	57
Post-Form IV	2	3	2	3	2
	(81)	(68)	(112)	(65)	(73)
Clerical and secretarial					
Standards 1–4	3	3	0	1	0
Standards 5–6	6	4	1	0	1
Standards 7–8	48	34	17	13	9
Forms I–IV	43	59	77	67	65
Post-Form IV	0	0	5	19	25
	(43)	(63)	(192)	(144)	(118)
Other non-manual					
Standards 5–6	0	0	6	0	0
Standards 7–8	25	12	7	0	4
Forms I–IV	37	44	45	22	0
Post-Form IV	38	44	42	78	96
	(16)	(25)	(55)	(49)	(45)
All					
None	17	6	2	3	4
Standards 1–4	27	13	6	4	4
Standards 5–6	17	9	7	6	5
Standards 7–8	23	39	31	22	21
Forms I–IV	13	27	47	47	48
Post-Form IV	3	6	7	18	18
	(246)	(209)	(485)	(381)	(405)

The same differences in the educational attainment of employees appear in Table 5.27, which looks at particular occupations. In each occupation, the distribution of employees by level of education has shifted upwards. Among factory labourers with 15 and more years of employment, 78 per cent have no more than Standard 4 education, compared with only 3 per cent among those with seven or fewer years in employment. For semi-skilled factory machine operators, the proportion with that level of education in these two cohorts is 57 per cent and 7 per cent, respectively. A similar pattern is found in other occupations. Perhaps the most striking difference between cohorts is among messengers, where the proportion with secondary education has risen from 4 to 79 per cent.

These data illustrate very clearly the process of filtering down as the supply of educated labour increases. With the expansion of education, a higher level of education comes to be required of entrants into a particular occupation than was required in the past. Putting it the other way round, a particular level of education will obtain entry only to an occupation lower in the hierarchy than was the case in the past.

It is true that some part of the change will be the consequence of individuals rising in the occupational hierarchy, from unskilled to skilled manual employment, for instance, during the course of their employment careers. However, we can be confident that promotion from one occupation to another as workers acquire employment experience is not the major explanation. First, Table 5.26 shows a remarkable increase in educational attainment from one entry-cohort to another. It is unlikely that there has been any significant change over time in the occupational distribution as a whole. With the educational composition of the labour force changing and its occupational composition stable over time, filtering down has inevitably occurred. The fact that it is concentrated among recent cohorts reflects the job protection which incumbents have enjoyed against better-educated entrants to the labour-market, or the skills which they have acquired on the job. Secondly, there is evidence that movement up the occupational hiearchy does not occur on a large scale through movement from one employer to another (see Table 5.60). Thirdly, a comparison of Tables 5.25 and 5.26 for Kenya with the equivalent Tables 8.25 and 8.26 for Tanzania (Chapter 8) indicates the much greater extent to which filtering down has occurred in Kenya, reflecting the more rapid expansion of educational enrolments in Kenya. Here we are comparing equivalent cohorts in two countries with very similar overall occupational distributions.[2] The difference must be due to the greater extent of filtering down in Kenya and cannot contain any element of occupational promotion with experience.

---

[2] Compare the 'All' levels of education section of Table 5.25 with that of Table 8.25.

Table 5.27 *Kenyan Employees by Particular Occupations and Years of Employ-ment Experience: Distribution by Education*

Occupation and education	Years of experience		
	0–7	8–14	15 and over
Factory Labourer			
None	0	17	21
Standards 1–4	3	17	57
Standards 5–6	12	8	0
Standards 7–8	29	50	22
Forms I–IV	56	8	0
	(41)	(12)	(14)
Semi-skilled factory machine operator			
None	0	0	17
Standards 1–4	7	16	40
Standards 5–6	11	9	23
Standards 7–8	38	41	20
Forms I–IV	44	34	0
	(45)	(32)	(30)
Messenger			
None	3	0	35
Standards 1–4	0	0	22
Standards 5–6	3	15	4
Standards 7–8	15	50	35
Forms I–IV	79	35	4
	(33)	(20)	(23)
Clerk			
Standards 1–4	0	0	11
Standards 5–6	0	0	0
Standards 7–8	6	17	39
Forms I–IV	69	83	50
Post-Form IV	25	0	0
	(111)	(53)	(18)
Secretary/typist			
Standards 1–4	0	0	10
Standards 5–6	0	0	0
Standards 7–8	24	24	30
Forms I–IV	73	70	60
Post-Form IV	3	6	0
	(37)	(47)	(10)
Government administrator			
Forms I–IV	..	56	100
Post-Form IV	..	44	0
		(9)	(8)

C. Filtering Down and Wages

In the previous section the phenomenon of 'filtering down' was identified. The present section examines the ways in which this phenomenon affects the wage structure. There are considerable differences in average earnings by occupation at each educational level, as well as on account of educational differences between occupations. For instance, average earnings in the manual occupations rise from Shs 578 in the unskilled to Shs 975 per month in the skilled grade. The clerical and secretarial occupation averages Shs 1620 and other non-manual categories no less than Shs 3415. To take one particular level of education, whether a Forms I–IV-leaver is employed as an unskilled labourer or as a clerk makes a difference of over Shs 1000 to his monthly pay. The filtering down of the more educated might therefore be expected to reduce their pay in absolute terms, and probably in relation to that of the less educated (Table 5.28).

These expectations are borne out by the evidence. Table 5.4 shows that, with very few exceptions, absolute earnings at any particular educational level are lower for the more recent cohorts to the labour-market. The average earnings of Forms I–IV-leavers increase with length of employment experience, being for employees with over 14 years of experience more than three times those for employees with under 4 years. And Table 5.29 (derived from Table 5.4) shows that wage dispersion by level of education is narrower for those entering in more recent than in more distant periods. For employees who entered the labour-market before 1966, the range of the wages by education up to Forms I–IV is from 39 to 169 per cent of the cohort average; for those who entered in the most recent period, the corresponding range is only from 52 to 81. For the most recent cohort the range for all but the post-Form IV group is very narrow. The mean deviation of the distribution of wages by education falls steadily from Shs 828 for the earliest cohort to Shs 460 for the latest.

It would be wrong to attribute these results entirely to the process of filtering down. As Tables 5.29 and 5.30 show, there is a similar but weaker tendency for average earnings to be lower and dispersion to be narrower for the more recent cohorts within the occupational category 'manual'. The higher wages of the earlier cohorts must in part be due to their accumulation of skills as they acquired employment experience. The greater wage dispersion of the earlier cohorts could partly reflect a tendency for the more educated to acquire more skills than the less educated in the course of their working careers.

Table 5.30 shows that the narrowing of the range of wages by education has not been accompanied by a clear narrowing by occupation. There has been a narrowing within the manual categories, the ratio of skilled to

Table 5.28. *Kenyan Employees by Education and Occupation: Mean Wage (Shs per month)*

Occupation	Education							All
	None	Standards 1–4	Standards 5–6	Standards 7–8	Forms I–IV	Post-Form IV		
Manual								
Unskilled	616	613	565	552	566	..		578
	(52)	(39)	(39)	(78)	(71)			(279)
Semi-skilled	525	745	681	718	686	..		694
	(24)	(63)	(37)	(84)	(69)			(277)
Skilled	726	901	981	920	1033	1968		975
	(14)	(39)	(45)	(171)	(114)	(9)		(392)
Clerical and secretarial	..	..	718	1424	1606	2116		1620
			(8)	(105)	(374)	(66)		(558)
Other non-manual	..	..	..	2610	3185	3707		3415
				(13)	(53)	(107)		(175)
All	609	786	746	979	1432	3222		1352
	(90)	(147)	(132)	(450)	(685)	(183)		(1688)

Table 5.29. *Kenyan Employees by Occupation and Year Entering Labour Force: Mean Wage for Each Level of Education as Percentage of Mean Wage for All Levels; Mean Wage for All Levels of Education (Shs per month)*

Occupation and education	Year entering labour force				All
	Before 1966	1966–72	1973–6	1977–80	
All manual					
None	67	80	91	84	78
Standards 1–6	96	81	75	84	97
Standards 7–8	106	101	99	95	101
Forms I–IV	174	115	112	108	104
All	940	782	705	610	776
Clerical and secreterial					
Standards 7–8	92	64	93	58	88
Forms I–IV	111	105	93	78	99
Post-Form IV	..	158	134	174	134
All	2134	1673	1360	1271	1620
Other non-manual					
Forms I–IV	96	85	68	..	93
Post-Form IV	114	137	110	101	109
All	4377	3393	3349	2523	3415
All					
None	39	44	49	52	45
Standards 1–4	56	45	37	51	58
Standards 5–6	60	42	42	54	55
Standards 7–8	87	61	63	64	72
Forms I–IV	169	117	88	81	106
Post-Form IV	376	275	219	239	238
All	1621	1428	1306	990	1352

unskilled pay declining from 2 for the earliest to $1\frac{1}{2}$ for the latest cohort. But the mean deviation of the distribution (in terms of percentage of the mean wage) first rises from 47 per cent for the earliest cohort to 48 per cent for the next; it then falls to 43 per cent and 42 per cent, and rises to 55 per cent for the most recent cohort. There is no indication in these figures for a tendency to compression. However, the greater compression of wages by educational level in the case of recent cohorts is primarily due to their different occupational composition rather than a different occupational wage structure. And, as it was argued above, filtering down is likely to be responsible for the differences in occupational composition between cohorts.

Table 5.30. *Kenyan Employees by Year Joined Labour Force: Mean Wage for Each Occupation as Percentage of Mean Wage for All; Mean Wage for All Occupations (Shs per month)*

Occupation	Year joined labour force				
	Before 1959	1959–65	1966–72	1973–6	1977–80
Manual					
Unskilled	45	38	41	44	53
Semi-skilled	57	41	53	50	52
Skilled	88	58	63	66	82
Clerical and secretarial	167	117	117	104	138
Technical and semi-professional	..	..	141	169	..
Managerial and administrative	371	157	258	..	..
Professional	..	331	404	278	254
All	1378	1901	1428	1306	990

The fact that the relation between education and occupation is flexible and has been changing raises important questions for educational policy. Which educational level is 'best' for each occupation? One approach to this question is to examine the relationship between educational level and earnings within an occupation. However, it is not certain that the higher earnings of the more educated necessarily reflect greater productivity resulting from their additional education. The higher earnings might instead reflect the superior ability of those selected to proceed to the higher levels of the educational system, so that wages and educational attainment are both the consequence of the same underlying determinant. Alternatively, higher wages might be paid to the educated for non-economic reasons, for instance reflecting a feeling that it is right and proper for the more educated to be more highly paid.

Although the data cannot point to a choice between these competing hypotheses, they do provide evidence on the relation between educational level and earnings within an occupation (Table 5.28). As might be expected, there is no clear relationship in the case of unskilled and semi-skilled manual workers. In the skilled manual occupations, however, and particularly steeply in the non-manual occupations, average earnings increase with educational level. The process of filtering down causes a decrease in wages within an educational level but an increase in wages within an occupation. This evidence is consistent with the view that filtering down brings with it gains in productivity within an occupation.

Table 5.31. *Kenyan Employees by Year Education Completed and by Education; Distribution by Months between End of Education and Start of Wage-Employment*

Year education completed and education	Months between end of education and start of employment			
	0	1–6	7–12	13 and over
All				
Standards 1–4	18	2	9	71 (140)
Standards 5–6	22	6	19	53 (121)
Standards 7–8	29	11	17	43 (450)
Forms I–IV	32	23	22	23 (688)
Post-Form IV	58	28	12	2 (194)
1970 and earlier				
Standards 1–4	18	3	8	71 (115)
Standards 5–6	24	7	17	52 (98)
Standards 7–8	30	11	15	44 (314)
Forms I–IV	41	21	20	18 (296)
Post-Form IV	72	17	11	0 (46)
1971–79				
Standards 1–4	0	0	20	80 (10)
Standards 5–6	2	0	35	63 (17)
Standards 7–8	25	13	25	37 (123)
Forms I–IV	25	25	24	26 (384)
Post-Forms IV	53	31	14	2 (140)

D. Recruitment and the Role of Education: Actual and Perceived

The less educated the employee the longer it takes him to get his first wage-job. Table 5.31 shows that 58 per cent of those with post-Form IV education obtained their first job without delay, compared with only 18 per cent of those who did not go beyond Standard 4. The percentage of Form IV-leavers who obtained immediate employment was even higher in 1970 and earlier, when 72 per cent obtained immediate employment, and 89 per cent were in work within six months. Since 1970 the proportion of employees with post-primary and with other levels of education who obtained work at once has fallen. The figure is still high, except for those with little education, and all but 2 per cent of those with post-Form IV education obtained work within a year, whereas a much higher proportion of those in the lower levels of educational attainment had a long time to wait.

Table 5.32. *Kenyan Employees by Occupation, Sector of Employment, and Years of Employment Experience: Percentage in Casual Employment*

Occupation
  Manual
    Unskilled   32 (314)
    Semi-skilled   13 (290)
    Skilled   19 (413)
  Clerical and secretarial   3 (555)
  Technical and semi-professional   0 (43)
  Managerial and administrative   1 (46)
  Professional   2 (91)
  All   13 (1752)

Sector of employment
  Agriculture   0 (92)
  Manufacturing   10 (453)
  Construction   49 (239)
  Commerce   7 (307)
  Transport   36 (21)
  Private services   6 (638)

Years of Employment experience
  0–3   25 (401)
  4–7   13 (378)
  8–14   8 (477)
  15–21   8 (205)
  22 and over   7 (242)

Casual workers are a significant proportion of the work-force in manual occupations. Only 3 per cent of clerical and secretarial employees are in casual employment, but 19 per cent of skilled manual workers are casual and 32 per cent of the unskilled. Almost all the casual workers are men: there are very few female casual workers in any occupation. In all sectors of employment, except construction and transport, casual workers are a small proportion of all employees (Table 5.32).

For all but the higher occupations, casual employment is important as a preliminary to regular employment. Nearly half of the unskilled manual workers in regular employment started as casual workers, and the figure is nearly 40 per cent for skilled workers. Even among clerical and secretarial employees, nearly a quarter began as casual workers. There are wide differences in the proportion between sectors of employment. Rather few employees with post-primary education started as casual workers, but for those with less education the proportion of regular employees who started as casuals is quite high, ranging from 37 to 46 per cent. The proportion of regular employees who started as casuals has varied over time, but with

Table 5.33. *Kenyan Regular Employees by Occupation, Sector of Employment, Education, and Year Entered Wage-Employment: Percentage Starting as Casual Employees*

Occupation		
Manual		
Unskilled	47	(209)
Semi-skilled	42	(249)
Skilled	38	(327)
Clerical and secretarial	23	(527)
Technical and semi-professional	9	(44)
Managerial and administrative	6	(48)
Professional	5	(87)
Sector of employment		
Agriculture	15	(89)
Manufacturing	42	(403)
Construction	72	(126)
Commerce	32	(281)
Transport	86	(14)
Private services	14	(579)
Education		
None	38	(84)
Standards 1–4	44	(120)
Standards 5–6	46	(102)
Standards 7–8	37	(377)
Forms I–IV	26	(626)
Post-Form IV	8	(182)
Year entered wage-employment		
1977–80	26	(295)
1973–76	38	(317)
1966–72	30	(432)
1959–65	26	(184)
Before 1959	28	(227)
All	30	(1456)

no particular trend (Table 5.33). The conclusion that casual work is to an important extent a step on the road to regular employment is strengthened by the evidence that a quarter of the labour force who have employment experience of 3 years or less are in casual employment, compared with only 13 per cent of those with 4 to 7 years' experience, and less than 10 per cent of those with even more experience than that (Table 5.32).

In only a few firms are casual employees a large proportion of the work-force. Only 3 per cent of firms have more than a half of their

Table 5.34. *Distribution of Kenyan Firms by Percentage of Employees in Regular Employment*

Percentage of employees in regular employment	Percentage of firms
0–50	3
51–75	11
76–90	33
91–100	53
	(57)

Table 5.35. *Kenyan Employees by Employment Status and for Regular Employees by Employment Status at Time Employment Started: Distribution by Method of Job Application*

Method of application	Regular employees' starting employment		Casual Employees
	Regular	Casual	
At the gate	17	47	58
Letter replying to advertisement	20	7	6
Unsolicited letter	25	9	7
Through relative or friend	24	30	22
Through government employment exchange	5	2	1
Other	9	5	6
	(1040)	(693)	(233)

workers in casual employment, and only 11 per cent have more than a quarter (Table 5.34).

There is a marked difference between regular and casual employees in the way they get their jobs. Applying for a job 'at the gate' is an important procedure for casual workers, but not for regulars. Nearly half of the regular employees who started as casual workers applied for their job in this way, as did more than a half of those at present in casual employment. The most important method for regular employees was application to the employer by letter, either unsolicited or in reply to an advertisement. Personal introductions, through a relative or friend, are important both for casual and for regular workers (Table 5.35).

Application 'at the gate' is important for manual workers and unimportant for those in other occupations. Application by letter was the most important way in which non-manual employees obtained their jobs. Personal introductions are important for manual and clerical, but not for other non-manual employees. It follows from the association between education and occupation that the most important ways of getting a job among those with the lower levels of education are 'at the gate' and by personal introductions, and for those with the higher levels of education, application by letter (Table 5.36).

The tables have shown the close relationship between education and occupation. It is a relationship perceived clearly by employees. A high proportion with education of Standards 7–8 and above believe they would not have got their job if they had had less education (Table 5.37).

E. Education and the Qualifications for Jobs: Employee Perceptions

The belief that they are qualified for a better job is widespread among employees. The trend in each occupation is for the proportion holding this belief to increase with their level of education. Only 6 per cent of unskilled manual workers with Standards 1–4 education believe they are qualified for a better job, but this figure rises to 85 per cent for those with secondary education. Only half of clerical employees with no more than complete primary education believe they are over-qualified whereas that belief is held by 88 per cent of clerical workers who have education beyond Form IV (Table 5.38). The existence of this phenomenon is not surprising when filtering down is at work. Those who have 'filtered down' see persons with less education in superior jobs, and they know that their own job used to be done by persons with less education than themselves.

Table 5.39 presents in a different way the relation between the belief and education. For unskilled workers the years of education of those who believe they are over-qualified in their present occupations range between 121 per cent and 176 per cent of the average years of education for unskilled workers, according to the time at which the workers entered wage-employment. For all other occupations the difference between the education of those who believe they are over-qualified and the generality of workers in their occupation is much less than that, suggesting that the validity of the belief is stronger for unskilled manual workers than for others.

The belief that they are over-qualified for their present job affects very different proportions of employees in the different occupations who are seeking a better job, and in general the higher the occupation in the hierarchy the more of those looking for a better job believe that they are over-qualified. For manual workers the proportion ranges only between 59 and 64 per cent; the non-manual workers who are looking for a better job and who believe they are over-qualified for their present job amount to between 79 and 100 per cent of the total (Table 5.40).

The existence of such high proportions of employees who believe they are qualified for a better job at once raises the question of why they are in

Table 5.36a. *Kenyan Employees by Occupation: Distribution by Method of Job*
          Application

Method of application	Occupation						
	1	2	3	4	5	6	7
At the gate	48	47	35	13	7	0	0
Letter replying to advertisement	1	3	15	24	39	31	20
Unsolicited letter	8	5	16	30	22	26	34
Through relative or friend	35	36	27	20	14	17	13
Through government employment exchange	4	4	2	5	6	8	6
Other	4	5	5	8	12	18	27
	(321)	(290)	(410)	(564)	(52)	(49)	(93)

Note: 1: Manual, unskilled; 2: Manual, semi-skilled; 3: Manual, skilled; 4: Clerical and secretarial; 5: Technical and semi-professional; 6: Managerial and administrative; 7: Professional

their present job. That no better job is available might be an obvious answer, and it turns out that this is the reason for those in most occupations. For unskilled and semi-skilled manual workers 70 per cent and 81 per cent, respectively, are in their present job because no better is available. For skilled manual workers and the lower grades of non-manual workers the percentage is in the 60s. For the upper grades of non-manual workers, however, a majority are in their present job for some other reason than that no better is available (Table 5.41). Relatively few employees are in a job for which they believe they are over-qualified in order to gain experience (Table 5.42).

The proportion who accept that no better job is available declines with the level of education, but not dramatically (Table 5.41).

F. Formal Training by Employers

One way in which a worker can acquire skill is through training provided by the employer. Skill can also be acquired through experience. And education is a major way in which future workers are endowed with skills of a more general kind. These three mechanisms for the acquisition of skills can be both complements and substitutes. Training can combine

Table 5.36b. *Kenyan Employees by Education: Distribution by Method of Job Application*

Method of application	Education					
	None	Standards 1–4	Standards 5–6	Standards 7–8	Forms I–IV	Post-Form IV
At the gate	54	52	56	37	16	3
Letter replying to advertisement	0	2	3	12	19	32
Unsolicited letter	0	2	3	13	28	36
Through relative or friend	39	35	35	32	22	7
Through government employment exchange	3	2	1	3	5	6
Other	4	7	2	3	10	16
	(119)	(158)	(137)	(466)	(704)	(199)

Table 5.37. *Kenyan Employees who Started as Regular Employees by Education and Occupation: Percentage who Think They Would Not Have Been Employed if They Had Received Less Education*

Education	Occupation	
	Manual	Non-manual
Below Standard 7	26	..
	(136)	
Standards 7–8	61	81
	(151)	(70)
Forms I–IV	57	88
	(116)	(296)
Post-Form IV	..	79
		(140)

with experience to provide skill, and education may be necessary if a worker is to be able to benefit from training. In modern technology, for instance, both training and experience are necessary for the acquisition of skill, and neither are of any use unless the worker has attained a certain level of education. On the other hand, there are some skills which can be acquired by experience, or obtained more quickly through training, and both training and experience may make up to some degree for deficiencies in a worker's education.

The importance of skills, and of the interrelationships of the various ways in which they may be acquired, arises from their effect on workers' productivity and wages. These labour-market effects of educational expansion are the major theme of this study. The role of training as either complementing or substituting for education must therefore be examined. Whether it is a substitute for or a complement to education, training may increase productivity and wages, but the effect on the structure of wages will be very different if it is the one rather than the other. It was shown in an earlier section of this chapter that differential educational attainment is associated with wage–income inequality. If training is used as a substitute for education it will work to diminish the degree of inequality, whereas if it is provided as a complement to education it will tend to increase it.

Some 80 per cent of the total sample had not attended a training course provided by their current employer.[3] The proportion of those provided

---

[3] The information on training presented in the tables all concerns training by the present employer. There is no information on training provided by previous employers, though the high proportion of the labour force without a previous employer (see section G) suggests that training by the present employer may be taken as an approximate representation of the total picture.

Table 5.38. *Kenyan Employees by Occupation and Education: Percentage who Believe They Are Qualified for a Better Job*

Occupation	Education				
	Standards 1–4	Standards 5–6	Standards 7–8	Forms I–IV	Post-Form IV
Manual					
Unskilled	6	48	60	85	..
	(43)	(38)	(79)	(76)	
Semi-skilled	16	12	41	77	..
	(61)	(36)	(85)	(72)	
Skilled	16	18	46	72	63
	(43)	(46)	(176)	(115)	(10)
Clerical and secretarial	..	40	51	67	88
		(8)	(104)	(378)	(64)
Other non-manual	..	..	40	65	68
			(15)	(55)	(120)

Table 5.39. *Kenyan Employees by Occupation and Year of Entry into Wage-Employment: Average Years of Education of Those who Believe They Are Qualified for a Better Job as Percentage of Average Years of Education of All*

Occupation	Year of entry into wage-employment					All
	Before 1959	1959–65	1966–72	1973–6	1977–80	
Manual						
Unskilled	176	..	122	136	121	140
	(34)		(53)	(56)	(104)	
Semi-skilled	..	160	116	108	121	131
		(31)	(70)	(59)	(56)	
Skilled	138	110	113	111	110	117
	(78)	(67)	(110)	(65)	(71)	
Clerical and secretarial	104	100	101	106	102	103
	(43)	(62)	(188)	(143)	(117)	
Technical and semi-professinal	..	..	107	102	..	111
			(22)	(11)		
Managerial and administrative	..	105	98	..	..	102
		(11)	(19)			
Professional	..	..	..	105	98	102
				(33)	(35)	

Table 5.40. *Kenyan Employees Seeking Better Job by Occupation: Percentage who Believe They Are Over-Qualified*

Occupation		
Manual		
Unskilled	64	(106)
Semi-skilled	59	(96)
Skilled	62	(105)
Clerical and secretarial	80	(144)
Technical and semi-professional	82	(17)
Managerial and administrative	100	(9)
Professional	79	(18)

Table 5.41. *Kenyan Employees who Believe They Are Over-Qualified in Present Job by Occupation and Education: Percentage who Are in Present Job because No Better Available*

Occupation	Education				All	
	Standards 5–8		Post-primary			
Manual						
Unskilled	66	(62)	75	(67)	70	(134)
Semi-skilled	87	(39)	77	(53)	81	(100)
Skilled	68	(91)	64	(84)	66	(190)
Clerical and secretarial	64	(50)	61	(308)	61	(358)
Technical and semi-professional	..		77	(30)	66	(35)
Managerial and administrative	..		45	(33)	44	(34)
Professional	..		41	(50)	41	(50)
All	67		62		64	

Table 5.42. *Kenyan Employees who Believe They Are Over-Qualified by Employ-ment Status: Distribution by Reason for Being in Present Job*

Reason for current employment	Employment status	
	Regular	Casual
To gain experience	16	9
Better job not available	64	71
Other	20	20
	(791)	(100)

Table 5.43. *Kenyan Employees by Occupation: Percentage Provided with Training Course*

Occupation		
Manual		
Unskilled	<1	(311)
Semi-skilled	4	(288)
Skilled	29	(405)
Clerical and secretarial	32	(558)
Managerial and administrative	43	(49)
Technical and semi-professional	40	(50)
Professional	37	(91)
All	22	(1752)

with a course increases fairly steadily through the order in which the occupations are listed in Table 5.43.

Training, it seems, is given predominantly by the larger establishments, and by only some of these (Table 5.44). More than half the trained employees in the sample are employed in only 9 per cent of the establishments, and those establishments employ a quarter of the total employees. Three-quarters of the trained employees are employed in 16 per cent of the establishments, which employ a little over a third of the total employees. There are no trained employees in 40 per cent of the establishments, which employ a quarter of all employees.

Private firms on average have only 16 per cent of their employees trained, compared with a third in government establishments and public corporations and a quarter in local-authority establishments. But as there are correlations between ownership, size, and economic activity of the establishment, it is not at all clear what role is played by ownership itself. There are large differences between economic activities in the proportion

Table 5.44. *Percentage of Total Trained Kenyan Employees with Percentage of Establishments in which They Are Employed and Percentage of All Employees Employed in Those Establishments*

Percentage of trained employees	Percentage of establishments	Percentage of all employees
55	9	26
75	16	37
100	60	76
(387)	(57)	(1174)

Note: The number of trained employees is summed establishment by establishment, in order of decreasing absolute number of trained employees. When 55% of trained employees has been accumulated, only 9% of all establishments have been counted, and those establishments employ 26% of all employees.

Table 5.45. *Kenyan Establishments by Ownership and Economic Activity: Percentage of Employees Trained*

Ownership		
Private	16	(1100)
Public corporation	34	(295)
Local authority	25	(73)
Government	32	(287)
Economic activity		
Agriculture	14	(93)
Manufacturing	23	(453)
Construction	9	(243)
Commerce	11	(306)
Transport	0	(21)
Private services	33	(640)

of employees who have been given training by the employer. There is, of course, some correlation between sector of economic activity and the employment of persons in particular occupations, and the differences between occupations in the training provided will, therefore, affect the amount of training provided in different economic sectors (Table 5.45).

The sample is not large enough for a full analysis of the relationship between the employee's level of education and whether he or she has been given a training course. The skilled manual workers who have been given a course have more education than those who have not had a course, and the same is true of clerical and secretarial employees. For

Table 5.46. *Kenyan Employees by Occupation and Education: Percentage with Training Course*

Education	Occupation		All
	Skilled manual	Clerical and secretarial	
None	7 (18)	0 (0)	1 (116)
Standards 1–4	8 (43)	0 (5)	3 (157)
Standards 5–6	6 (47)	0 (8)	3 (135)
Standards 7–8	32 (176)	21 (104)	19 (465)
Forms I–IV	40 (115)	34 (374)	31 (688)
Post-Form IV	72 (10)	48 (65)	39 (196)

Table 5.47. *Kenyan Employees by Occupation and Whether Provided with a Training Course: Mean Years of Education*

	Occupation		All
	Skilled manual	Clerical and Secretarial	
Course(s)	8.8 (118)	11.1 (179)	10.2 (298)
No Course	6.6 (285)	10.0 (377)	8.5 (662)

occupations as a whole there is a clear positive relation between the level of education and the proportion provided with a training course (Tables 5.46 and 5.47). There seems from this evidence to be no attempt to provide training courses as a substitute for education.

Training courses have been given to only a fifth of all employees. There is not much indication that in-service training has been used as a substitute for pre-service education. If anything, those with more education have been given more training and those in 'higher' occupations have the most training. Trained employees are concentrated in a relatively few establishments; a good many establishments have none, as do certain economic activities. Establishments have provided the same amount of training in recent as in earlier periods.

These, in the most summary form, are the conclusions that may be drawn from the tables discussed so far. The tables which follow show data on the relation between training and wages.

Table 5.48 looks at the wage of those at each level of education who have and who have not taken a training course. The wage of those who have taken a course is substantially greater, at some educational levels enormously greater, than that of employees who have not had a course,

Table 5.48. *Kenyan Employees by Education, Occupation, and Whether Have Had a Training Course: Mean Wage (Shs per month)*

	Training course	
	Taken	Not taken
Education		
Standards 7–8	1295	916
	(87)	(370)
Forms I–IV	1871	1218
	(212)	(462)
Post-Form IV	2889	3412
	(75)	(108)
All	1923	1160
	(384)	(1332)
Occupation		
Manual		
Semi-skilled	830	691
	(12)	(273)
Skilled	2317	887
	(116)	(282)
Clerical and secretarial	1793	1549
	(179)	(374)

and the same is true for employees in the occupations listed in the table. Three-quarters of the employees who have taken a course have a wage greater than Shs 1000 compared with only 31 per cent of those who have not taken a course.

At every level of education, skilled manual employees who have been trade-tested have a much higher wage than those who have not (Table 5.49), and the grade of pass in the test is positively correlated with the employee's wage (Table 5.50). The evidence suggests that, at least for the employee, training pays, and that it adds to the inequality of pay which is generated by differences in educational attainment.

G. Education and Labour Mobility

The job-mobility rate, that is, the number of employers per year in employment, is low (Table 5.51). Fifty-three per cent of the labour force have had no employer other than the one in their present job. Only 16 per cent have a mobility rate of more than 0.2. The higher levels of education have a higher proportion with rates both of zero and of more than 0.2. Even those who have been in employment for 30 years or more

Table 5.49. *Kenyan Skilled Manual Employees who Have and who Have Not Taken Trade Test by Education: Mean Wage (Shs per month)*

Education	Taken trade test	Not taken trade test
Standards 1–4	1273	667
	(15)	(24)
Standards 5–6	1164	831
	(21)	(22)
Standards 7–8	1022	782
	(98)	(72)
Forms I–IV	1171	683
	(80)	(33)
All	1124	767
	(226)	(166)

Table 5.50. *Kenyan Skilled Manual Employees by Grade of Trade-Test Pass: Mean Wage (Shs per month)*

Grade of pass		
Grade 1	1470	(93)
Grade 2	1163	(84)
Grade 3	884	(87)

Table 5.51. *Kenyan Employees by Education: Distribution by Rate of Job Mobility*

Education	Job-mobility rate[a]			
	0	Greater than 0, not greater than 0.1	Greater than 0.1, not greater than 0.2	Greater than 0.2
None	35	37	19	9 (86)
Standards 1–4	33	33	17	17 (143)
Standards 5–6	53	23	12	12 (134)
Standards 7–8	54	17	16	13 (446)
Forms I–IV	58	11	15	16 (688)
Post-Form IV	52	7	14	27 (182)
All	53	16	15	16 (1682)

[a] Job-mobility rate: Number of previous employers divided by years in wage-employment.

Table 5.52. *Kenyan Employees by Year Education Completed: Distribution by Number of Previous Employers*

Number of previous employers	Year education completed				All
	1950 and earlier	1951–60	1961–70	1971–9	
0	35	39	52	64	53
1	18	28	27	24	26
2	12	17	12	7	11
3 or more	35	16	9	5	10
	(92)	(236)	(562)	(694)	(1744)

Table 5.53. *Kenyan Employees by Number of Previous Employers and by Reason for Leaving Last Job: Distribution by Number of Times Out of Wage-Employment*

Reason for leaving job and times out of wage-employment	Number of previous employers			
	1	2	3	4 and more
Lost job				
0	50	38	30	56
1	44	24	31	13
2	4	29	19	9
3 and more	2	9	20	22
	(111)	(54)	(36)	(23)
Chose to leave				
0	77	62	69	61
1	19	17	12	21
2	4	15	13	5
3 and more	0	6	6	13
	(292)	(110)	(41)	(56)

have had relatively few employers. More than a third of employees who completed their education in 1950 and earlier have had only the single employer, and less than half have had more than one previous employer (Table 5.52). The evidence indicates a very low rate of labour turnover in Kenya.

Table 5.53 shows that a relatively high proportion of job-changes were made without an intervening period out of employment, even when the employees lost their job rather than chose to leave. More than three-quarters of those with one previous job who chose to leave it moved into their present job without an intervening period of unemployment, but so did half of those who lost their job. Table 5.54 shows that a high

Table 5.54. *Kenyan Employees by Years Since First Wage-Job: Distribution by Total Months Out of Wage-Employment*

Total months out of wage-employment	Years since first wage-job					All
	0–3	4–7	8–14	15–21	More than 21	
0	96	83	81	81	70	86
1–6	2	7	4	3	1	4
7–12	2	6	6	3	4	4
More than 12	0	4	9	13	25	8
	(402)	(373)	(469)	(202)	(227)	(1674)

Table 5.55. *Kenyan Employees by Education: Percentage Leaving Previous job Voluntarily*

Education		
None	60	(67)
Standards 1–4	59	(116)
Standards 5–6	62	(60)
Standards 7–8	64	(198)
Forms I–IV	77	(272)
Post-Form IV	83	(82)
All	69	(786)

proportion of employees have experienced no unemployment, and that only for employees who entered the labour force more than 21 years ago have a significant proportion had more than a year in total out of wage-employment.

A high proportion of the employees who had had a previous employer left their previous job voluntarily, particularly of those with post-primary education (Table 5.55). Between 80 and 90 per cent of those who chose to leave their job received a higher wage in their next job, but so did more than 70 per cent of those who lost their job (Table 5.56). The proportion of employees who are seeking a better job is higher among the manual than the non-manual workers, except for those whose education was most recently completed (Table 5.57).

In sum, the evidence shows that once persons have entered the wage-labour force they stay there. They have not withdrawn for long periods into urban or rural self-employment, nor have they suffered such periods of unemployment.

Table 5.58 deals with the relatively few employees who have been out

Table 5.56. *Kenyan Employees by Reason for Leaving Previous Job: Percentage who Received Pay Rise after Changing Job*

Reason for leaving last job	
Lost job	72
	(238)
Chose to leave	85
	(525)

Table 5.57. *Kenyan Employees[a] by Year Education Completed and Occupation: Percentage Seeking Better Job*

Occupation	Year education completed				All
	Before 1965	1965–9	1970–4	1975–9	
Manual	23	33	45	28	29
	(75)	(54)	(29)	(29)	(188)
Non-manual	14	19	17	46	21
	(35)	(36)	(6)	(13)	(91)
All	20	28	40	33	26

[a] Employees who completed primary education but have had no further education and who are in their first wage-job.

Table 5.58. *Kenyan Employees who Have Been Out of Wage-Employment by Education: Distribution by Main Activity When Out of Employment*

Activity	Education			All
	Below Standard 7	Standards 7–8	Post-primary	
Work on parents' *shamba*	57	48	20	42
Non-agricultural self-employment	6	11	15	10
Looking for employment	15	27	41	27
Other	22	14	24	21
	(112)	(71)	(95)	(278)

of employment. More of those with primary education spent their time working on their parents' *shamba* as their main activity than in any other activity. The proportion for whom this was the main activity declines with education to only 20 per cent for those with post-primary education.

Looking for employment was the most important activity of those with post-primary education. The figures suggest, therefore, that being unemployed, as distinct from not working, is a characteristic more of the higher educated than of the less educated. Perhaps it is only they who both can afford to be unemployed and have the incentive to wait for and the expectation of obtaining a better-paid job.

The time spent in the last job is shorter for the more educated than for the less educated, for those in small firms than in large firms, and for those in private employment than in the employment of government and public corporations. Among the economic sectors, employees in construction and manufacturing stayed for a rather shorter time than those in other sectors. Employees in electricity and water and in wholesale and retail trade stayed the longest (Table 5.59).

A high proportion of employees were in the same occupation in their previous job. Not many move up the hierarchy of occupations in changing their job. For instance, only 19 per cent of skilled manual workers were in semi-skilled or unskilled work in the previous job (Table 5.60). There is no strong relationship between the economic sector of the firm of previous employment and that of the firm in which employees are at present engaged.

H. Summary

There is a close relationship between an employee's wage and his or her educational attainment. As a consequence, the educational distribution of wages is highly unequal. The relationship between the wage and the employee's occupation is also close. The educational and occupational spread of wages is not greatly altered when bonus and overtime payments are taken into account. Other benefits provided by employers tend to reinforce the relation between education and income, though their provision is in fact widespread. The number of dependants compounds the educational inequality of earnings as the better educated have on average fewer dependants that the less well educated.

The level of education of the employee and his or her occupation are closely related. Nevertheless, as many as a quarter of the employees in unskilled manual jobs have secondary education.

Higher wages are paid for experience, and the time spent in wage-employment is closely associated with the wage paid. Men are mostly

Table 5.59a. *Kenyan Employees with Previous Job by Level of Education: Mean Years in Last Job*

	Education					All
None	Standards 1–4	Standards 5–6	Standards 7–8	Forms I–IV	Post-Form IV	
4.9	4.6	3.7	2.8	3.1	2.8	3.4
(64)	(97)	(59)	(196)	(268)	(86)	(769)

Table 5.59b. *Kenyan Employees with Previous Job by Size of Firm in Last Job: Mean Years in Last Job*

	Size of firm	
Fewer than 50	50–499	500 and more
3.1	3.0	4.3
(349)	(235)	(116)

Table 5.59c. *Kenyan Employees with Previous Job by Type of Employer in Last Job: Mean Years in Last Job*

	Type of employer	
Private	Public corporation	Government
3.0	5.1	4.0
(506)	(43)	(167)

Table 5.59d. *Kenyan Employees with Previous Job by Sector of Employment in Last Job: Mean Years in Last Job*

			Sector of employment				
1	2	3	4	5	6	7	8
3.2	2.8	6.5	2.3	4.2	3.6	3.6	3.3
(56)	(109)	(25)	(80)	(83)	(64)	(84)	(179)

Note: 1: Agriculture and forestry;   2: Manufacturing;   3: Electricity and water;   4: Construction;   5: Wholesale and retail trade;   6: Transport and communications;   7: Finance and insurance;   8: Social and personal services

Table 5.60. *Kenyan Employees with Previous Job by Occupation in Current Job: Distribution by Occupation in Last Job*

Occupation in last job	Occupation in current job				
	Manual, unskilled	Manual, semi-skilled	Manual, skilled	Clerical and secretarial	Other
Manual					
Unskilled	60	18	14	7	0
Semi-skilled	17	63	5	5	2
Skilled	4	3	71	1	5
Clerical and secretarial	16	15	7	74	12
Other	3	1	3	13	81
	(132)	(131)	(199)	(248)	(84)

paid more than women, but for some levels of education it is the other way round.

Employees who were at mission schools before 1960 are paid more than those who were at government schools, but for employees who left school after that the relationship is the reverse. Former pupils of government secondary schools have done better than their peers who were at private schools. Employees who obtained a Primary School Certificate are paid more than those who did not, and the gap has been increasing over time. There is a strong relationship between earnings and performance in the secondary school Form IV examination, but not with the Form VI examination.

Casual employees are paid less than regulars. Manual workers do better in public corporations than with other employers; and clerical workers are paid less by government than by other employers.

Over time, the level of education of employees in each particular occupation has risen, or, to put it the other way round, the occupation entered by those with a given level of education has been lower in the hierarchy, illustrating the process of 'filtering down' that has occured with the increase in the supply of educated employees. It is perhaps worth saying at once, because the opposite view is so common, that the filtering-down process is probably to be welcomed rather than deplored. The common view possibly springs from the misguided notion that it is a waste for the educated to be engaged in menial tasks, or rather tasks that were previously performed by the uneducated, or those of less education. But that view is an example of those rigid and inappropriate expectations which, it is suggested below, are not held by the employees themselves. The desirability or otherwise of filtering down should be judged by its effect on productivty. If the more educated are more productive in the jobs they are entering—and the fact that employers prefer them to the less educated may be some evidence to that effect—then filtering down is a desirable and beneficial process.

The effect of filtering down on wages is to lower the wage for any level of education and to compress the differential for education, reducing over time the premium received by the more educated.

The narrowing of the range of wages by education has not been accompanied by a narrowing of the range by occupation and the compression of the educational distribution of the wage for recent cohorts of employees has been primarily the consequence of a change in the education–occupation structure. That is, employees with a particular level of education are in lower-paid jobs than in the past. It has not been the consequence of a change in the wage–occupation structure. That is, it has not been the result of a narrowing of the range between highly and lowly paid jobs.

It takes longer for an employee to get his first job the less educated he is. Although fewer secondary school-leavers enter employment immediately than in the past, not many of them have a long wait. It takes much longer for those with less education, but the time it takes for primary school-leavers to obtain work has been decreasing over time. The explanation may be a change in school-leavers' expectations. It is possible that their expectations have adjusted to the opportunities available, and school-leavers are not prepared to wait around without work for a better job than they are likely to get. If this is the explanation, it provides an interesting comment on the widely held view that the process of education inculcates rigid expectations in the educated.

Casual labour is quantitatively important, and for manual workers an important prelude to regular employment. Casual workers mostly get their jobs by application 'at the gate'. Personal introductions are an important method of recruitment for manual workers and for clerical employees. For higher-level jobs written application is the most important method of recruitment.

The relationship between education and occupation is clearly perceived by employees, a high proportion of those with education of Standards 7–8 and above believing that they would not have got their job if they had had less education. But the belief that they are qualified for a better job is widespread, and increases with the level of education. The majority of workers believe they are in their present job because no better is available and only a few are in it to gain experience.

The provision of training by employers is not widespread; it is not used as a substitute for pre-service education. But for those workers who are provided with training it is a good thing, as it is correlated with substantially higher pay.

The amount of movement between jobs is small: employees tend to stay in their jobs, and there is no simple pattern of movement according to level of education. When employees do change jobs a high proportion do so without a break in employment. They generally go into the kind of work they left, and there is little upward movement in the occupational hierarchy through changing employers. A high proportion of employees who leave their jobs do so voluntarily.

6

Who Gets Schooling
in Kenya?

The educational attainments of the employees in Nairobi as set out in Chapter 4 are to a large degree the consequence of the expansion of the educational system in Kenya, particularly during the years since Independence in 1963. This expansion did not take place uniformly in the different sectors of education, nor did it select at random those who were to be educated.

As primary school places are broadly speaking available to all, the question of selection for education, of deciding who goes to school and who does not, is especially concerned with secondary education. Selection at random is not, of course, to be seriously considered. Life may be a lottery, but selection for post-primary education could not nominally be so. Nominally it is by merit: access to the highly valued places in government secondary schools[1] is according to performance in the highly competitive Certificate of Primary Education examination, which was introduced in 1966 to select for admission to maintained secondary schools as well as to provide a terminal primary school examination (Kenya 1979a). However, if life is a lottery and the distribution of ability is on the same basis, it might be expected that success in the examinations would be distributed independently of such extraneous considerations as family background and the type of primary school attended. In reality, no one would expect that to be the case, but the interesting and important questions include how much is it not the case: in what way and to what extent does the selection for education diverge from a random distribution of ability?

---

[1] Private and *harambee* schools charge high fees but they are generally inferior to the maintained schools. Unaided schools tend to have poorer facilities (e.g. most do not have the laboratories and equipment to offer science subjects in the EACE examinations), a higher proportion of untrained teachers, and very few have upper-secondary classes. In the mid-1970s, fees for *harambee* secondary schooling for day-pupils ranged from Shs 450 p.a. to around Shs 1200; in low-cost government day schools they were between Shs 300 and 400, and about twice that in boarding schools.

Table 6.1. *Kenyan Employees by Father's Education: Distribution by Own Educa-*
         tion

Employee's education	Father's education		
	None	Primary	Post-primary
None	12	0	0
Standards 1–6	22	10	3
Standards 7–8	30	24	12
Forms I–IV	33	50	39
Post-Form IV	3	16	46
	(1015)	(591)	(154)

And the question can equally be asked of access to the unaided secondary schools.

This chapter attempts to provide answers to those questions. The data enable answers to be provided to 'how much?' and 'in what way?', but not to the question 'why?' The data show relationships but not causation, though in places some suggestions about causation are hazarded.

Section A deals with the way the educational level reached by the employees varies with the education of their parents. The way in which the reasons for discontinuing education at a particular point vary with the period of time, the level of education reached, and the education of the employees' parents are set out in section B. The ways in which the size and location of the employees' families vary with the level of education of the employees are dealt with in section C.

Section D repeats the analysis between generations of section A, but for the employees and their children, instead of for the employees and their parents. Attitudes to, and expenditures on, the education of children, as they vary with education and income, are examined in sections E and F. Section G investigates the extent to which occupation and wages are affected by family background, independently of education. A summary is provided in section H.

A. Education of Employees: Variation with the Education of Their Parents

There is a strong correlation between father's education and the level of education achieved by the employee. From Table 6.1 it is clear that, as the father's level of education increases, the percentage of children attaining high levels of education increases. Of the employees whose fathers had no education, 36 per cent had at least secondary education them-

Table 6.2. *Kenyan Employees by Own Education: Distribution by Father's Education*

Employee's education	Father's education			
	None	Primary	Post-primary	
None	98	2	0	(119)
Standards 1–4	87	12	1	(157)
Standards 5–6	67	30	3	(134)
Standards 7–8	66	30	4	(463)
Forms I–IV	48	43	9	(693)
Post-Form IV	16	47	37	(194)

selves, whereas for those whose fathers had primary education the corresponding figure is 66 per cent, and for those whose fathers had secondary or post-secondary education it is as much as 85 per cent. These percentages can be seen as roughly indicating the probability, given the education of the father, of getting at least to secondary school, and clearly for children from well-educated family backgrounds the probability is very high. This means that the children of fathers with less than secondary education are competing for the residual secondary school places remaining after the children of fathers with secondary education have in effect claimed their places. The size of the secondary school system, and hence the size of the residual, is therefore a crucial determinant of the probability of children from less-privileged family backgrounds going to secondary school.

In Kenya the growth of the unaided sector of secondary education has been the response to the scarcity of places relatively to the high demand for them in government schools, and accounts for the quite high proportion achieving secondary education, even from the less-educated households. But the differential effect of father's education is felt in the quality as well as the quantity of education. Although a relatively high proportion of primary school-leavers go on to secondary education, even when they are from less-educated households, to a relatively large extent they go to the lower-quality unaided schools. Fifty-four per cent of employees who went to secondary school and whose fathers were uneducated went to government secondary schools, as compared with 70 per cent of those whose fathers had secondary education or more. As there is a close relationship between education and income, these figures imply that the children of poor households attend disproportionately the high-cost unsubsidized schools.

Table 6.2 tells the same story as Table 6.1, by showing the different levels of education of the father when employees are grouped by their

Who Gets Schooling in Kenya?

Table 6.3. *Kenyan Employees whose Fathers Had Primary Education by Mother's Education: Distribution by Own Education*

Employee's education	Mother's education	
	None	Primary
None	1	0
Standards 1–6	17	2
Standards 7–8	27	20
Post-primary	55	78
	(317)	(261)

own educational attainment. The percentage of employees with uneducated fathers declines strongly as the level of education of employees rises and, conversely, the percentage of fathers with primary, secondary, or post-secondary education rises with the level of education of employees.

For example, 98 per cent of employees with no education had fathers with no education, while only 16 per cent of those with post-Form IV education had uneducated fathers. A person with a high level of education from a low socio-economic background, being one of very few, will therefore be competing for jobs mostly with people who have similar educational qualifications but a higher socio-economic background, with all the advantages this may bring. Hence, upwardly mobile school-leavers may be at a disadvantage in the job-market compared with their educational peers. Evidence about this is presented in a later section.

Table 6.3 shows that, controlling for father's education, mother's education has an independent effect on the probability of going to secondary school. Thus 55 per cent of the children of fathers with primary education whose mothers had no education went on to secondary or higher education, while 78 per cent of those whose mothers also had primary education did so.

Table 6.4 shows very clearly the strong positive relation between the education level of one parent (holding the other parent's education constant) and the years of education[2] of the employee. Increasing either the mother's or the father's education from none to primary (holding the other parent constant at none) raises the mean length of education of the child by over two years and, similarly, raising either parent from primary to secondary and over (keeping the other parent with primary) raises the mean length of education of the employee by a year and a half. Interac-

[2] Years of education are calculated from level of education attained, hence those who repeated classes would have spent more years in school than the years of education variable indicates.

Table 6.4. *Kenyan Employees by Mother's Education and Father's Education: Mean Years of Education*

Father's education	Mother's education		
	None	Primary	Post-primary
None	6.9	9.3	..
	(959)	(45)	
Primary	9.0	10.5	12.0
	(317)	(258)	(6)
Post-primary	11.0	12.0	13.1
	(55)	(65)	(24)

tion effects are captured along the diagonal, showing the beneficial effect of increasing both parents' education. The difference in years of education of the employee between the socio-economic extremes of both parents with zero education and both with post-primary education is very high, namely over six years. To that difference must be added the effect of family background on the type and quality of secondary school attended, which has already been remarked upon.

The effect of mothers' education, independently of that of fathers, on the education of children has already been noted. But, in practice, mothers' education is not independent of that of fathers. It has frequently been observed that people tend to choose marriage partners with similar socio-economic characteristics. This behaviour has been called 'assortative mating'. Clearly the probability of children gaining access to secondary school and, more generally, the degree of inequality in the distribution of educational opportunity by socio-economic background will be strongly affected by the propensity of individuals to marry their educational peers. The next generation will have the most unequal distribution of educational opportunity if there is perfectly assortative mating, the educated marrying the educated; the distribution will be less unequal if there is random mating, and most equal if there is anti-assortative mating, the educated marrying the uneducated.

Tables 6.5 and 6.6 show the relationships between the educational levels of the employees' parents. Thus, Table 6.5 shows that 95 per cent of employees whose fathers had no education had mothers with no education, 54 per cent of those with primary-educated fathers had mothers with no education, and only 37 per cent of those whose fathers had post-primary education had uneducated mothers. Eighteen per cent of employees whose fathers had post-primary education had mothers of that educational level, compared with a mere 1 per cent when fathers had only primary education and none when the fathers were uneducated.

Table 6.5. *Kenyan Employees by Father's Education: Distribution by Mother's Education*

Mother's education	Father's education		
	None	Primary	Post-primary
None	95	54	37
Primary	5	45	45
Post-primary	0	1	18
	(1011)	(585)	(149)

Table 6.6. *Kenyan Employees by Mother's Education: Distribution by Father's Education*

Father's education	Mother's education		
	None	Primary	Post-primary
None	72	12	8
Primary	24	70	18
Post-primary	4	18	74
	(1335)	(374)	(36)

These patterns are strongly suggestive of assortative mating. If mating were random, for each category of father's education the educational distribution of the mother would be the same and equal (or close) to the distribution of education among women in the population of Kenya.

Table 6.6 tells the other side of the same story. It shows, for instance, that 72 per cent of employees with uneducated mothers had uneducated fathers, whereas only 12 per cent of those with primary-educated mothers, and no more than 8 per cent of those with mothers of post-primary education, had uneducated fathers.

The behaviour illustrated in the tables is somewhere between perfectly assortative mating and random mating. Perfectly assortative mating is anyway not possible because there are far fewer educated women than men. However, Table 6.6 shows that nearly 90 per cent of the rather small pool (23 per cent) of women with education are married to educated men, i.e. it suggests that, if males and females were similarly allocated across educational groups, mating would be more nearly perfectly assortative. Given the advantages of having an educated parent, and particularly two educated parents, the propensity of educated individuals to have educated spouses will reinforce the unequal distribution of educational opportunities for the next generation. It is therefore of interest to try to assess the trend in assortative mating over time with the extension of education to more of the population. Some evidence is presented in section C, where a comparison is made of marriage patterns of the employees with those of their parents.

To examine the change in intergenerational mobility over time which results from the expansion of education, employees are divided in Table 6.7 into two cohorts, those aged 30 or less and those aged more than 30.

At the beginning of this section it was suggested that the probability of children from less-educated families going to secondary school depended on the size of the secondary school system, and hence on the size of the residual once the children from well-educated families had secured places. In Kenya, the residual of secondary school places has grown quite significantly, and this is reflected in Table 6.7.

In both age-groups the educational attainment of employees is related to that of their fathers. In both groups more than 80 per cent of employees whose fathers had post-primary education have it themselves, whereas the proportion is lower for employees whose fathers had only primary education and still lower for those whose fathers were uneducated. But the differences are much smaller for the younger than for the older group. In the younger group, 72 per cent of employees whose fathers were primary-educated have post-primary education, as do 54 per cent of those whose fathers were uneducated; among the older group, post-primary education has been achieved by only 53 per cent of those with primary-educated fathers and by no more than 22 per cent of those with uneducated fathers.

The narrowing of the influence of fathers' education, however, seems to have been largely confined to junior secondary education. The gap in the proportion of employees with post-Form IV education remains wide in the younger group. For those with secondary-educated fathers it is 43 per cent, for those with primary-educated fathers 18 per cent, and for those with uneducated fathers 5 per cent.

There has again been a move towards equality at the other end of the educational ladder, in the proportion having no more than the first 6 standards of primary school: the proportion has fallen from 46 per cent of those with uneducated fathers in the older group of employees to 19 per cent in the younger. Nevertheless, the divergence within the younger group remains wide as the proportion is only 2 per cent for those from the most-educated backgrounds.

The average years of education (Table 6.8) tell the same story. The figure is virtually the same for the two age-cohorts, except that it is higher in the younger cohort by two years when both parents are uneducated, and by one year when one parent is uneducated and the other has primary education. As a result of the increase in years of education for

Table 6.7. *Kenyan Employees by Age and Father's Education: Distribution by Own Education*

Employee's age and father's education	Employee's education				
	Standard 6 or less	Standards 7–8	Forms I–IV	Post-Form IV	Post-primary
30 years and under					
None	19	27	49	5	54 (455)
Primary	6	22	54	18	72 (388)
Post-primary	2	10	45	43	88 (105)
Over 30 years					
None	46	32	20	2	22 (559)
Primary	18	29	43	10	53 (204)
Post-primary	4	15	29	52	81 (49)
All ages					
None	34	30	33	3	36 (1014)
Primary	10	24	51	15	66 (592)
Post-primary	3	12	39	46	85 (154)

Table 6.8. *Kenyan Employees by Age and Parents' Education: Mean Years of Education*

Parents' education	Employee's age	
	30 years and under	Over 30 years
Both none	8.1	6.0
	(414)	(544)
One none, one primary	9.3	8.4
	(242)	(120)
Both primary	10.6	10.3
	(176)	(82)
One none, one post-primary	11.1	11.1
	(41)	(18)
One primary, one post-primary	11.7	12.6
	(52)	(20)
Both post-primary	13.1	13.1
	(11)	(13)
All	9.3	7.2

those with two uneducated parents, the difference between the two extremes of parental education is 7 years in the older group and only 5 years in the younger.

This analysis indicates that the expansion of education over the last 20 years or so has not removed the relationship between family background and the chances of moving to the top of the educational ladder, and to get beyond junior secondary school it is a great advantage to come from a well-educated family (Table 6.1). Nevertheless, the data suggest that intergenerational mobility has greatly increased with educational expansion.[3]

B. Reasons for Discontinuing Education

The replies to the questionnaire showed that around 90 per cent of employees had wanted to continue their formal education at the time they left it. There was no significant variation according to age or level of education, except that the percentage of those with post-Form IV education was in the seventies instead of the nineties. Evidently, as more

---

[3] For those who obtain employment in the urban formal sector, that is. All these statements, it must be kept in mind, are based on information about his relatively small and privileged group.

Table 6.9. *Kenyan Employees who Desired to Continue Their Education by Period at which Education Ceased: Distribution by Reason for Not Continuing*

Reason for not continuing	Period education completed			
	1931–50	1951–60	1961–70	1971–80
Educational	6	12	15	26
Economic	87	81	78	62
Other	7	7	7	12
	(89)	(229)	(506)	(583)

education becomes available, people's desires and expectations expand in step, so that the excess demand for education is undiminished.

If so many had wanted to continue their education beyond the stage at which it ceased, why had they not continued? There are two main sets of reason. One is educational, particularly examination failure but also the absence of a local school. Other reasons may be classed as economic: inability to pay school fees, the direct cost of education, and inability to do without the income (monetary or non-monetary) which would accrue from working instead of attending school, the indirect cost of education. In addition there is a variety of other reasons. Table 6.9 shows how the relative importance of these different reasons has changed over time. Until the 1970s the reasons were overwhelmingly economic, and predominantly the direct cost of school fees. In the last decade, educational reasons, particularly examination failures (of the 26 per cent in 1971–80 who did not continue for educational reasons, 23 per cent was because of examination failure), have become somewhat more important, and so has the undifferentiated 'other' category.

The impression given by the data is that over the last ten years access to schooling has become more meritocratic, but it is still to a very large degree dependent on ability to pay fees. Clearly children from well-educated backgrounds must pass the examinations more often to explain the high correlation reported in section A between father's and own education. However, families with higher incomes are still at a great advantage over less well-off families in ensuring secondary education for their children, for if they fail to make the government secondary school they can pay for private education. Evidence that families (and especially the better off) are willing to pay for private schooling is reviewed in section E.

That lack of success in the national Form IV examinations is the major reason for not continuing to Forms V and VI is given direct confirmation

Table 6.10. *Kenyan Employees by Form IV Examination Result: Percentage Reaching Form VI*

Examination result	Percentage reaching Form VI
Division 1	77
	(102)
Division 2	30
	(152)
Division 3	4
	(196)

Table 6.11. *Kenyan Employees by Father's Education: Distribution by Form IV Examination Result*

Examination result	Father's education		
	None	Primary	Post-primary
Division 1	7	18	35
Division 2	24	24	34
Division 3	38	34	16
Division 4	22	17	12
Fail	6	6	3
Did not sit	3	1	0
	(225)	(285)	(95)

in Table 6.10. The percentage going on to Form VI declines monotonically with the results in the examination.

Table 6.11 shows a strong relationship between success in the examination and the education of the father, so it seems that it is very hard for children from less-educated backgrounds not only to get into secondary school, but to do well once they are there. In contrast, in Table 6.12 there is only a weak correlation between results in the national Form VI examination and fathers' education. The children of primary-educated fathers do better than those of uneducated fathers, but they also do better than children whose fathers had post-primary education. The weak relationship is consistent with the notion that the Form IV examination selects the most able and determined pupils to continue to Form VI, whatever the family background, and that, whatever the form of influence of family background on Form IV candidates, it no longer operates by the time they take the Form VI examination.

Table 6.12. *Kenyan Employees with Passes in Form VI Examination by Father's*
Education: Distribution by Number of Passes

Number of passes	Father's education		
	None	Primary	Post-primary
1	19	15	22
2 or more	81	85	78
3 or more	46	58	43
4 or more	7	11	6
	(22)	(55)	(48)

C. Education of Employees and Size and Location of Their Families

Section A recorded the high degree of assortative mating by education level of employees' parents. Table 6.13 shows that such behaviour is also very strong for the employees themselves. There is a strongly declining monotonic relationship between the level of education of employees and the percentage having spouses with no education, and a strongly increasing and monotonic relation between the level of education of employees and the percentage having spouses with secondary or more education. For example, 86 per cent of men with no education have wives with no education, while only 28 per cent of those with primary education and 11 per cent of those with secondary education or more have wives with no education. This is strong evidence for assortative mating. If mating were random the percentage with wives with no education would be the same across male education categories, and equal to the percentage of women with no education in the Kenyan population.

There is a difference in the pattern for men and women. Only 23 per cent of women, but 55 per cent of men, with secondary and post-secondary education had spouses with primary education or less. Only 8 per cent of men, but 67 per cent of women with primary education had spouses with secondary or post-secondary education. This difference in the extent of assortative mating may be because women are reluctant to marry beneath themselves educationally, or because men are reluctant to marry women better educated than themselves. More plausibly, it is because of the scarcity of educated women and relative abundance of educated men.

In section A it was suggested that assortative mating may have in-

Table 6.13. *Kenyan Employees by Sex and Education: Distribution by Education of Spouse*

Employee's sex and spouse's education	Employee's education		
	None	Primary	Post-primary
All employees			
None	86	28	11
Primary	14	60	38
Post-primary	0	12	51
	(84)	(570)	(549)
Male employees			
None	86	29	11
Primary	14	63	44
Post-primary	0	8	45
	(81)	(537)	(460)
Female employees			
None	..	20	17
Primary	..	13	6
Post-primary	..	67	77
		(33)	(89)

creased over time as more women were educated. Twenty or so years ago, so few women were educated that many well-educated men would have been unable to find a well-educated wife. Today the number of educated women is much larger relative to the number of educated men, and so there is increased potential for assortative mating. Evidence that this is so comes from a comparison of Tables 6.13 and 6.5, which show that only 18 per cent of employees whose fathers had post-primary education also had mothers of that educational level, whereas 45 per cent of male employees with post-primary education have wives with the same education. In other words, the extent of assortative mating has increased from 18 per cent in one generation to 45 per cent in the next. Similarly, 45 per cent of employees whose fathers had primary education had mothers with primary education, whereas 63 per cent of male employees have primary-educated wives. Both changes indicate a move towards fully assortative mating.

There is a very strong monotonic relationship between the level of education of male African employees with one wife and the percentage having their wife with them in Nairobi rather than in the country. The same relation holds for the level of wages: only 25 per cent of those in the lowest wage-group, but over 60 per cent of those with Shs 1500 a month or more, have their wife in Nairobi. The high cost of living in Nairobi is likely to be part of the explanation and, given the extent of assortative mating, educated men tend to have educated wives for whom there are job opportunities in the city.

The same pattern holds for the location of children: the percentage of children located in Nairobi rises strongly and monotonically as the level of education and income of the employee rises; over 60 per cent of employees earning Shs 3000 or more per month have their first child educated in Nairobi, while this is the case for only 14 per cent of those earning Shs 500 per month. As educational opportunities are much greater in Nairobi than elsewhere, this difference in location compounds the disadvantages of those born to uneducated households.

D. Education of Employees' Children: Variation with the Education of Employees

The tables in this section are like those of section A which looked at the first and second generations, but they look at the educational attainment of the third generation (children of employees) in relation to that of the second and the first. The third is not strictly comparable with the earlier generations, however, because it is an urban sample with parents employed in the urban wage-sector. The second generation was predominantly rural born and educated, with parents employed in agriculture, and at least part of any improvement in educational opportunities to the third generation can be explained by the urban location. Part of the benefit of education for the second generation may be the opportunity to raise children in an urban location. The tables are also not strictly comparable with those of section A because most of the children have not completed their education, hence caution must be exercised when making statements about educational opportunity.

Employees have very few eligible children who are totally without schooling. For employees with education above Standard 6 the proportion is below 10 per cent, whereas for those with less education it ranges from 10 to 19 per cent. Table 6.14 shows that the education of the parent makes no difference to the years of education acquired by the first child under the age of 11 years, and it may be guessed that the abolition of fees for the first four years of primary school in 1974 has equalized educational opportunities for young children. The table also shows that it makes some difference to the years of education of the first child aged 15 or over, and a smaller difference for those aged between 11 and 14.[4]

---

[4] Years of education are calculated from class level reached in school. This would not equal years spent in school if some classes were repeated.

Table 6.14. *Kenyan Employees by Own Level of Education, Age of First Child and Whether Education of Child Continuing: Mean Years of Education of First Child*

Whether education continuing and age of first child	Employee's education					
	None	Standards 1–4	Standards 5–6	Standards 7–8	Forms I–IV	Post-Form IV
All						
6–10	3.1 (7)	2.5 (22)	2.3 (26)	2.8 (99)	2.8 (129)	2.1 (23)
11–14	5.3 (9)	5.4 (21)	6.6 (22)	6.0 (79)	6.4 (49)	8.7 (7)
15 and more	9.4 (45)	9.6 (76)	9.7 (32)	11.6 (75)	12.0 (38)	‥
Education completed						
15 and over	9.3 (17)	9.7 (35)	8.9 (14)	12.5 (19)	12.9 (13)	‥
Education continuing						
15 and over	10.5 (25)	9.6 (40)	10.3 (18)	11.3 (55)	11.5 (25)	‥

Table 6.15. *Kenyan Employees and Spouses by Education and by Age of First Child: Mean Years of Education of First Child*

Education of both parents	Age of first child		
	6–10	11–14	15 and over
None	..	..	9.3
			(33)
Primary	2.5	6.3	10.5
	(69)	(67)	(90)
Post-primary	2.8	7.8	12.4
	(72)	(14)	(8)

There is a difficulty about these figures of the length of education of the employees' children. They are concerned with the same relationships, those between the education of parents and children, as were analysed in section A, but there, where relationships were between first and second generations, and the child was the employee, all children had completed their education. In this section, where the relationship is between second and third generations, between employee and child, less than 40 per cent of the children have completed their education, and there is no way of knowing the final educational attainment of the rest. The figures for average length of education of those whose education is continuing therefore understate what it will be when they have completed, and the small difference, of just one year, that exists at present between top and bottom may be biased.

Table 6.15 shows the effects of the education of both parents on the years of education of the child, which is significant for the 11-year-olds and onwards. Table 6.16 shows the difference[5] between the attainment of secondary school by the children of parents with or without secondary education themselves.

E. Attitudes to the Education of Children: Variation with Employees' Education and Income

It is evidence of the importance attributed to education that a high proportion of employees say that they will pay to send a son to secondary school if he fails to gain a place at a government school (or make him repeat primary school so as to have another chance at gaining a place in a government school). And there is no strong relationship between that

---

[5] Though perhaps still subject to the bias already discussed.

Table 6.16. *Kenyan Employees with First Child Aged 15 or More who Has Completed Education by Own Education: Distribution by Education of First Child*

Education of employee	Education of child		
	Below secondary	Secondary	Post-secondary
None	43	57	0 (45)
Primary	32	59	9 (183)
Post-primary	12	69	19 (42)

proportion and either education or income (Table 6.17). The percentages are much the same for daughters as for sons. Of course, this is again the answer to a hypothetical question, and practice may not conform to stated intention. Over 80 per cent of the children who have completed their education and whose fathers were not educated beyond primary school did not themselves proceed to secondary school, which suggests a considerable departure from the stated intentions of the fathers.

F. Expenditure on Children's Education: Variation with Employees' Education and Income

The total cost of children's education increases strongly as the number of children in school increases (Table 6.18). As the level of education of the employee rises, and as the wage rises, his or her total spending on education also rises, but as a percentage of the wage it falls, and for the highest educational level it is less than half that of the lowest (Table 6.19). An employee's expenditure on education is affected by the number of children paid for, including those of the 'extended family'. Table 6.19 shows that the expenditure per child by level of education and by level of income does not rise in step with total expenditure, indicating that educational expenditure per child is more equally distributed than total educational expenditure.

Of course, the income variable used is the employee's wage and this is only a rough indicator of family resources as other members of the family (for example, the spouse) may be working and there may also be non-wage income (for example, from the *shamba*). Nevertheless, the high proportion of wage income spent by those with the lowest wage is very striking (Tables 6.19 and 6.20). Table 6.21 makes plain the high cost of secondary education even for those in government schools, where the fees are lower than in private schools. The high expenditure on a child in

Table 6.17. *Kenyan Employees by Education and by Wage: Distribution by Act-*
ion if Son Could Not Go to Government Secondary School

	Action by parent		
	Pay fees at private secondary school	Make son repeat primary	Other
Education			
None	65	19	16 (115)
Primary	57	24	19 (734)
Forms I–IV	54	33	13 (668)
Post-Form IV	64	20	16 (180)
Wage (Shs per month)			
0–1000	56	27	17 (988)
1001–2000	53	30	17 (395)
Over 2000	68	20	12 (285)

Note: The question put was 'If after leaving primary school your son could not continue to a government secondary school, what would you do?'

Table 6.18. *Kenyan Employees by Number of Children in School: Mean Expendi-*
ture on Education (Shs p.a.)

Number of children in school	Expenditure
1	500
2	1348
3	1405
4	2112
5	2641
6 and over	2986

government school is noteworthy, and information to provide a detailed explanation is not available. It is to be emphasized that school fees are only part of the cost of a child's education, and additional expenditures, on books, uniforms and particularly on boarding charges, may be greater for a child at a government school than at a private or *harambee* school. The higher expenditure on a child at a government than at a private school is partly the result of the distribution of pupils between the different employee income classes, because in most individual income classes expenditure is greater on a pupil at a private than at a government school. It was remarked in Chapter 4 that a very high proportion of the more senior secondary school pupils are at government schools, and it

Table 6.19. *Kenyan Employees by Education and Wage: Mean Expenditure (Shs p.a.) on Education of Children in School, Total, per Child, as Percentage of Income*

	Expenditure		
	Total	Per child	% of income
Education			
None	1279	699	21.2
	(78)	(86)	(80)
Standards 1–6	1550	581	18.2
	(183)	(198)	(105)
Standards 7–8	1553	608	11.5
	(263)	(276)	(77)
Forms I–IV	2020	829	10.8
	(224)	(228)	(263)
Post-Form IV	3578	1962	10.2
	(34)	(41)	(43)
Wage (Shs per month)			
0–500	1113	614	18.3
	(122)	(132)	(117)
501–750	1116	515	14.3
	(183)	(195)	(182)
751–1000	1257	421	13.9
	(141)	(144)	(144)
1001–1500	1580	604	14.7
	(125)	(132)	(135)
1501–2000	1566	572	8.2
	(69)	(70)	(70)
2001–3000	3151	1044	12.1
	(79)	(82)	(84)
Over 3000	4483	2047	10.1
	(56)	(64)	(67)

Note: The percentages are of the incomes of those reporting the data for this table. The incomes are not identical with those of the larger sample reported in Table 5.5.

is probable that supplementary expenditures required for senior pupils are much larger than those required for children in the lower grades of secondary school.

Despite the attitudes to the education of daughters reported in the previous section, Table 6.22 suggests that expenditure is discriminatory. Although the same amount is spent on boys and girls for primary education, at junior-secondary level a gap has opened, and for post-Form IV education the amount spent on the first child, if a boy, is twice that spent

Table 6.20. *Kenyan Employees by Wage and Educational Level of First Child in School: Mean Percentage of Employee's Income Spent on Education of First Child*

Wage (Shs per month)	Educational level of first child	
	Primary	Secondary
0–500	6.2	30.4
	(70)	(20)
501–750	3.9	20.1
	(93)	(35)
751–1000	3.6	16.5
	(72)	(23)
1001–1500	3.3	12.6
	(53)	(23)
1501–2000	3.6	8.6
	(26)	(11)
2001–3000	4.3	6.2
	(36)	(21)
Over 3000	4.8	5.2
	(17)	(15)

Table 6.21. *First Child of Kenyan Employees in School by Type of School Attended: Mean Expenditure by Employees on Education of First Child (Shs p.a.)*

Type of school	Expenditure	
Government primary	327	(506)
Private primary	1551	(31)
Government secondary	1859	(84)
Private secondary	1705	(58)

Table 6.22. *Kenyan Employees' First Child by Education and Sex: Mean Cost of Education in Year (Shs)*

Education of first child	Male	Female	All
Standard 4 and below	414	386	400
	(170)	(171)	(341)
Standards 5–8	320	330	324
	(142)	(107)	(249)
Forms I–IV	1412	1223	1337
	(116)	(75)	(191)
Post-Form IV	3236	1515	2641
	(15)	(8)	(22)
All	738	568	662
	(442)	(361)	(803)

on a girl. The difference might be expected to be the other way round, because girls go disproportionately to the more expensive schools. Female enrolment at maintained schools is 32 per cent, at assisted schools 50 per cent, and at unaided schools 45 per cent (Kenya 1979*a*), and yet expenditure on a girl is less than on a boy. Unfortunately, the survey data do not suggest how it is that girls come cheaper.

G. The Independent Effect of Family Background on Occupation and Wages

Family background is a major determinant of an employee's educational attainment, and hence a major indirect determinant of his or her occupation and earnings. But family background may have an effect on economic status independently of its effect on educational attainment. There are various reasons why this might be so: employers may discriminate in favour of people from well-educated backgrounds because of snobbery, they may believe that people from educated backgrounds possess valuable non-cognitive traits and personality attributes, there may be nepotism at work, or well-educated parents may be able to use their urban, white-collar contacts to get the best jobs for their offspring. People from less-favourable family backgrounds may have lower career aspirations, and may be less informed about job opportunities. Some of these reasons imply market imperfections. An alternative approach would explain the possibility that people from favourable family backgrounds do better in the job-market entirely by reference to differences in 'human capital'. Formal education is a major contributor to the formation of human capital in the form of a productive worker. But other investments, both before school and outside school (for example, better health resulting from better nutrition and hygiene), are of importance, and are likely to be much greater in educated households, especially where the mother is educated. These investments both facilitate access to and reinforce cognitive development at school. They may also have an independent effect on productivity in the job-market. The use in this study of years of education as a proxy for investment in 'human capital' ignores not only these pre-school and non-school investments, but also differences in the quality of schooling, a major component of the effectiveness of investment in human capital and one which is likely to be correlated positively with family background.

To detect the independent effect of family background on occupation and income, it is necessary to control for educational attainment. This is done in Table 6.23, and the general tendency is clear: employees are less likely to be in manual occupations, whatever their own education, the

Table 6.23. *Kenyan Employees by Education, and Father's Education: Distribution by Occupation*

Employee's education and father's education	Employee's occupation			
	Manual	Clerical	Other	
Employee's education				
Standards 5–8				
Father's education				
None	81	18	1	(393)
Primary	75	19	6	(182)
Post-primary	63	26	11	(21)
Forms I–IV				
Father's education				
None	41	48	11	(333)
Primary	37	59	4	(291)
Post-primary	25	66	9	(56)
Post-Form IV				
Father's education				
None	21	35	44	(31)
Primary	5	43	52	(92)
Post-primary	0	21	79	(70)

more educated their fathers. For instance, employees with Standards 5–8 education are in manual occupations to the extent of 81 per cent when their fathers were uneducated, whereas ony 75 per cent of those with primary-educated fathers, and 63 per cent of those whose fathers had post-primary education, are manual workers. Similarly, for employees with junior secondary education, the proportion in manual occupations falls from 41 per cent to 37 per cent and to 25 per cent as the education of the fathers rises from none to primary to post-primary. The wage of an employee also tends to be higher the higher the educational attainment of his father, particularly for employees with post-Form IV education and long work experience (Table 6.24).

Other benefits of having a father with secondary education are displayed in Table 6.25. For employees in both educational groups distinguished in the table, a higher proportion obtained employment immediately after leaving school, and a smaller proportion had more than a year to wait, when their fathers had had a secondary education than when their fathers were of a lower educational status. It also appears (Table 6.26) that a higher proportion of employees who had had more than one job changed jobs without an intervening spell of unemployment if their fathers were secondary-educated than if they came from families with a lower level of education.

Table 6.24. *Kenyan Employees by Education, Years of Employment Experience, and Father's Education: Mean Wage (Shs per month)*

| Father's education | Employee's education and experience | | | |
| | Forms I–IV | | Post-Form IV | |
	0–7 yrs	More than 7 yrs	0–7 yrs	More than 7 yrs
None	897	1854	2299	2617
	(162)	(168)	(17)	(11)
Primary	1024	1976	2724	3879
	(165)	(125)	(62)	(21)
Post-primary	1106	1952	2598	6395
	(36)	(24)	(49)	(22)

Table 6.25. *Kenyan Employees by Education and Father's Education: Distribution by Time between End of Education and Start of Wage-Employment*

| Employee's education and time between end of education and start of wage-employment (months) | Father's education | | |
	None	Primary	Post-primary
Standards 5–8			
Zero	24	33	44
1–12	28	27	34
More than 12	48	40	22
	(374)	(172)	(19)
Form I–IV			
Zero	31	32	39
1–12	44	46	45
More than 12	25	22	16
	(331)	(287)	(59)

Table 6.26. *Kenyan Employees with Previous Wage-Employment by Education and Father's Education: Percentage Continuously Employed*

| Father's education | Employee's education | |
	Standards 5–8	Forms I–IV
None	56	66
	(200)	(140)
Primary	58	68
	(78)	(117)
Post-primary	89	72
	(12)	(32)

In summary, the data suggest that family background does have some direct effect on an individual's economic success, independently of his or her educational attainment. A favourable family background may also help an individual to get an urban wage-job more quickly, and to be less likely to suffer spells of unemployment, because of superior contacts or information.

H. Summary

There is a strong positive correlation between the level of education of fathers and the level achieved by their children. The mother's education has an independent effect in the same direction. The correlation operates with respect to the quality as well as to the quantity of education.

There is an independent relationship between mothers' and childrens' education, but because of assortative mating the education of fathers and mothers are not independent, and this pattern of mating reinforces the link between the education of parents and that of their children. With the increase in the number of educated women, assortative mating has been increasing. The same relationships are found between employees and their children as between the children of employees and employees, that is, between the third and second generation as between the second and the first.

The strong correlation between the education of adjacent generations means that a high proportion of children of parents with secondary education achieve that level of education themselves. It follows that the opportunities for those from less-educated families of achieving secondary education depend on the size of the secondary school entry, and hence on the size of the residual once the children of well-educated families have secured places. The growth of the secondary school system has resulted in that residual being large. Although the relationship between family background and the chance of climbing to the top of the educational ladder has not disappeared, as a result of the expansion in secondary school places upward mobility from one generation to the next has greatly increased.

Around 90 per cent of employees had wished to continue their education beyond the stage they reached. Over time, educational reasons for failing to continue have become more important, and economic reasons less important, so that the system has become more meritocratic. Nevertheless, the advantage of an educated and higher-income family background persists.

Just as almost everyone wanted to have more education than they had in fact achieved, so all employees want their children to have more education than they had themselves. A high proportion of all employees, irrespective of education, occupation, and income, say they would pay for private education if their children fail to obtain a place at a government secondary school. Employees' expenditure on education rises with their income, but the proportion of income spent declines. Family background is related to economic success not only through its effects on educational attainment: there is a correlation between family background and economic success for employees of the same educational attainment.

7

Education and Rural–Urban Links in Kenya

This chapter deals with the migration of rural dwellers to the urban labour-market in Nairobi and their integration into it. Migrants are defined as those who came to the city aged 14 or more. Section A presents the demographic characteristics of migrant employees, including their regions of origin; in section B educational characteristics of the migrants are reviewed and compared with those of non-migrants. The process of the migrants' integration into the urban labour-market and the role of education therein are the topics of section C. Continuing links with the rural areas, including support for dependants outside Nairobi, intentions to return to area of origin and possession of a *shamba*, are discussed in section D. Section E provides a brief summary of findings. As these issues concern African employees, and not Asians or Europeans, the data refer only to them.

A. Demographic Characteristics of Urban Migrant Employees

The high proportion of Nairobi employees who are migrants has already been remarked upon (Chapter 4 and Table 4.4). Of the non-migrants, only 3 per cent were actually born in the city, the others arriving as children. Half the migrants arrived in the last decade, and all but 5 per cent since 1950.

Most migrants (defined as those arriving at age 14 or over) arrived young, 88 per cent before the age of 27 and 41 per cent before they were 20. Women arrived younger than men, 53 per cent being under 20 as compared with 40 per cent of the men, with mean ages of 20.1 and 21.3, respectively (Table 7.1).

Nearly 40 per cent of Nairobi wage-employees were born in nearby Central Province and another 19 per cent in Eastern Province. Eighteen

Table 7.1. *Kenyan African Migrant Employees by Sex: Distribution by Age on Arrival in Nairobi; Mean Age*

| | Age on arrival (years) | | | | | | Mean | |
	14–16	17–19	20–2	23–6	27–35	Over 35		
Male	12	28	31	17	9	3	21.3	(1217)
Female	18	35	27	11	8	2	20.1	(181)
All	12	29	30	16	9	3	21.2	(1398)

per cent came from Nyanza, remote but well served by transport. Thus Central Province was disproportionately represented in the flow of migrants to Nairobi, while the Rift Valley and the Coast and North-Eastern Provinces were particularly under-represented. The location of these provinces with respect to Nairobi may not be explanation enough, but it is certainly part of the explanation (see Map 1, p. xxxiii). Other differences between provinces, including differences in the cultural attitudes of the population and the availability of land, doubtless also have an effect.

There have been some changes over time in the origin of migrants by province and it seems that more recent migrants have been increasingly from the nearby rather than the more distant provinces. Women tend to have come less far than men, with a higher share from Central Province.

B. Educational Characteristics of Migrants

Migrant employees have on average fewer years of education (8.1) than non-migrants (10.3). As many as 73 per cent of non-migrants had some post-primary education, compared with 47 per cent of migrants. However, the average years of education of arriving migrants who are wage-employees rose quickly to 8.6 years for those arriving in 1966–70, from only 2.3 years for those arriving in the 1940s. Since 1966–70, however, there has been no further increase. In each period women have tended to have more years of education than men (Table 7.2), which must mean, given the lower education of women in the population as a whole (see Chapter 4), that it is the more-educated women who migrate.

Most migrants completed their education before migrating (see Chapter 4 and Tables 4.13 and 7.3), and of those who did not, most arrived in the city young and subsequently attained one of the higher levels of education. For example, no more than 29 per cent of migrant employees with post-Form IV education who arrived younger than 20 had completed

Table 7.2. *Kenyan African Migrant Employees by Year of Arrival in Nairobi and Sex: Mean Years of Education*

Year of arrival in Nairobi	Males		Females		All	
1941–50	2.3	(14)	..		2.3	(14)
1951–60	3.8	(58)	..		3.7	(60)
1961–65	5.9	(156)	..		6.0	(161)
1966–70	8.5	(429)	9.0	(72)	8.6	(500)
1971–75	8.9	(289)	9.8	(58)	9.0	(347)
1976–80	8.6	(320)	8.8	(47)	8.6	(367)
All	8.0	(1271)	9.1	(183)	8.1	(1454)

Table 7.3. *Kenyan Educated African Migrant Employees by Education and Age on Arrival in Nairobi: Percentage who Completed Their Education before Migrating*

Education	Age on arrival				All
	14–19	20–2	23–6	27 and over	
Standards 1–4	91	89	100	97	93
	(46)	(27)	(20)	(29)	(122)
Standards 5–6	100	83	93	94	94
	(42)	(23)	(28)	(16)	(109)
Standards 7–8	80	92	95	87	87
	(178)	(123)	(59)	(48)	(408)
Forms I–IV	59	90	93	100	77
	(245)	(185)	(108)	(21)	(559)
Post-Form IV	29	56	46	79	48
	(42)	(46)	(23)	(24)	(115)
All	69	86	91	91	81
	(553)	(404)	(228)	(128)	(1313)

their education before migrating, compared with 79 per cent of those aged 27 and over.

Most migrants who attain relatively high levels of education are young on arrival in the city. Whereas 50 per cent of persons with no education arrived at 23 years of age or more, and 40 per cent of persons with education of Standards 1–4, only 23 per cent of migrants with lower-secondary education arrived at that age (Table 7.4). Nevertheless, since some persons with little education come to Nairobi quite young, the average age of arrival differs little by level of education.

Table 7.4. *Kenyan African Migrant Employees by Education: Distribution by Age on Arrival in Nairobi; Mean Age on Arrival*

Age on arrival (years)	Education						All
	None	Standards 1–4	Standards 5–6	Standards 7–8	Forms I–IV	Post-Form IV	
14–16	13	21	15	10	13	11	13
17–19	22	17	23	34	31	26	29
20–22	15	22	21	30	33	40	30
23–26	11	16	26	14	19	11	17
27 and over	39	24	15	12	4	12	11
	(82)	(122)	(109)	(408)	(559)	(115)	(1398)
Mean age on arrival	25.0	22.5	22.0	21.0	20.2	21.4	21.2

The average time taken to get a job after completion of education was far shorter for persons born in Nairobi (9.5 months) than for those who came as children (22.9 months) or for migrants (23.7 months). It was also shorter for migrants who finished their education in Nairobi (10.9 months) than for those who finished before migrating (26.8 months). Differences of these kinds exist for most levels of education.

The distribution of activities between completing education and taking up employment is markedly different according to whether the migrants completed their education before or after migrating. For the former group, 46 per cent of the average time of 26.8 months was spent working on a *shamba* and 22 per cent unemployed, looking for employment. For migrants who completed their education after migrating, the corresponding figures are 31 per cent and 42 per cent.

C. Migrants' Process of Adjustment on Arrival: The Role of Education

For migrants who finished their education before migrating, the average interval before finding an independent source of income after they arrived in the city is 7.2 months. Something over half (57 per cent) of them found an independent income immediately or within a month, another 31 per cent had found one within a year, and the remaining 12 per cent took over a year. Education helped to keep this waiting period short: for persons with Standards 1–4 the average is 12.7 months, while for those with post-Form IV it is 4.8 months. In general, a source of income was found more quickly by older than by younger migrants for any given level of education, perhaps reflecting a greater tendency for the older to migrate only if some job possibility were relatively assured (Table 7.5). The length of the search for an independent source of income on arrival shows no clear trend over time, either in the sample as a whole or for specific levels of education.

A large majority (80 per cent) of migrants who had completed their education before migrating had had as their first source of independent income in Nairobi either the job they held at the time of the survey or a similar job with a different employer. There had been little movement from job to job. Only 5 per cent entered self-employment (Table 7.6).

D. Ties with Rural Areas: Variation by Level of Education

Employees in Nairobi have strong ties with the rural areas; most have migrated from them and even the few who have not tend to have con-

Table 7.5. *Kenyan African Migrant Employees who Completed Their Education before Migrating by Education, Age on Arrival, and Sex: Mean Time (months) to Find an Independent Source of Income after Arrival in Nairobi*

Education	Age on arrival in Nairobi				Sex	
	14–19	20–6	27 and over	All	Male	Female
Standards 1–4	14.1	13.7	9.5	12.7	12.6	51.8
	(37)	(39)	(28)	(103)	(118)	(6)
Standards 5–6	11.2	6.0	4.1	7.5	9.5	9.9
	(33)	(41)	(17)	(92)	(93)	(3)
Standards 7–8	11.9	6.7	3.6	8.4	7.9	12.7
	(133)	(149)	(42)	(322)	(316)	(24)
Forms I–IV	6.5	5.0	2.0	5.3	5.2	6.8
	(140)	(259)	(25)	(424)	(368)	(73)
Post-Form IV	4.2	5.8	2.8	4.8	3.2	12.8
	(12)	(28)	(11)	(51)	(43)	(8)
All	9.6	6.2	4.4	7.2	7.3	10.8
	(360)	(521)	(129)	(1010)	(940)	(114)

siderable links with them. Frequently the spouse and children live there, and remittances are made for their support and for the support of other relatives; about a third of the employees own a *shamba*.

Spouses and Children Outside Nairobi

Only a minority of married employees have a spouse with them in Nairobi, the proportion being much higher for female than male employees. In total, about 40 per cent of spouses live in Nairobi (though it is 65 per cent for non-migrants) and more than half live on the employee's *shamba* (Table 7.7). The proportion of spouses on the *shamba* falls with the level of education beyond Standards 5–6, from 70 per cent to 9 per cent for those with post-Form IV education. The proportion rises with age from 37 per cent for those aged 15–30 to 80 per cent for those over 40 years of age (Table 7.8). The location of children is quite similar to that of spouses. A somewhat higher percentage of the children of older employees than of their spouses are in Nairobi, probably reflecting the existence of children who are now on their own and have moved to the city. The proportion of wives and children in Nairobi varies considerably by province of origin (excluding Nairobi) from a low of 26 per cent for Eastern Province to 50 per cent for Nyanza.

The proportion of wives and children in Nairobi is significantly lower

Table 7.6. *Kenyan African Migrant Employees who Completed Their Education before Migrating by Education: Distribution by First Independent Source of Income in Nairobi*

Source of independent income	Education					All
	Standards 1–4	Standards 5–6	Standards 7–8	Forms I–IV	Post-Form IV	
Current employer	41	54	60	72	53	62
Similar job with another employer	31	24	18	13	25	18
Other wage-job	21	16	20	10	16	15
Self-employment	7	6	2	5	6	5
	(106)	(87)	(267)	(377)	(51)	(888)

Table 7.7. *Kenyan African Employees by Education and Migrant Status: Percentage of Spouses in Nairobi and on the* Shamba

Education	Non-migrant			Migrant			All	
	Nairobi	*Shamba*		Nairobi	*Shamba*		Nairobi	*Shamba*
None	..	..		19	71	(94)	20	70
Standards 1–4	..	..		18	71	(128)	19	69
Standards 5–6	..	..		24	72	(92)	26	70
Standards 7–8	71	29	(31)	27	62	(334)	30	59
Forms I–IV	59	24	(49)	57	35	(379)	57	34
Post-Form IV	100	0	(12)	85	11	(66)	87	9
All	65	25	(108)	39	52	(1093)	41	50

(34 per cent) for employees who own a *shamba* than for those without one (53 per cent), but even for the latter a high proportion of spouses are in the rural areas. Owning a *shamba* is associated with having a larger family, especially for employees aged 30 or less.

Support for Relatives Outside Nairobi

Nearly all employees in the sample provide support for relatives outside Nairobi, reflecting the fact that many have spouses and children and nearly all the rest have siblings or parents outside Nairobi. These remittances averaged Shs 2736 for the year before the survey, and constituted nearly a fifth of the income reported. For those who provided such support (i.e. excluding those providing none) the average amount was Shs 3150 or 23 per cent of income.

The percentage of employees providing support and the amount they provide depends on the nature of their original ties with the countryside. Adult migrants are more likely to provide support (92 per cent) than those who arrived as children (78 per cent) or than those born in Nairobi (51 per cent), and the income used in this way constitutes 21 per cent, 15 per cent, and 5 per cent respectively of the total income of these groups (Table 7.9). While average support rises with both earnings and education, the percentage of income so used falls as the level of education rises (from about 30 per cent for those with none to 10 per cent for those with post-Form IV education) and as the level of earnings rises (from 35 per cent for those earning less than Shs 500 per month to 11 per cent for those earning above Shs 3000) (Table 7.10). As the support is used to a considerable extent to pay for essentials, it might be expected that the share of income used in this way would be highest for low income-

Table 7.8. *Kenyan African Employees by Age and Education: Percentage of Spouses in Nairobi and on the Shamba*

Age	Education									
	None		Primary		Forms I–IV		Post-Form IV		All	
	Nairobi	Shamba	Nairobi	Shamba	Nairobi	Shamba	Nairobi	Shamba	Nairobi	Shamba
15–30	67	33 (15)	37	50 (183)	58	32 (242)	91	6 (35)	52	37
31–40	20	80 (15)	27	64 (237)	54	37 (143)	88	12 (25)	39	52
41 and over	10	88 (57)	12	82 (159)	33	60 (30)	..	.. (4)	14	80
All	22	77 (87)	26	65 (579)	55	36 (415)	84	11 (64)	39	52

Note: When percentages do not add to 100 it is because spouses are reported as elsewhere, other than Nairobi or *shamba*.

Table 7.9. *Kenyan African Employees by Education and Migrant Status: Percentage who Support Relatives Outside Nairobi and Percentage of Income Used in that Way*

Education	Non-Migrant				Migrant		All	
	Born Nairobi		Born elsewhere					
	% supporting	% of income	% supporting	% of income	% supporting	% of income	% supporting	% of income
None	..	..	..	..	94 (106)	30 (88)	93 (115)	30 (98)
Standards 1–4	..	..	..	..	93 (139)	28 (114)	92 (148)	28 (122)
Standards 5–6	..	..	87 (6)	..	92 (121)	25 (110)	91 (130)	26 (118)
Standards 7–8	..	..	79 (28)	18 (27)	93 (413)	22 (380)	91 (449)	21 (416)
Forms I–IV	56 (23)	5 (18)	84 (61)	14 (56)	93 (565)	20 (508)	90 (660)	19 (591)
Post-Form IV	48 (12)	3 (13)	40 (13)	6 (13)	85 (112)	12 (100)	76 (139)	10 (126)
All	51 (44)	5 (44)	78 (115)	15 (109)	92 (1455)	21 (1299)	90 (1641)	19 (1473)

Table 7.10. *Kenyan African Employees by Wage and Education: Percentage of Income Used to Support Relatives Outside Nairobi*

Wage (Shs per month)	Education						All
	None	Standards 1–4	Standards 5–6	Standards 7–8	Forms I–IV	Post-Form IV	
0–500	43 (41)	38 (32)	32 (23)	30 (72)	33 (64)	··	35 (232)
501–750	24 (40)	32 (49)	26 (46)	25 (136)	26 (110)	··	26 (391)
751–1000	25 (11)	21 (22)	30 (21)	21 (90)	25 (116)	19 (14)	24 (276)
1001–1500	··	27 (13)	30 (13)	24 (62)	22 (129)	13 (27)	23 (249)
1501–2000	··	··	··	21 (24)	14 (67)	16 (10)	16 (111)
2001–3000	··	··	··	15 (21)	13 (67)	11 (39)	13 (131)
Over 3000	··	··	··	10 (8)	15 (39)	7 (32)	11 (83)
All	30 (98)	28 (122)	26 (118)	21 (416)	19 (591)	10 (126)	19 (1473)

earners, particularly as they have closer ties to rural areas, with a higher share of their spouses and children living there. For those with low incomes, the share used for support outside Nairobi tends to be unrelated to the employee's education. For higher income-earners, the share is unaffected by education until the secondary level is reached, when it is associated with a lower share, in part due no doubt to the more urban life-style of persons with secondary, especially post-Form IV, education, as reflected in the higher share of spouses and children living in Nairobi.

As female employees are much less likely than males to have members of their immediate family outside Nairobi, fewer of them provide support (79 per cent compared with 91 per cent) and on average they provide much less support (Shs 1655 compared with Shs 2855, and 11 per cent compared with 21 per cent of their income). For respondents from most provinces the share of income used for remittances is between 18 per cent and 22 per cent, the exceptions being Nairobi (4 per cent) and Eastern Province (26 per cent).

Support for relatives outside Nairobi mainly takes the form of remittances of money: in nearly 60 per cent of cases money was the sole form of support, in 37 per cent it was used together with purchase of goods, and in only 3 per cent of cases was there no money involved in the process. The provision of both money and goods, rather than money alone, increases with the total level of support. In the great majority of cases part of the remittance is used for food (84 per cent) and in nearly 60 per cent of cases some is used for education. Both farm improvements and house construction are imporant uses (a third and a quarter of cases) whereas land acquisition is infrequent (5 per cent of cases). The purposes for which support is used does not vary widely by level of education, or by earnings, except that construction is more likely to be a use for respondents with earnings above Shs 3000 than for other groups (20–31 per cent). Farm improvement was also most likely for the top earnings category (54 per cent) and less so for the others (29–33 per cent). Use of remittance funds for land acquisition was also most frequent in the top income category (12 per cent contrasting with 2–6 per cent for other groups).

The close links that Nairobi employees have with a rural area gives them a choice of location for the education of their children. The place chosen is closely related to earnings and education. Seventy-two per cent of employees earning Shs 500 a month or less had their first child educated in the rural areas; for employees with earnings above Shs 3000 a month the proportion is only 14 per cent. The proportion falls from 63 per cent for employees with no education to 7 per cent for those with post-Form IV education (Table 7.11). The migrant status of the employee is also important: employees born in Nairobi do not educate their children in the rural areas, while those who arrived in the city as children do

Table 7.11. *Kenyan African Employees^a by Wage, Education, and Migrant Status: Percentage of Cases where First Child Educated in the Rural Area*

	Education						All
	None	Standards 1–4	Standards 5–6	Standards 7–8	Forms I–IV	Post-Form IV	
Wages (Shs per month)							
0–500	76	87	78	63	69	··	72
	(21)	(15)	(9)	(30)	(16)		(91)
501–750	63	56	74	49	48	··	55
	(19)	(34)	(19)	(73)	(21)		(167)
751–1000	43	33	82	54	48	··	53
	(7)	(15)	(11)	(56)	(27)		(116)
1001–1500	··	85	60	55	36	··	50
		(13)	(10)	(49)	(44)		(121)
1501–2000	··	··	··	52	27	··	39
				(21)	(30)		(62)
2001–3000	··	··	··	15	28	9	21
				(20)	(44)	(11)	(77)
Over 3000	··	··	··	25	17	33	14
				(8)	(23)	(12)	(43)
All	63	62	70	50	36	7	48
	(49)	(81)	(56)	(257)	(205)	(29)	(678)
Migrant status							
Non-migrants	··	50	67	27	17	··	28
		(6)	(6)	(22)	(23)		(60)
Migrants	63	65	67	51	38	7	49
	(46)	(75)	(52)	(233)	(180)	(27)	(614)

^a Only employees whose first child has been or is being educated.

Table 7.12. *Kenyan African Employees with Children in School Last Year by Wage and Place of Children's Education: Mean Cost of Education per Child (Shs per year)*[a]

Wage (Shs per month)	Place of education	
	Nairobi	Rural area
0–500	443	391
	(37)	(164)
501–750	641	288
	(100)	(220)
751–1000	502	375
	(74)	(170)
1001–1500	586	509
	(103)	(146)
1501–2000	656	610
	(54)	(51)
2001–3000	1093	729
	(82)	(43)
Over 3000	1668	436
	(67)	(15)
All	803	414
	(518)	(808)

[a] Figures include up to three children for each employee, beginning with the oldest.

so in 41 per cent of cases, making a mean for non-migrants of 28 per cent. Migrants do so to the extent of 49 per cent. These patterns for the first child seem to be essentially the same for the second and third children.

The cost of a child's education is on average about twice as high in Nairobi as in the rural areas (Table 7.12). The average outlay tends to rise with the level of the respondent's earnings, especially when the child is educated in Nairobi. The cost differential between Nairobi and the rural areas in considerable for employees earning Shs 1000 and less, and for those earning above Shs 2000. The data strongly suggest that one reason children are educated in the rural areas is that it is so much cheaper. The relatively low cost in the rural areas must strongly motivate lower-income employees to educate their children there, though it is probable that the figures are biased.by the effect of a higher proportion of costly secondary pupils in Nairobi and of cheaper primary pupils in a rural area.

Possession of a Shamba

A little more than a third of all respondents had a *shamba*. The proportion having a *shamba* varies with age from 8 per cent of employees aged

Table 7.13. *Kenyan African Employees by Education, Age, and Migrant Status: Percentage with* Shamba

	Age				All
	15–20	21–30	31–40	41 and over	
Education					
None	..	41	39	71	57
		(29)	(23)	(65)	(117)
Primary	0	26	52	77	46
	(19)	(283)	(257)	(168)	(727)
Forms I–IV	17	19	37	68	26
	(35)	(439)	(168)	(34)	(676)
Post-Form IV	0	12	56	40	20
	(14)	(105)	(27)	(5)	(151)
All	9	21	46	73	36
	(68)	(856)	(475)	(272)	(167)
Migrant status					
Non-migrant	15	18	38	64	25
	(13)	(117)	(29)	(14)	(173)
Migrant	8	22	47	73	38
	(51)	(732)	(439)	(254)	(1476)

15–20 to 73 per cent of those aged 41 and over (Table 7.13). Shamba ownership is negatively associated with education. For instance, 57 per cent of those with no education had a *shamba*, compared with 20 per cent of those with post-Form IV education (Table 7.13).

Migrants are more likely to have a *shamba* than non-migrants (Table 7.13). Many more males have *shambas* (41 per cent) than females (12 per cent); a striking 83 per cent of males over 50 have *shambas*. A greater proportion of employees from Western, Eastern and Nyanza Provinces have *shambas* (46–9 per cent) than those from Nairobi (24 per cent), Central (27 per cent), Rift Valley (31 per cent), and Coast (20 per cent) Provinces.

Seventy per cent of all *shamba* owners acquired them by inheritance, nearly a quarter by purchase, and the rest by a variety of other means. Purchase appears to be especially frequent for persons in the prime earning years of 31–40. Purchase is more important and inheritance less so the higher the level of income and education (Table 7.14).

The median *shamba* size is 3–4 acres, with a substantial 12 per cent being more than 10 acres, so that the mean size of holding for employees having a *shamba* is 10.6 acres. There seems to be no systematic relationship between average *shamba* size and level of either education or

Table 7.14. *Kenyan African Employees with Shamba by Wage and Education: Distribution by Method of Shamba Acquisition*

Method of *shamba* acquisition	Wage (Shs per month)						Education		
	0–750	751–1500	1501–2000	2001–3000	Over 3000	All	None	Primary	Secondary
Inheritance	81	68	80	31	40	69	80	73	60
Settlement scheme	4	2	0	6	0	3	3	3	4
Purchase	10	25	17	59	58	23	7	21	31
Other	5	5	3	4	2	5	10	3	5
	(261)	(208)	(38)	(51)	(45)	(599)	(70)	(333)	(202)

wage, except that employees with both the highest education and the highest wage (there were only 15 in a sample of 580) had *shambas* with a mean size of 143 acres. Four of the largest *shambas* in the sample are in the Rift Valley and average 500 acres.

Loans were used by about 26 per cent of employees who purchased a *shamba*, and much more frequently by the higher-income groups: of those with earnings above Shs 2000 a month over 40 per cent utilized such loans, compared with only 17 per cent of those with incomes under Shs 1500. The difference in *shamba* ownership between the older and the younger groups suggests that the process of acquiring a *shamba* is an interesting aspect of an employee's economic career. As the great majority of *shamba* owners acquired them by inheritance, the ownership difference between the older and younger groups of employees is explained largely by the fact that the younger have not yet inherited. The difference in the proportion owning a *shamba* may also be the consequence of a decline in the availability of land, so that a higher proportion of the older group had land when they were young than of the present younger group. The importance of inheritance in the acquisition of a *shamba* also implies that *shamba* size is likely to be smaller for the younger than for the older group, and smaller still for the next generation, as *shambas* are divided between the sons of the deceased. Large *shambas* are likely, in fact, to have been acquired by the richer employees from several owners of small *shambas*.

Links with the Shamba

The widespread tendency for employees to have their spouses and children on the *shamba* creates an expectation of ties of other kinds, such as frequent visits, remittances to family members in the rural area, and productive expenditures on the *shamba*.

The frequency of visits, however, is not strikingly high: the median is about 4 per year while the mean is 8.4. A few employees (4 per cent) did not visit at all, but 20 per cent visited no more than once.

The number of visits is closely related to province of birth, which in most cases will be the province in which the *shamba* is located. Few persons from Western and Nyanza Provinces make more than 4 visits per year (11 per cent), while much higher proportions do so from the Rift Valley (68 per cent), Central Province (87 per cent) and Eastern Province (67 per cent) (Table 7.15). The average number was 14 for Central Province, 13 for Eastern Province, 6 for the Rift Valley and only 3 or 4 for the other, more distant provinces. The number of visits to the *shamba* is related to the location of the spouse: the median number was 2 for employees with a spouse in Nairobi only, 5 for those with a spouse on the

Table 7.15. *Kenyan African Employees with* Shamba *by Province of Birth: Distribution by Number of Visits to the* Shamba *during the Previous Year; Mean Number of Visits*

Number of visits	Province of birth						All
	Central	Eastern	Nyanza	Rift Valley	Western	Other	
0	2	2	6	8	4	5	4
1	4	8	26	8	27	42	16·
2	3	8	33	8	31	12	16
3–4	4	15	24	8	27	17	16
5–23	39	34	10	34	8	24	25
24–97	35	33	0	8	3	0	18
More than 97[a]	13	0	1	26	0	0	5
	(161)	(135)	(120)	(23)	(102)	(33)	(573)
Mean[b]	13.5	12.8	2.9	6.2	3.4	3.6	8.4

[a] Includes respondents who live on the *shamba*.
[b] Excludes persons making more than 97 visits.

shamba only, and 3 for the unmarried. Very few of the respondents who visited the *shamba* every two weeks or more had spouses in Nairobi. On the other hand, even when no more than one visit was made in the year, the spouse was more frequently on the *shamba* than in Nairobi.

Production and Decision-Making on the Shamba

Most *shambas* (73 per cent) are worked entirely by members of the owner's family. Non-family workers are more common on *shambas* of the more-educated owners, and 83 per cent of owners with post-Form IV education employ them. In fact, 29 per cent of such owners have four or more such workers. It is clear that a small share of *shamba* owners, mostly with post-Form IV education, have large *shambas* which are commercial in nature, as reflected by the employment of several paid workers (Table 7.16).

Plans to Return to the Rural Area

Over 90 per cent of migrant employees plan to live in the country on retirement (Table 7.17). It is lower for persons with post-Form IV than for those with less education, but still very high, and for persons with high wages than for those with low wages. More than 80 per cent of employees born in Nairobi also plan to retire to the country.

Table 7.16. *Kenyan African Employees by Education: Percentage with* Shamba; *Use of Employed Workers*

Education	% with *shamba*	% employing workers
None	58	13
	(120)	(60)
Standards 1–4	57	12
	(150)	(72)
Standards 5–6	59	26
	(121)	(65)
Standards 7–8	40	21
	(464)	(169)
Forms I–IV	26	39
	(675)	(141)
Post-Form IV	20	83
	(150)	(23)
All	37	27
	(1680)	(532)

Table 7.17. *Kenyan African Migrant Employees by Education: Percentage who Plan to Return to the Rural Area*

Education	
None	95
	(104)
Standards 1–4	95
	(132)
Standards 5–6	98
	(121)
Standards 7–8	95
	(404)
Forms I–IV	93
	(552)
Post-Form IV	85
	(111)
All	94
	(1423)

E. Summary

The great majority of Nairobi employees are migrants from the rural areas; all but a few arrived recently, and most arrived young. They came disproportionately from the areas nearer to Nairobi.

Migrants have less education than non-migrants, but their educational level rose rapidly between the 1940s and the period 1966–70. Except for those who attained the higher levels of education, most migrants completed their education before they migrated. It took longer for migrants than for others to find a job after they had finished their education, and longer for migrants who had finished it before they migrated than for those who had completed it in Nairobi. Doubtless, this latter relationship is affected by the fact that migrants who completed their education in Nairobi were those who attained the higher levels of education.

The majority of migrants who had completed their education when they migrated found an independent source of income immediately they had arrived in the city. The more educated and the older the migrant, the shorter was the average delay before employment was taken up. A large majority had their current job, or a similar one, as their first employment after they arrived.

Migrants retain strong ties with the rural areas, and the majority of their spouses live there and not in Nairobi. The spouse is more frequently in Nairobi, however, the higher the employee's income and level of education. Most employees provide support for relatives in the rural area, and these take up a relatively high proportion of the donor's income, though the proportion declines as income rises.

The great majority of the lower paid and of the less educated have their children educated in the rural areas, where education is very much cheaper than in Nairobi.

Ownership of a *shamba* varies directly with age and inversely with education. Migrants are more likely to have a *shamba* than non-migrants. The distribution of *shambas* by size is very skewed; a high proportion of owners of large *shambas* obtained them with the help of bank loans. Owners do not visit their *shambas* very frequently, particularly when they are a long way from Nairobi. Most *shambas* are worked entirely by members of the owner's family.

Almost all migrants intend to return to the rural areas at some time in the future. Even a high proportion of those born in Nairobi say that they intend to move there.

8

Educational Attainment and the Urban Labour-Market in Tanzania

Chapter 4 documented the rise in the educational level of the urban wage-labour force in Dar es Salaam, providing information on the changing supply of educated labour. The present chapter brings the demand for educated labour into relation with that supply. It follows the pattern of Chapter 5 and answers a range of questions about the effect of the greater expansion in the supply of, than in the demand for, educated labour.

Section A presents evidence on the existing relationship between the educational level of employees and the size of their wage, as it is affected by a number of other variables. It is a cross-section analysis, providing a picture of the situation at the time of the survey. Changes over time are introduced in section B, which is concerned with 'filtering down', and provides data on different entry-cohorts to show changes over time in the relationship between level of education and occupation. Section C looks at the effect of 'filtering down' on the relative wages paid in different occupations. The role of education in recruitment is dealt with in section D, and employees' own perception of their qualifications for employment in section E. Section F is concerned with the training provided by employers, and in section G data on job mobility are presented. The results of the analysis are summarized with comments in section H.

A. The Relationship between Education, Occupation, Wages, and Inequality

Table 8.1 shows, first of all, the close relationship between the level of education of an employee and his or her wage. A monthly wage of Shs 750 or less is received by almost three-quarters of the employees who had no education. A smaller proportion of the educated at successively higher

Table 8.1. *Tanzanian Employees by Education: Distribution by Wage; Mean Wage by Sex*

Wage (Shs per month)	Education					
	None	Standards 1–4	Standards 5–6	Standards 7–8	Forms I–IV	Post-Form IV
0–750	73	72	62	63	32	10
751–1000	11	14	19	17	17	14
1001–1500	12	10	11	13	23	22
1501 and over	4	4	8	17	28	54
Mean	708	684	813	805	1210	1754
Mean (males)	729	695	841	837	1282	1830
Mean (females)	409	439	452	617	1001	1215
(All)	(177)	(237)	(117)	(551)	(467)	(189)
(Females)	(12)	(10)	(8)	(81)	(119)	(23)

levels of education fall in this wage-group. But the dramatic change occurs when secondary education is reached: 63 per cent of those who completed primary education earn Shs 750 or less, whereas only 32 per cent of those with secondary education up to Form IV are in that wage-group, and only 10 per cent of those with education beyond Form IV. The same story is told by the figures of the average wage of each educational group. A few years of primary education do not make much difference. In fact, the mean wage for men with education up to Standard 4 is lower than that for the entirely uneducated. Those with additional primary education do better, but the sharp rise in the wage comes for those with secondary education, and particularly education beyond Form IV, for which group the mean wage is more than double that for employees who completed primary school but had no further education.

The relationship between education and occupation of employees in Dar es Salaam is clearly evident in Table 8.2. The average years of education of the employees in the different occupations increase consistently through the order in which the occupations are listed. At the extremes, the professional employee has more than $3\frac{1}{2}$ times the years of education of the unskilled manual worker. Correspondingly, the proportion of employees with secondary education increases through the same hierarchy of occupations from 5 per cent for the unskilled and semi-skilled to virtually universal secondary education for the managerial, administrative, and professional employees. Only in manual occupations are any workers entirely without education, and in those the proportion declines with skill from approaching one-third for the unskilled to only a little more than a tenth for the skilled employee. A sharp jump in the proportion of employees with secondary education occurs from 15 per cent for skilled manual workers to 66 per cent for clerical and secretarial employees.

Table 8.3 shows the relationship between wages and occupation: the distribution of wages shifts upwards through the hierarchy of occupations from unskilled manual employment. Eighty-five per cent of unskilled manual employees have a monthly wage of not more than Shs 750. For semi-skilled manual employees the proportion is 75 per cent, for skilled employees 55 per cent, for clerical and secretarial employees 39 per cent, and so on. Correspondingly, there is a consistent rise in the proportion of employees receiving more than Shs 1500, from zero among the unskilled to 82 per cent of employees in the professions. The figures for the mean wage tell the same story.

The longer the time spent in employment, the higher the wage. This is true for all levels of education taken together and for each taken separately (Table 8.4). (The same is true for long service with the current employer.) Length of employment experience is evidently a very important influence on the employee's wage.

Table 8.2. *Tanzanian Employees by Occupation: Distribution by Education; Mean Years of Education*

Occupation	Mean years of education	Education					
		None	Standards 1–4	Standards 5–6	Standards 7–8	Forms I–IV	Post-Form IV
Manual							
Unskilled	3.99	29	33	9	24	5	0 (289)
Semi-skilled	5.19	16	24	12	43	4	1 (282)
Skilled	6.04	11	18	14	42	13	2 (364)
Clerical and secretarial	9.99	0	1	1	32	53	13 (577)
Technical and semi-professional	11.29	0	0	2	23	39	36 (71)
Managerial and administrative	12.78	0	0	0	2	49	49 (88)
Professional	14.21	0	0	0	3	24	73 (52)
All	7.69	10	13	7	32	27	11 (1760)

Table 8.3. Tanzanian Employees by Occupation: Distribution by Wage; Mean Wage by Sex

Wage (Shs per month)	Occupation							All
	Manual, unskilled	Manual, semi-skilled	Manual, skilled	Clerical and secretarial	Technical and semi-professional	Managerial and administrative	Professional	
0–750	85	75	55	39	10	6	0	51
751–1000	10	14	18	21	10	2	0	16
1001–1500	5	10	16	24	27	13	18	16
Over 1500	0	1	11	16	53	79	82	17
Mean	556	642	905	1035	1647	2351	2174	990
Mean (males)	573	650	907	1115	1683	2528	2259	1017
Mean (females)	428	497	..	838	1360	1485	1545	832
(All)	(286)	(281)	(357)	(571)	(71)	(89)	(52)	(1707)
(Females)	(34)	(15)	..	(164)	(8)	(15)	(6)	(245)

Table 8.4. *Tanzanian Employees by Occupation, Education, and Years of Employment Experience: Mean Wage (Shs per month)*

Occupation and education	Years of employment experience				All
	0–3	4–7	8–14	15 and over	
All manual					
None	513	503	623	901	699
	(27)	(24)	(34)	(61)	(147)
Standards 1–6	508	584	617	983	716
	(22)	(51)	(104)	(105)	(313)
Standards 7–8	550	633	797	1056	683
	(124)	(80)	(93)	(26)	(323)
Form I–IV	551	945	1212	1527	983
	(29)	(9)	(24)	(7)	(71)
Post-Form IV	781	..	..	..	826
	(8)				(9)
All	544	616	742	985	719
	(240)	(164)	(256)	(200)	(860)
Clerical and secretarial					
Standards 7–8	580	624	994	1213	881
	(33)	(34)	(79)	(30)	(175)
Forms I–IV	718	902	1204	1627	1043
	(82)	(63)	(109)	(30)	(285)
Post-Form IV	925	1332	1969	..	1230
	(38)	(8)	(14)		(64)
All	740	845	1174	1393	1018
	(153)	(104)	(203)	(76)	(537)
Other non-manual					
Forms I–IV	798	2157	1759	2253	1942
	(9)	(12)	(23)	(37)	(82)
Post-Form IV	1194	2107	2192	3153	2151
	(10)	(27)	(48)	(9)	(94)
All	1028	2113	2000	2487	2047
	(23)	(39)	(77)	(56)	(195)
All					
None	511	502	623	967	732
	(27)	(24)	(34)	(66)	(151)
Standards 1–4	513	596	628	873	685
	(38)	(43)	(62)	(76)	(220)
Standards 5–6	492	501	613	1194	815
	(14)	(8)	(45)	(43)	(110)
Standards 7–8	570	635	923	1333	797
	(162)	(120)	(182)	(63)	(527)
Forms I–IV	687	1086	1292	1953	1202
	(122)	(85)	(164)	(76)	(446)
Post-Form IV	954	1930	2121	2612	1726
	(56)	(35)	(64)	(12)	(167)
All	643	880	1094	1329	984
	(420)	(314)	(551)	(335)	(1621)

Table 8.5. *Tanzanian Employees by Occupation and Education: Mean Wage, Overtime, and Bonus (Shs per month)*

	Wage	Overtime	Bonus	Total
Occupation				
Manual				
Unskilled	556	85	6	647
	(286)	(282)	(270)	
Semi-skilled	642	110	6	758
	(281)	(276)	(278)	
Skilled	905	198	3	1106
	(357)	(350)	(358)	
Clerical and secretarial	1035	108	18	1161
	(571)	(567)	(558)	
Technical and semi-professional	1647	63	8	1718
	(71)	(71)	(64)	
Managerial and administrative	2351	96	..	2447
	(89)	(86)		
Professional	2174	7	1	2182
	(52)	(52)	(52)	
Education				
None	708	116	2	826
Standards 1–4	684	90	8	782
Standards 5–6	813	210	4	1027
Standards 7–8	805	141	9	955
Forms I–IV	1210	114	..	1324
Post-Form IV	1754	36	15	1805

There is also a consistent relationship between the wage and the occupation for each level of education: for each level of education the wage increases as one moves up the hierarchy of occupations.

Overtime and bonus payments to some degree offset the inequality of the distribution of the monthly wage by level of education. Table 8.5 shows the wage, overtime payments, and the annual bonus converted to a monthly basis, and the sum of these three, for each level of education. Overtime particularly benefits those with Standards 5–6 education, and pushes their earnings well above the earnings of employees who remained at school until completing primary education. Those with post-Form IV education do least well from overtime, and though they do relatively better from the annual bonus the amounts received from that are small. As a result of these additional payments the magnitude of the jump in earnings between those with primary and with secondary education is somewhat diminished, and the relative position of employees with post-

Form IV education is made less predominant. Nevertheless, the general pattern of inequality remains. Overtime and bonus payments vary with occupation. They widen the earnings differential within the manual grades, and somewhat narrow it between the manual and non-manual and within the non-manual grades, but the effect is small.

Direct monetary payments are not the only form of employee compensation. Other benefits are provided by employers which may be neutral with respect to the education level of the employee, or they may reinforce or offset the association between wages and education. Table 8.6 shows the extent to which the employer provides free or subsidized benefits in addition to the wage. The tendency is for the percentage receiving these benefits to rise with the level of education. The only benefits in which the trend runs the other way are in the provision of subsidized rations and in contributions to the National Provident Fund, but the significance of the trend in this latter benefit is outweighed by the much higher proportion among the more educated for whom the employer contributes to other pension schemes. On balance, the provision of these benefits enhances the relationship between the level of education and the wage.

There is also a tendency for the proportion of the labour force receiving the benefits to rise through the hierarchy of occcupations, as does the wage itself. The provision of non-wage benefits is not, therefore, an equalizing influence on 'employee compensation'. Unskilled manual workers do particularly badly in the receipt of most of the benefits. On the other hand, semi-skilled manual workers appear to do particularly well. In fact, the extent to which benefits are provided in all occupations is a more striking feature of the tables than the extent to which they are provided mostly to the higher paid. For skilled manual workers the provision of benefits tends on the whole to be greater the higher the educational level of the employee, but the relationship is weak or non-existent for clerical and secretarial employees.

Some benefits in addition to the wage are provided to a very different extent by firms in different ownership. An annual bonus, for instance, is provided to a significant number of employees only in the private sector, whereas annual leave is provided to virtually all employees in the governmental sector but to a significantly smaller extent by private firms. Broadly, the provision of benefits is more widespread for employees in parastatal and government than in private employment.

Table 8.1 is informative about the relative wages of men and women. The relationship between education and the wage holds for both, in fact more strongly for women than for men, but at every level of education the women are paid a great deal less than the men. The margin is largest for those with little education—the wage for uneducated women is only

Table 8.6a. *Tanzanian Employees by Education, All Occupations: Percentage Receiving Various Benefits from Employer*

Benefit	Education						All
	1	2	3	4	5	6	
Annual bonus	8	17	13	17	20	12	16
	(152)	(212)	(111)	(502)	(441)	(178)	(1598)
Paid annual leave	72	76	83	82	97	94	86
	(172)	(230)	(118)	(539)	(457)	(193)	(1713)
Rations	21	25	24	18	12	9	17
	(172)	(232)	(118)	(556)	(465)	(193)	(1741)
Medical treatment	66	69	77	76	83	91	77
	(176)	(231)	(116)	(552)	(467)	(193)	(1740)
Transport	27	32	39	40	36	41	36
	(172)	(234)	(118)	(552)	(466)	(186)	(1733)
NPF	61	67	60	53	44	27	51
	(173)	(231)	(114)	(533)	(456)	(191)	(1703)
Pension, other	18	20	27	38	63	74	44
	(171)	(228)	(114)	(526)	(456)	(193)	(1692)
Loans	58	73	71	77	91	93	79
	(171)	(230)	(114)	(537)	(454)	(189)	(1699)

Note: 1: None; 2: Standards 1–4; 3: Standards 5–6; 4: Standards 7–8; 5: Forms I–IV; 6: Post-Form IV

56 per cent of that for men—and the smallest for those with secondary education up to Form IV, where the women receive 78 per cent of the men's wage.

The differential between the wage for men and women can be investigated further by standardizing for occupation and seniority. It is not possible to make the comparison over the whole range of occupations because the number of women in the sample is too few, but there are a number of comparisons that can be made. Table 8.9 shows that in any given occupation, at every educational level for which a comparison is possible, the average wage for the men is significantly greater than that for the women. It is shown elsewhere that employment experience has a large effect on the wage paid, those with experience being paid substantially more than recent recruits to the labour-market, so that it is possible that women are paid less because they are more junior. Again this hypothesis cannot be tested across the full range of occupations and years of employment experience, but Table 8.7 provides evidence over part of the range. It shows that in six out of seven cases, for the same length of experience and education, women are paid significantly less than men.

Table 8.6b. *Tanzanian Employees by Education, Particular Occupations: Percentage Receiving Various Benefits from Employer*

Benefit	Education						All
	1	2	3	4	5	6	
Skilled manual							
Annual bonus	17	9	10	6	11	0	9
Paid annual leave	71	76	87	68	92	100	76
Rations	34	23	19	16	28	29	19
Medical treatment	49	65	83	63	91	100	69
Transport	28	29	37	40	43	28	36
NPF	59	54	54	38	45	23	47
Pension, other	20	29	46	32	57	48	36
Loans	56	67	72	58	91	89	66
	(32–41)	(57–61)	(48–52)	(129–149)	(44–46)	(6–7)	(318–359)
Clerical/Secretarial							
Annual bonus	..	26	..	24	20	12	20
Paid annual leave	..	100	..	87	97	93	94
Rations	..	18	..	8	8	9	9
Medical treatment	..	80	..	80	79	94	81
Transport	..	52	..	38	31	55	37
NPF	..	100	..	53	40	34	44
Pension, other	..	49	..	47	63	69	58
Loans	..	100	..	91	92	97	92
		(8)		(172–185)	(279–300)	(71–76)	(538–576)

Note: 1: None; 2: Standards 1–4; 3: Standards 5–6; 4: Standards 7–8; 5: Forms I–IV; 6: Post-Form IV

Table 8.6c. *Tanzanian Employees by Occupation: Percentage Receiving Various Benefits from Employer*

Benefit	Occupation							All
	1	2	3	4	5	6	7	
Annual bonus	14	17	8	20	25	31	9	19
Paid annual leave	68	90	76	94	99	95	100	86
Rations	18	38	19	9	13	8	8	17
Medical treatment	65	84	69	81	93	86	88	77
Transport	31	43	36	37	30	42	29	57
NPF	56	76	47	44	42	44	14	51
Pension, other	17	26	36	58	65	79	75	43
Loans	61	80	65	92	94	95	77	79
	(239–287)	(266–281)	(318–359)	(538–575)	(69–71)	(84–88)	(49–52)	(1598–1741)

Note: 1: Manual, unskilled; 2: Manual, semi-skilled; 3: Manual, skilled; 4: Clerical and secretarial; 5: Technical and semi-professional; 6: Managerial and administrative; 7: Professional

Table 8.6d. *Tanzanian Employees by Ownership of Firm: Percentage Receiving Various Benefits from Employer*

Benefit	Private	Parastatal	Local government	Government	All
Annual bonus	34	7	0	1	16
Paid annual leave	72	94	100	94	86
Rations	13	28	0	7	17
Medical treatment	58	99	100	70	77
Transport	37	39	5	35	36
NPF	63	53	5	30	51
Pension, other	14	60	95	62	44
Loans	63	92	100	85	79
	(591–665)	(625–664)	(34–38)	(323–352)	(1598–1741)

Table 8.7. *Clerical and Secretarial Employees in Tanzania by Years of Employment Experience, Education, and Sex: Mean Wage (Shs per month)*

Education and employment experience (years)	Male	Female
Standards 7–8		
0–3	634	486
	(21)	(12)
4–7	663	532
	(23)	(10)
8–14	1113	792
	(50)	(29)
15 and over	974	609
	(15)	(5)
Forms I–IV		
0–3	697	767
	(57)	(25)
4–7	996	807
	(32)	(31)
8–14	1282	992
	(80)	(29)

Table 8.8. *Tanzanian Employees by Education and Sex: Distribution by Occupation*

Occupation	Education					
	Standards 7–8		Forms I–IV		Post-Form IV	
	Male	Female	Male	Female	Male	Female
Manual	69	24	20	3	6	0
Clerical	27	76	61	81	37	57
Other	4	0	19	16	57	43
	(469)	(79)	(338)	(119)	(169)	(23)

Nor does it seem likely that the difference results from women being in
occupations lower in the hierarchy than men with similar education. The
figures in Table 8.8 make it difficult to accept that as an explanation.
There may be other explanations, but it is difficult to avoid the conclusion
that for some reason women are paid less than men because they are
women.

Although the number of Asians in the sample is small, Table 8.10 is

Table 8.9. *Tanzanian Employees by Education, Occupation, and Sex: Mean Wage (Shs per month)*

Occupation and education	Male		Female		All
Manual, unskilled					
None	583	(73)	403	(10)	567
Standards 1–8	539	(166)	441	(21)	528
Manual, semi-skilled					
Standards 7–8	593	(110)	494	(10)	585
Clerical and secreterial					
Standards 7–8	954	(120)	651	(60)	875
Forms I–IV	1082	(189)	838	(87)	1060
Post-Form IV	1332	(59)	1133	(10)	1284

Table 8.10. *Tanzanian Employees by Ethnic Group and Education: Mean Wage (Shs per month)*

Education	African	Asian	
Standard 8 and below	753	1454	
	(1065)	(15)	
Forms I–IV	1166	1958	
	(434)	(28)	
Post-Form IV	1673	2871	
	(170)	(16)	
All	954	2081	
	(1669)	(59)	

pretty clear evidence that the wage of Asian employees is substantially larger than that of Africans with the same level of education.

Standardization for certain characteristics is also required if the differences between the wages of Africans and Asians shown in Table 8.10 are to be further investigated. Table 8.11 shows, for the few cases where the size of the sample is enough to make comparison possible, that the differential in favour of Asians in found for the same occupation and level of education.

No consistent relationship appears to exist between the type of primary school attended by an employee and his or her wage. Although the distribution in Table 8.12 of the wages of those educated at mission schools is more skewed towards the higher-wage groups than the distribution of those educated at government schools, and the mean wage is

Table 8.11. *Male Tanzanian Employees by Education, Occupation, and Ethnic Group: Mean Wage (Shs per month)*

Occupation and education	African	Asian
Clerical and secretarial		
Forms I–IV	1082	1768
	(189)	(13)
Technical and semi-professional		
Post-Form IV	1865	2257
	(19)	(6)
Professional		
Post-Form IV	1934	3709
	(30)	(6)

Table 8.12. *Tanzanian Employees with Primary Education Only by Type of Primary School Attended: Distribution by Wage; Mean Wage (Shs per month) by Year Leaving School*

Wage (Shs per month)	Primary school type	
	Government	Mission
500 and under	37	20
501–750	33	36
751–1000	14	24
1001–1500	11	15
Over 1500	5	5
Mean		
All Periods	710	822
	(482)	(172)
Before 1960	914	857
	(94)	(66)
1960–69	751	779
	(199)	(81)
After 1969	574	869
	(199)	(25)

higher, the association looks less clear when different age-cohorts are identified. Employees educated at mission schools have a large advantage over those educated at government schools where both groups completed their education after 1969, but the advantage is the other way, though smaller, for those who left school before 1960.

Table 8.13. *Tanzanian Employees with Secondary Education up to Form IV by Type of Secondary School First Attended: Distribution by Wage; Mean Wage (Shs per month)*

Wage (Shs per month)	Secondary school type		All[a]
	Government	Private	
0–1000	50	40	44
1001–1500	19	30	23
Over 1500	31	30	33
Mean	1203	1365	1292
	(281)	(157)	(478)

[a] Includes also Self-Help Secondary (mean Shs 1657, sample size 25) and Technical Secondary (mean Shs 1597, sample size 21).

Table 8.14. *Tanzanian Employees with Complete Primary but No Further Education by Period in which Education Completed: Mean Wage of Those With as Percentage of Mean Wage of Those Without Primary Certificate*

Period education completed			
1959 or earlier	1960–9	1970–9	All
258	108	108	111
(18/5)	(180/17)	(164/8)	(370/30)

Table 8.13 shows that those who attended private secondary schools have a rather higher wage than those who attended a government school. The difference is seen in the lowest, Shs 0–1000 wage-group, which contains 40 per cent of those who had been to private schools, compared with 50 per cent of those who had attended a government secondary school.

Employees who completed the full course of primary education and obtained a Primary Certificate are paid more than their peers who did not receive a certificate, though for most periods the difference is small and there are few who did not receive a certificate (Table 8.14). However, for those who completed their primary education before 1960, the wage for those with a certificate is $2\frac{1}{2}$ times the wage of those without one, though the numbers in that early period are so small that the statistic may not be of any significance.

The relationship between examination results and earnings is more

Table 8.15. *Tanzanian Employees who Completed Education at Form IV by Result in Form IV Examination and Period in which Education Completed: Mean Wage (Shs per month)*

Examination result	Period education completed			All
	1959 or earlier	1960–9	1970–9	
Div. 1	..	..	1840	2048
			(9)	(12)
Div. 2	2211	2155	1244	1692
	(9)	(24)	(37)	(73)
Div. 3	1765	1473	1024	1187
	(6)	(37)	(80)	(125)
Div. 4	..	1148	699	828
		(10)	(48)	(63)

Table 8.16. *Tanzanian Employees who Completed Education at Form IV by Form IV Examination Result and Occupation: Mean Wage (Shs per month)*

Occupation	Examination result			
	Div. 1	Div. 2	Div. 3	Div. 4
Skilled Manual	..	1416	1256	..
		(7)	(8)	
Clerical and secretarial	..	1380	1008	833
		(38)	(77)	(46)
Other non-manual	2736	2255	1767	..
	(7)	(27)	(31)	

strongly apparent with secondary school, Form IV-leavers than with primary school-leavers. Table 8.15 shows that each Division commands a higher wage that that below it, and this is true for each period identified, as well as for the sample as a whole. The pattern holds also for each occupation (Table 8.16) and for performance in particular subjects (Table 8.17). The possible interpretations of the relationship between examination results and wages have been discussed in Chapter 5.

The relationship between wages and the Form VI examination results, for those who did not proceed beyond secondary school, is less clear (Table 8.18). It is clear enough for those who took the examination before 1973: the more passes the higher the wage. There is no such consistent pattern for the later period. A possible explanation is that, in the relatively short time they have been in employment, there has not

Table 8.17. *Tanzanian Employees who Completed Education at Form IV by Grade of Form IV Examination Pass in Different Subjects: Mean Wage (Shs per month)*

Examination grade	Mathematics		English		Best science subject	
Excellent	2331	(9)	1905	(11)	1769	(12)
Very Good	1642	(39)	1614	(63)	1860	(21)
Good	1429	(58)	1188	(108)	1352	(86)
Satisfactory	1161	(71)	1164	(95)	1197	(59)
Fail	958	(107)	927	(40)	1034	(25)
All	1237	(299)	1250	(323)	1280	(248)

Table 8.18. *Tanzanian Employees With Complete Secondary but Without Post-Secondary Education by Result in Form VI Examination and Period in which Education Completed: Mean Wage (Shs per month)*

Result in examination	Period education completed			
	1972 or earlier		1973 or later	
1 pass	1928	(11)	1227	(11)
2 passes	2097	(22)	1358	(21)
3 passes	2344	(17)	1027	(26)
4 or more passes	3119	(8)	1182	(21)

been time for the quality of the more highly qualified to emerge, and to be reflected in their wage.

Casual employees, not unexpectedly, are paid substantially less than regular employees with the same education (Table 8.19). Those with post-Form IV education are an exception, and this may be something to do with professional workers who are in effect self-employed rather than regular employees. The lower-wage of the casual worker is also likely to be influenced by the 'seniority effect', workers being taken on as casual workers and becoming regular employees only after some time (see section D). The low wage of casual workers would reflect, therefore, their being the most junior employees, as well as their employment status as such.

The very wide differences in the wages paid to employees with the same education by establishments in different ownership is apparent from Table 8.20.[1] Parastatals pay more than other employers for the lower levels of education up to the end of primary school, and less than private

---

[1] The provision of benefits in addition to the wage has already been discussed.

Table 8.19. *Tanzanian Employees by Employment Status and Education: Mean Wage (Shs per month)*

Education	Employment status	
	Regular	Casual
None	795	531
	(119)	(56)
Standards 1–4	741	538
	(172)	(63)
Standards 5–6	898	591
	(83)	(29)
Standards 7–8	874	591
	(416)	(121)
Forms I–IV	1228	680
	(446)	(15)
Post-Form IV	1727	2281
	(181)	(7)

Table 8.20. *Tanzanian Employees by Occupation, Education, and Ownership of Firm: Mean Wage (Shs per month)*

Occupation and Education	Ownership of firm		
	Private	Parastatal	Government
Manual, unskilled			
None	454	765	395
	(45)	(32)	(6)
Standards 1–4	466	664	440
	(53)	(32)	(6)
Standards 5–6	447	658	..
	(15)	(7)	
Standards 7–8	509	577	484
	(32)	(34)	(8)
All	470	696	462
	(145)	(111)	(26)
Manual, semi-skilled			
None	527	951	..
	(16)	(24)	
Standards 1–4	595	827	679
	(37)	(23)	(6)
Standards 5–6	538	739	..
	(21)	(11)	
Standards 7–8	525	659	550
	(53)	(50)	(17)
All	558	760	574
	(132)	(112)	(36)

Table 8.20. *(Continued):*

Occupation and Education	Ownership of firm		
	Private	Parastatal	Government
Manual, skilled			
None	688	1336	..
	(28)	(10)	
Standards 1–4	721	1142	597
	(35)	(22)	(8)
Standards 5–6	700	1512	869
	(17)	(23)	(11)
Standards 7–8	715	1129	670
	(66)	(42)	(36)
All	726	1252	706
	(152)	(126)	(75)
Clerical and secretarial			
Standards 7–8	944	1132	664
	(74)	(41)	(50)
Forms I–IV	1377	1186	607
	(94)	(109)	(79)
Post-Form IV	2041	1270	704
	(10)	(51)	(9)
All	1228	1215	631
	(180)	(209)	(142)
Other non-manual			
Standards 7–8	1555	2937	..
	(8)	(9)	
Forms I–IV	2378	1918	1567
	(26)	(38)	(20)
Post-Form IV	3113	2164	1841
	(17)	(41)	(48)
All	2494	2137	1720
	(51)	(88)	(71)
All Occupations			
None	541	967	456
	(89)	(68)	(14)
Standards 1–4	578	883	572
	(127)	(83)	(23)
Standards 5–6	564	1157	737
	(54)	(43)	(17)
Standards 7–8	744	1000	650
	(233)	(184)	(109)
Forms I–IV	1536	1340	767
	(133)	(181)	(128)
Post-Form IV	2676	1610	1608
	(28)	(99)	(61)
All	909	1177	850
	(664)	(657)	(352)

employers for education above the primary level. They pay more than the government for the first stage of secondary education, but for employees with post-Form IV education the government has caught up with the parastatals. Government pays less than private employers for most levels of education, and for post-primary education enormously so—employees with education at Forms I–IV receive in government service only half what is paid by the private employer. The table also shows that the parastatals pay much higher wages than other employers for some occupations, but rather less for others. Manual employees do very well in the parastatals. Unskilled workers earn some 40 per cent more than with other employers, and in fact they receive more than other employers pay their semi-skilled employees. In contrast, secretarial and managerial wages are lower in the parastatals than in private employment.

All occupations in government employment fare badly as compared with the parastatals, and non-manual occupations are also substantially worse paid in government than in private employment. Manual employees, on the other hand, are paid roughly the same by government and private employers. Another notable difference in the wages paid by the different classes of employer is the inferior position of clerical and secretarial employees in parastatals and government in relation to skilled manual workers. In private employment, in contrast, the clerical and secretarial wage is 70 per cent above that of skilled manual workers. These various differences in the wages paid by firms in different types of ownership are an indication, perhaps, of the differential effectiveness of the Tanzanian government's incomes policy.

The relationship between the level of education and the wage is fairly well maintained when employees are classified according to the size of the firm in which they are employed, though there are rather more aberrations from the relationship in the larger than in the smaller firms. There is no single pattern in the relationship between the size of the firm and the wage paid to employees with a given level of education. For those with no more than Standard 4, the wage is higher the larger the firm. That pattern is approximated for those with the higher levels of primary education, but for those with Forms I–IV and post-Form IV education the relationship is more nearly the reverse (Table 8.21). These results partly reflect differences in the distribution of firm size by type of ownership.

The degree of inequality in employment income associated with the different educational attainment of employees is affected by the number of dependants an employee supports. Table 8.22 indicates that dependants are an equalizing influence, in that the better paid have more of them than the poorer paid. The mean wage of the top group is ten times that of the bottom group, whereas the average wage per dependant for the top group is only seven times that of the bottom group.

Table 8.21. *Tanzanian Employees by Size of Firm and Education: Mean Wage (Shs per month)*

Education	Size of firm (no. of employees)			
	1–99	100–99	200–499	500 and over
None	484	549	626	927
	(25)	(26)	(59)	(62)
Standards 1–4	561	587	632	836
	(45)	(37)	(71)	(83)
Standards 5–6	596	551	648	1080
	(15)	(25)	(22)	(52)
Standards 7–8	887	616	765	900
	(40)	(103)	(157)	(243)
Forms I–IV	1668	1027	1375	1101
	(51)	(52)	(91)	(266)
Post-Form IV	3049	1738	1255	1778
	(15)	(18)	(45)	(111)
All	1120	758	894	1092

In relation to education, however, the number of dependants does not fall into an equalizing pattern. Table 8.23 shows that the more educated have fewer dependants than the less educated. Certainly, the more educated are younger than the less educated, and have had less time to accumulate dependants, but even within the same age-group they have fewer dependants (Table 4.16). As a result, the existence of dependants is a disequalizing influence on the relation between education and wages. The mean wage of employees with post-Form IV education is $2\frac{1}{2}$ times that of the uneducated (Table 8.1); for the wage per dependant the corresponding figure is 4 (Table 8.23).

B. The Changing Relation between Education and Occupation: Filtering Down

The next step in the analysis of the links between education and the labour-market is to set out the data on the relationship between the education and the occupations of employees, both at one time and as it has changed over time, the latter to provide evidence on 'filtering down'.

The length of education of those joining the wage-labour force has risen over time (Table 8.24). Table 8.25 shows a clear change over time in the occupational distribution of employees with each particular level of education. For every level of education, jobs lower in the hierarchy of

Table 8.22. *Tanzanian Employees by Wage: Average Number of Full and Part Dependants, Average Number of Full Dependants, and Average Wage (Shs per month) Per Full Dependant*

Wage (Shs per month)	Wives and children			Persons		
	Av. no. of full and part dependants	Full dependants		Av. no. of full and part dependants	Full dependants	
		Av. no.	Av. wage		Av. no.	Av. wage
0–500	2.13 (398)	1.94	215	4.67	3.02	138
501–750	3.08 (467)	2.76	222	5.56	4.01	153
751–1000	3.36 (258)	2.89	300	6.10	4.21	206
1001–1500	3.54 (272)	3.16	393	6.16	4.47	278
1501–2000	3.81 (122)	3.32	515	6.45	4.92	348
2001–3000	4.44 (138)	3.94	614	6.54	4.95	489
Over 3000	4.70 (31)	2.74	1458	6.75	4.13	967
All	3.16 (1686)	2.79	355	5.69	4.02	247

Table 8.23. *Tanzanian Employees by Education: Average Number of Full and Part Dependants, Average Number of Full Dependants, and Average Wage (Shs per month) Per Full dependant*

Education	Wives and children			Persons		
	Av. no. of full and part dependants	Full dependants		Av. no. of full and part dependants	Full dependants	
		Av. no.	Av. wage		Av. no.	Av. wage
None	4.40 (174)	4.15	176	6.03	5.05	145
Standards 1–4	3.95 (225)	3.71	185	6.32	4.78	143
Standards 5–6	4.79 (116)	4.14	197	7.79	6.10	134
Standards 7–8	2.72 (546)	2.34	341	5.55	3.63	220
Forms I–IV	2.68 (452)	2.26	532	5.39	3.57	337
Post-Form IV	2.38 (186)	2.00	863	4.73	3.07	562
All	3.15 (1699)	2.77	355	5.72	4.02	245

Table 8.24. *Tanzanian Employees by Date of Joining Labour Force: Mean Years of Education*

Date of joining labour force		
Before 1961	6.19	(314)
1961–70	7.76	(469)
After 1970	8.13	(971)

occupations are more important for more recent entrants to the labour-market than for earlier entrants. For those in the three lowest educational categories distinguished in the table, a higher proportion of more recent than of earlier recruits are in unskilled employment. For those with no more than Standard 6 education, 53 per cent of those who first entered wage-employment in 1977–80 are in unskilled jobs, compared with only 14 per cent of those who entered before 1959.[2]

For those employees who completed primary school but did not continue education (Standard 7–8 leavers) there is a rise over time in the proportion in unskilled manual occupations, but the change appears most clearly as a consistent decline in the proportion engaged in non-manual occupations: the figure is 62 per cent in clerical and other non-manual occupations for those who entered the labour-market before 1959 and only 22 per cent for the most recent recruits. Employees with post-primary education have become increasingly engaged in clerical/secretarial occupations and decreasingly in managerial and administrative employment: between the first and last cohorts distinguished in Table 8.25 the percentage of those who had been to secondary school who are in clerical jobs increases from 27 per cent to 69 per cent, and the percentage who are in managerial and administrative jobs falls from 46 per cent to 4 per cent.

The same pattern of change, which is seen in Table 8.25 as a lower position in the hierarchy of occupations for more recent entrants to the labour-market with a given level of education, is seen in Table 8.26 as a rise in the level of education of employees in a particular occupation. Only 2 per cent of unskilled manual workers who entered wage-employment before 1959 have more than Standard 6 education, compared with more than half of the most recent cohort. It is the same with the other manual occupations. Only 5 per cent of the semi-skilled workers who entered employment before 1959 have complete primary education,

---

[2] These figures and those in the next paragraph are derived from the percentages for the separate education groups in Table 8.25.

Table 8.25. *Tanzanian Employees by Education and Year of First Wage-Job: Distribution by Occupation*

Education and occupation	Year of first wage-job				
	Before 1959	1959–65	1966–72	1973–6	1977–80
None					
Manual, unskilled	16	36	61	72	57
Manual, semi-skilled	43	32	12	28	9
Manual, skilled	37	32	27	0	34
Clerical and secretarial	4	0	0	0	0
	(39)	(25)	(34)	(24)	(28)
Standards 1–4					
Manual, unskilled	24	33	62	31	54
Manual, semi-skilled	30	25	23	36	23
Manual, skilled	40	28	13	33	23
Clerical and secretarial	6	14	2	0	0
	(38)	(39)	(61)	(43)	(39)
Standards 5–6					
Manual, unskilled	4	0	26	43	42
Manual, semi-skilled	17	20	37	57	40
Manual, skilled	67	80	36	0	18
Clerical and secretarial	7	0	1	0	0
Technical and semi-professional	5	0	0	0	0
	(34)	(10)	(44)	(7)	(15)
Standards 7–8					
Manual, unskilled	2	3	7	17	19
Manual, semi-skilled	6	10	21	29	22
Manual, skilled	30	31	24	24	37
Clerical and secretarial	39	54	45	30	19
Technical and semi-professional	14	2	3	0	3
Managerial and administrative	9	0	0	0	0
	(25)	(38)	(178)	(114)	(170)

Table 8.25. *(Continued)*

Education and occupation	Year of first wage-job				
	Before 1959	1959–65	1966–72	1973–6	1977–80
Forms I–IV					
Manual, unskilled	0	3	0	0	10
Manual, semi-skilled	1	0	3	1	6
Manual, skilled	9	9	13	10	9
Clerical and secretarial	30	45	69	74	67
Technical and semi-professional	3	5	8	6	6
Managerial and administrative	45	28	6	7	2
Professional	12	10	1	2	0
	(27)	(49)	(157)	(85)	(121)
Post-Form IV					
Manual, semi-skilled	0	..	0	0	5
Manual, skilled	0	..	1	0	8
Clerical and secretarial	20	..	23	23	70
Technical and semi-professional	15	..	12	16	6
Managerial and administrative	48	..	35	20	10
Professional	17	..	29	41	1
	(10)	..	(64)	(35)	(59)
All					
Manual, unskilled	10	15	15	17	20
Manual, semi-skilled	21	15	14	20	15
Manual, skilled	36	26	18	16	23
Clerical and secretarial	15	30	38	34	36
Technical and semi-professional	4	2	5	4	4
Managerial and administrative	11	9	6	4	2
Professional	3	3	4	5	0
	(173)	(166)	(537)	(310)	(433)

Table 8.26. *Tanzanian Employees by Occupation and Year of First Wage-Job: Distribution by Education*

Education and occupation	Year of first wage-job				
	Before 1959	1959–65	1966–72	1973–6	1977–80
Manual, unskilled					
None	37	38	25	32	18
Standards 1–4	54	55	45	25	24
Standards 5–6	7	2	14	6	7
Standards 7–8	2	5	16	37	37
Forms I–IV	0	0	0	0	14
	(17)	(23)	(84)	(54)	(88)
Manual, semi-skilled					
None	46	34	5	11	4
Standards 1–4	32	41	18	26	14
Standards 5–6	16	8	21	7	9
Standards 7–8	5	17	50	55	57
Forms I–IV	1	0	6	1	11
Post-Form IV	0	0	0	0	5
	(35)	(24)	(76)	(61)	(64)
Manual, skilled					
None	23	18	10	0	9
Standards 1–4	24	25	9	28	9
Standards 5–6	37	19	17	0	3
Standards 7–8	12	28	43	54	64
Forms I–IV	4	10	20	18	11
Post-Form IV	0	0	1	0	4
	(62)	(42)	(96)	(50)	(99)
Clerical and secretarial					
None	6	1	0	0	0
Standards 1–4	9	10	0	0	0
Standards 5–6	9	0	0	0	0
Standards 7–8	37	41	39	32	21
Forms I–IV	31	45	54	60	52
Post-Form IV	8	3	7	8	27
	(26)	(50)	(204)	(105)	(156)
Other non-manual					
Standards 5–6	3	0	0	0	0
Standards 7–8	16	4	8	0	17
Forms I–IV	52	92	31	33	39
Post-Form IV	29	4	61	67	44
	(31)	(24)	(77)	(40)	(23)
All					
None	22	16	6	8	7
Standards 1–4	22	23	11	13	9
Standards 5–6	20	6	8	3	3
Standards 7–8	14	23	33	38	39
Forms I–IV	16	30	30	27	28
Post-Form IV	6	2	12	11	14
	(173)	(166)	(553)	(315)	(433)

whereas for the most recent recruits the figure is 57 per cent. The proportion of skilled workers with complete primary education is 12 per cent for the earliest, and 64 per cent for the latest cohort.

The change is as striking with clerical-secretarial employees. Seventy-nine per cent of those who most recently entered wage-employment have at least secondary education, compared with 39 per cent who had their first job before 1959. In the higher occupations, the change takes the form of a shift in the distribution between the first stage of secondary school and post-Form IV education. Although the change in the distribution from cohort to cohort is erratic, there is a significantly higher proportion of employees with post-Form IV education among the most recent than among the earliest entrants into employment.

The same differences in the educational attainment of employees appear in Table 8.27, which looks at particular occupations. In each occupation the distribution of employees by level of education has shifted upwards. Among factory labourers with 15 and more years of employment, 57 per cent have no education, compared with only 10 per cent among those with seven or fewer years in employment. For semi-skilled factory machine operators, the proportions with no education in these cohorts are 33 per cent and 5 per cent, respectively, and with Standards 1–4, 43 per cent and 13 per cent. A similar pattern is found in the other occupations. Perhaps the most remarkable difference between cohorts is among messengers: none had more than Standard 4 education in the earliest cohort; in the most recent cohort 62 per cent have secondary education.

These data illustrate very clearly the process of filtering down as the supply of educated labour increases. With the expansion of education, a higher level of education comes to be required of entrants into a particular occupation than was required in the past. Putting it the other way round, a particular level of education will obtain entry only to an occupation lower in the hierarchy than was the case in the past. Some part of the change will be the consequence of individuals rising in the occupational hierarchy, from unskilled to skilled manual employment, for instance, during the course of their employment careers, but the reasons for discounting such promotion as a major explanation of the change were set out in Chapter 5, which also remarks on how much further filtering down has gone in Kenya than in Tanzania.

C. Filtering Down and Wages

In the previous section the phenomenon of 'filtering down' was identified. How does the phenomenon affect the wage structure? There are consider-

Table 8.27. *Tanzanian Employees by Particular Occupations and Years of Employment Experience: Distribution by Education*

Occupation and education	Years of experience		
	0–7	8–14	15 and over
Factory labourer			
None	10	33	57
Standards 1–4	23	20	29
Standards 5–6	13	27	14
Standards 7–8	47	20	0
Forms I–IV	7	0	0
	(30)	(16)	(7)
Semi-skilled factory machine operator			
None	5	15	33
Standards 1–4	13	20	43
Standards 5–6	10	14	10
Standards 7–8	64	50	14
Forms I–IV	8	1	0
	(39)	(27)	(21)
Messenger			
None	0	24	36
Standards 1–4	0	47	64
Standards 5–6	0	12	0
Standards 7–8	38	17	0
Forms I–IV	62	0	0
	(16)	(17)	(11)
Clerk			
Standards 1–4	0	0	11
Standards 5–6	0	0	5
Standards 7–8	28	40	46
Forms I–IV	55	58	32
Post-Form IV	17	2	6
	(111)	(80)	(37)
Secretary/typist			
Standards 7–8	27	56	50
Forms I–IV	73	36	50
Post-Form IV	0	8	0
	(41)	(25)	(8)
Government administrator			
Forms I–IV	0	22	80
Post-Form IV	100	78	20
	(7)	(18)	(15)

able differences in average earnings by occupation at each educational level, as well as on account of educational differences between occupations. For instance, average earnings in the manual occupations rise from Shs 541 in the unskilled to Shs 913 per month in the skilled grade. The clerical and secretarial occupation receives on average Shs 1018 and other non-manual categories no less than Shs 2038. At both the Standards 7–8 and Forms I–IV levels of education, for instance, there is one dividing line between the unskilled or semi-skilled jobs and the skilled manual jobs, and another between the clerical or secretarial jobs and the other non-manual jobs. The filtering down of the more educated can therefore be expected to reduce their pay in absolute terms, and probably in relation to that of the less educated (Table 8.28).

These predictions are borne out by the evidence. Table 8.4 shows that, for all occupations combined, absolute earnings at any particular educational level are lower for the more recent cohorts of entrants to the labour-market. Average earnings of Standards 7–8 and of Form I–IV-leavers increase monotonically with length of employment experience, being for employees with over 14 years of experience more than double those for employees with under 4 years. The mean deviation of the distribution of wages by education (calculated from the data in Table 8.4) is Shs 379 for the earliest cohort; for the subsequent cohorts it falls to Shs 356, Shs 343, and, strikingly, Shs 108 for the most recent. And Table 8.29 (derived from Table 8.4) also shows that wage dispersion by level of education is narrower for those who entered in more recent than in more distant periods. For employees who entered the labour force before 1966, the range of wages by education is from 66 per cent to 197 per cent of the cohort average; for entrants during the period 1977–80 the corresponding range is from 77 to 148. Even more striking is the range for all except the highest level of education: only from 77 per cent to 107 per cent of the cohort average. The premium paid for most differences in education narrowed greatly, though there is still a substantial premium (148 per cent as against 107 per cent of the mean wage) for those with post-Form IV education over the level below.

It would be wrong to attribute these results entirely to the process of filtering down. As Tables 8.29 and 8.30 show, there is a similar tendency for average earnings to be lower for the more recent cohorts even within occupational groups, and for their dispersion also to be narrower within the manual but not the non-manual group. The higher wages of the earlier cohorts must in part be due to their accumulation of skills as they acquired employment experience. The greater wage dispersion of the earlier cohorts could partly reflect a tendency for the more educated to acquire more skills than the less educated in the course of their working careers.

Table 8.28. *Tanzanian Employees by Education and Occupation: Mean Wage (Shs per month)*

Occupation	Education						All
	None	Standards 1–4	Standards 5–6	Standards 7–8	Forms I–IV	Post-Form IV	
Manual							
Unskilled	569	532	513	545	494	..	541
	(68)	(93)	(23)	(67)	(12)		(263)
Semi-skilled	785	697	609	581	655	..	646
	(38)	(58)	(34)	(113)	(12)		(259)
Skilled	837	856	1102	829	1118	..	913
	(51)	(57)	(48)	(142)	(46)		(339)
Clerical and secretarial	..	..	..	881	1043	1230	1018
				(175)	(285)	(64)	(573)
Other non-manual	..	..	..	1955	1942	2151	2038
				(16)	(82)	(94)	(194)
All	732	685	815	797	1202	1726	984
	(151)	(220)	(110)	(527)	(446)	(167)	(1621)

Table 8.29. *Tanzanian Employees by Occupation and Year Entering Labour Force: Mean Wage for Each Level of Education as Percentage of Mean Wage for All Levels; Mean Wage for All Levels of Education (Shs per month)*

Occupation and education	Year entering labour force				All
	Before 1966	1966–72	1973–6	1977–80	
All Manual					
None	91	84	82	94	97
Standards 1–4	100	84	97	94	92
Standards 5–6	107	83	82	90	112
Standards 7–8	155	107	103	101	94
Forms I–IV	..	165	153	101	136
All	985	742	616	544	724
Clerical and Secretarial					
Standards 7–8	87	85	74	78	87
Forms I–IV	117	103	107	97	102
Post-Form IV	..	168	158	125	121
All	1393	1174	845	740	1018
Other non-manual					
Standards 7–8	..	67	..	..	96
Forms I–IV	91	88	102	79	95
Post-Form IV	127	110	100	116	105
All	2487	2000	2113	1028	2038
All					
None	73	57	57	79	74
Standards 1–4	66	57	68	79	70
Standards 5–6	90	56	57	77	83
Standards 7–8	100	84	72	89	81
Forms I–IV	147	118	123	107	122
Post-Form IV	197	194	219	148	175
All	1329	1094	880	643	984

Table 8.30 shows that a narrowing of the range of wages by occupation has accompanied the narrowing of the range of wages by education, at any rate in terms of a comparison between the earliest and latest cohorts. But there is no consistent trend for a compression of the distribution of wages by occupation. The mean deviation of the distribution (in terms of percentage of the mean wage) is 30 per cent for the earliest cohort and 23 per cent for the next; it then rises to 30 per cent and 35 per cent, and falls to 19 per cent for the most recent cohort. To the extent that there has been compression of the distribution in the case of a particular cohort, it

Table 8.30. *Tanzanian Employees by Year Joined Labour Force: Mean Wage for Each Occupation as Percentage of Mean Wage for All; Mean Wage for All Occupations (Shs per month)*

Occupation	Year joined labour force				
	Before 1959	1959–65	1966–72	1973–6	1977–80
Manual					
Unskilled	38	71	54	58	71
Semi-skilled	61	70	62	64	76
Skilled	91	81	86	89	103
Clerical and secretarial	113	104	108	96	115
Technical and semi-professional	130	..	163	196	143
Managerial and administrative	186	192	196	328	183
Professional	..	..	193	195	..
All	1414	1239	1094	880	643

means there has been a change not only in the occupational composition of the cohort, but also in the occupational wage structure. This in turn could reflect the greater influence of market forces on the pay of entrants to the labour-market, or the willingness of those in better jobs to accept some sacrifice in pay during their period of training or learning on-the-job.

The fact that the relation between education and occupation is flexible and has been changing raises important questions for manpower planning of the sort which is practised in Tanzania. Which educational level is 'best' for each occupation? As was explained in Chapter 5, it is not certain that the higher earnings of the more educated necessarily reflect greater productivity resulting from their additional education. Nevertheless it is instructive to examine the effect of educational level on earnings within an occupation (Table 8.28). In the manual occupations, earnings are seen to rise somewhat with educational level, although the main distinction is between those with and without post-primary education. The relation is stronger in the case of clerical and secretarial jobs, and it is generally more evident with standardization for length of employment experience as in Table 8.4. This is because such standardization eliminates the neutralizing effect that the lesser average employment experience of the more educated has on wages. The evidence is consistent with the view that filtering down brings with it gains in productivity within an occupation.

Table 8.31. *Tanzanian Employees by Year Education Completed and by Educa-*
tion: Distribution by Months between End of Education and Start of
Wage-Employment

Year education completed and education	Months between end of education and start of employment			
	0	1–6	7–12	13 and over
All				
Standards 1–4	17	4	8	71 (141)
Standards 5–6	17	9	5	69 (76)
Standards 7–8	29	10	17	44 (430)
Forms I–IV	55	17	16	12 (366)
Post-Form IV	69	16	10	5 (157)
1970 and earlier				
Standards 1–4	16	4	6	74 (125)
Standards 5–6	11	10	7	72 (61)
Standards 7–8	25	11	15	49 (264)
Forms I–IV	60	17	8	15 (178)
Post-Form IV	79	9	4	8 (53)
1971–79				
Standards 1–4	0	0	36	64 (10)
Standards 5–6	44	10	0	46 (8)
Standards 7–8	34	8	20	38 (177)
Forms I–IV	50	16	24	10 (183)
Post-Form IV	64	20	13	3 (103)

D. Recruitment and the Role of Education: Actual and Perceived

The less educated the employee the longer it takes him to get his first wage-job. Table 8.31 shows that 69 per cent of those with post-Form IV education obtained their first job without any delay, compared with only 17 per cent of those who did not go beyond Standard 6. The percentage of post-Form IV-leavers who obtained immediate employment was even higher in 1970 and earlier, when 79 per cent obtained immediate employment and 88 per cent were in work within six months. Since 1970 the proportion of employees with post-primary education who obtained work at once has fallen. The figure is still high, and all but 3 per cent obtained work within a year, but a much higher proportion of those in the lower levels of educational attainment had a long time to wait. However, the

Table 8.32. *Tanzanian Employees by Occupation, Sector of Employment, and Years of Employment Experience: Percentage in Casual Employment*

Occupation		
Manual		
Unskilled	32	(285)
Semi-skilled	15	(269)
Skilled	31	(354)
Clerical and secretarial	8	(495)
Technical and semi-professional	0	(71)
Managerial and administrative	0	(88)
Professional	3	(51)
All	17	
Sector of Employment		
Agriculture	0	(20)
Mining	7	(106)
Manufacturing	8	(420)
Public utility	0	(38)
Construction	88	(221)
Commerce	5	(34)
Transport	4	(480)
Private services	9	(38)
Public services	10	(346)
Years of employment experience		
0–3	38	(423)
4–7	15	(315)
8–14	9	(545)
15–21	6	(163)
22 and over	5	(172)

proportion of those with Standards 5–6 and 7–8 education who obtained work immediately was higher in 1971–9 than in the earlier period.

Casual workers are a significant proportion of the work-force in manual occupations. Only 8 per cent of clerical and secretarial employees are in casual employment, but 31 per cent of skilled manual workers are casual and 32 per cent of the unskilled. There are very few female casual workers in any occupation. In all sectors of employment, except construction, casual workers are a small proportion of all employees (Table 8.32).

For all but the higher occupations, casual employment is important as a preliminary to regular employment. Nearly three-quarters of the unskilled manual workers in regular employment started as casual workers, and the figure is nearly 50 per cent for skilled workers. Even among clerical and secretarial employees, as many as 20 per cent began as casual workers. There are wide differences in the proportion between sectors of employment. Rather few employees with post-primary education started as casual workers, but for those with less education the proportion of regular employees who started as casuals is high, ranging from 47 to 65 per cent. However, the proportion of regular employees who started as casuals has fallen over time, from 39 per cent of those who entered employment before 1966 to 25 per cent of those who started work between 1977 and 1980 (Table 8.33). The conclusion that casual work is to an important extent a step on the road to regular employment is strengthened by Table 8.32. This table shows that more than a third of the labour force who have employment experience of 3 years or less are in casual employment, compared with only 15 per cent of those with 4 to 7 years' experience, and much smaller percentages of those with even more experience than that.

In only a few firms are casual employees a large proportion of the work-force. Only 9 per cent of firms have more than a half of their workers in casual employment, and only 17 per cent have more than a quarter (Table 8.34).

There is a marked difference between regular and casual employees in the way they get their jobs. Applying for a job 'at the gate' is an important procedure for casual workers, but not for regulars. A third of the regular employees who started as casual workers applied for their job in this way, as did two-thirds of those at present in casual employment. The majority of regular employees applied to the employer by letter, either unsolicited or in reply to an advertisement. Personal introductions, through a relative or friend, are more important for casual than for regular workers, and a significant proportion of the latter were allocated their job by the government (Table 8.35).

Application 'at the gate' is important for manual workers and unimportant for those in other occupations. Application by letter and government allocation are the two most important ways in which non-manual employees obtained their jobs. Personal introductions are important for manual, but not for non-manual employees. It follows from the association between education and occupation that the most important ways of getting a job among those with the lower levels of education are 'at the gate' and by personal introductions, and for those with the higher levels of education, application by letter and government allocation. The latter is of particular importance for those with post-Form IV education, more than half of whom obtained their job in this way (Table 8.36).

The tables in this and earlier sections have shown the close relationship between level of education and occupation. It is a relationship perceived clearly by employees. A high proportion with education of Standards 7–8 and above believe they would not have got their job if they had had less education. But education does not seem to be a passport to the job of

Table 8.33. *Tanzanian Regular Employees by Occupation, Sector of Employment, Education, and Year Entered Wage-Employment: Percentage Starting as Casual Employees*

Occupation		
Manual		
Unskilled	73	(186)
Semi-skilled	54	(231)
Skilled	47	(245)
Clerical and secretarial	20	(526)
Technical and semi-professional	7	(69)
Managerial and administrative	5	(87)
Professional	4	(51)
Sector of employment		
Agriculture	40	(20)
Mining	14	(102)
Manufacturing	47	(383)
Public utility	11	(38)
Construction	63	(27)
Commerce	55	(31)
Transport	40	(458)
Private services	5	(38)
Public services	22	(311)
Education		
None	60	(118)
Standards 1–4	65	(170)
Standards 5–6	62	(82)
Standards 7–8	47	(420)
Forms I–IV	13	(447)
Post-Form IV	5	(186)
Year entered wage-employment		
1977–80	25	(264)
1973–76	36	(268)
1966–72	38	(494)
1959–65	39	(153)
Before 1959	39	(161)
All	35	(1426)

their choice for those who are allocated to a job by the government. More than half of those who were allocated to a job by the government after completing the first stage of secondary education were put into the job of their first choice; for those with a higher level of education only 26 per cent were put into the job of their first choice. Within each of these educational groups, professional employees were allocated to the job of their first choice to a greater extent than employees in other occupations,

Table 8.34. *Distribution of Tanzanian Firms by Percentage of Employees in Regular Employment*

Percentage of employees in regular employment	Percentage of firms
0–50	9
51–75	8
76–80	5
81–90	16
91–100	62
	(63)

Table 8.35. *Tanzanian Employees by Employment Status and for Regular Employees Employment Status at Time Employment Started: Distribution by Method of Job Application*

Method of application	Regular employees' starting employment		Casual employees
	Regular	Casual	
At the gate	8	34	65
Letter replying to advertisement	23	13	5
Unsolicited letter	31	21	10
Through relative or friend	9	22	14
Through government employment exchange	4	4	0
Government allocation	22	2	4
Other	3	4	2
	(922)	(495)	(299)

but there is no consistent relationship between the employee's level in the occupational hierarchy and the satisfaction of his or her preference (Table 8.37).

E. Education and the Qualifications for Jobs: Employee Perceptions

The belief that they are qualified for a better job is widespread among employees. In each occupation the proportion holding this belief increases with their level of education: only 17 per cent of unskilled manual

Table 8.36*a*. *Tanzanian Employees by Occupation: Distribution by Method of Job Application*

Method of application	Occupation						
	1	2	3	4	5	6	7
At the gate	53	39	40	5	<1	0	6
Letter replying to advertisement	5	10	13	26	29	19	25
Unsolicited letter	14	19	17	41	16	28	5
Through relative or friend	20	24	16	7	10	3	0
Through government employment exchange	4	3	2	2	12	10	3
Government allocation	0	4	9	16	29	34	61
Other	4	1	3	3	4	6	0
	(288)	(278)	(363)	(569)	(69)	(86)	(52)

Note: 1: Manual, unskilled; 2: Manual, semi-skilled; 3: Manual, skilled; 4: Clerical and secretarial; 5: Technical and semi-professional; 6: Managerial and administrative; 7: Professional

workers believe they are qualified for a better job, but this figure rises to 85 per cent for those with secondary education. There is no consistent difference between employees with different lengths of time in wage employment; nor does the proportion vary consistently with the employee's position in the hierarchy of occupations (Table 8.38). The belief is stronger among regular employees than among casual workers.

Table 8.39 presents in a different way the relation between the belief and education. For unskilled workers the years of education of those who believe they are over-qualified in their present occupations range between 110 per cent and 149 per cent of the average years of education for unskilled workers, according to the time at which the workers entered wage-employment. For all other occupations the difference between the education of those who believe they are over-qualified and the generality of workers in their occupation is much less than that, suggesting that the validity of the belief is stronger for unskilled workers than for others.

The belief that they are over-qualified for their present job affects very different proportions of employees in the different occupations who are seeking a better job, and in general the higher the occupation in the hierarchy the more of those looking for a better job believe that they are over-qualified. For manual workers the proportion ranges between 39 and 53 per cent; of the non-manual workers who are looking for a better job,

Table 8.36b. *Tanzanian Employees by Education: Distribution by Method of Job Application*

Method of application	Education					
	None	Standards 1–4	Standards 5–6	Standards 7–8	Forms I–IV	Post-Form IV
At the gate	60	59	40	24	3	1
Letter replying to advertisement	4	4	8	19	27	17
Unsolicited letter	5	8	22	32	35	19
Through relative or friend	23	20	25	16	6	3
Through government employment exchange	4	4	0	1	5	5
Government allocation	1	2	1	4	21	53
Other	3	3	4	4	3	2
	(177)	(234)	(118)	(555)	(467)	(191)

Table 8.37a. *Tanzanian Employees who Started as Regular Employees by Educa-tion and Occupation: Percentage who Think They Would Not Have Been Employed if They Had Received Less Education*

Education	Occupation	
	Manual	Non-manual
Below Standard 7	31	50
	(93)	(8)
Standards 7–8	72	97
	(92)	(99)
Forms I–IV	73	90
	(45)	(281)
Post-Form IV	100	84
	(7)	(154)

Table 8.37b. *Tanzanian Employees Allocated Job by Government by Education and Occupation: Percentage Allocated Job of First Choice*

Form IV-leavers		
Clerical	50	(34)
Technical	57	(7)
Managerial	40	(10)
Professional	100	(6)
All	55	(60)
Form VI-leavers		
Clerical	13	(31)
Managerial	35	(17)
Professional	53	(15)
All	26	(68)

more than 80 per cent believe they are over-qualified for their present job, and for professional employees it is 100 per cent (Table 8.40).

The existence of such high proportions of employees who believe they are qualified for a better job at once raises the question of why they are in their present job. That no better job is available might be an obvious answer, but it turns out that a minority of employees who believe they are qualified for a better job believe that they are in their present job because nothing better is available. In every occupation, except that of unskilled manual worker, well under half, and for professional employees only a quarter, state that they are in their present job for that reason. The

Table 8.38. *Tanzanian Employees by Occupation and Education: Percentage who Believe They Are Qualified for a Better Job*

Occupation	Education				
	Standards 1–4	Standards 5–6	Standards 7–8	Forms I–IV	Post-Form IV
Manual					
Unskilled	17	41	47	85	..
	(92)	(21)	(69)	(11)	
Semi-skilled	22	44	52	53	..
	(60)	(34)	(118)	(12)	
Skilled	38	57	63	68	..
	(59)	(50)	(150)	(44)	
Clerical and secretarial	42	..	61	80	85
	(8)		(181)	(298)	(76)
Other non-manual	..	..	65	75	87
			(20)	(84)	(102)

Table 8.39. *Tanzanian Employees by Occupation and Year of Entry into Wage-Employment: Average years of Education of Those who Believe They Are Qualified for a Better Job as Percentage of Average Years of Education of All*

Occupation	Year of entry into wage-employment					All
	Before 1959	1959–65	1966–72	1973–6	1977–80	
Manual						
Unskilled	..	149 (8)	125 (15)	110 (11)	126 (25)	126
Semi-skilled	116 (11)	112 (8)	107 (31)	113 (26)	112 (24)	110
Skilled	106 (27)	106 (24)	107 (53)	106 (32)	98 (40)	104
Clerical and secretarial	110 (20)	105 (30)	103 (151)	106 (74)	101 (120)	104
Technical and semi-professional	103 (6)	..	103 (17)	102 (9)	105 (11)	103
Managerial and administrative	99 (16)	100 (12)	102 (17)	100 (13)	102 (6)	100
Professional	..	..	101 (15)	100 (16)	..	100

Table 8.40. *Tanzanian Employees Seeking Better Job by Occupation: Percentage who Believe They Are Over-Qualified*

Occupation		
Manual		
Unskilled	43	(65)
Semi-skilled	39	(60)
Skilled	53	(95)
Clerical and secretarial	83	(142)
Technical and semi-professional	83	(11)
Managerial and administrative	85	(25)
Professional	100	(10)

proportion who do accept that no better job is available declines with education from nearly 60 per cent for those with less than complete primary education, to only a third for those with secondary education and beyond (Table 8.41). More than 40 per cent of both regular and casual workers say that they are in their present job to gain experience (Table 8.42).

F. Formal Training by Employers

The interrelationships between education, experience, and training were discussed in Chapter 5, section F. Some 80 per cent of the total sample had not attended a training course provided by their current employer.[3] The proportion of those provided with a course increases steadily through the order in which the occupations are listed in Table 8.43.

Training, it seems, is given predominantly by the larger establishments, and by only some of these (Table 8.44). More than half the trained employees in the sample are employed in only 6 per cent of the establishments, and those establishments employ a quarter of the total employees. More than three-quarters of the trained employees are employed in 14 per cent of the establishments, which employ a little over half the total employees. There are no trained employees in a third of the establishments, which employ a fifth of all employees. In private establishments, however, there is no clear relationship between the size of the establish-

---

[3] The information on training concerns training by the present employer. See Chapter 5, note 3.

Table 8.41. *Tanzanian Employees who Believe They Are Over-Qualified in Present Job by Occupation and Education: Percentage who Are in Present Job because No Better Available*

Occupation	Education			All
	Below Standard 5	Standards 5–8	Post-primary	
Manual				
Unskilled	72	53	18	53
	(17)	(41)	(9)	(67)
Semi-skilled	34	30	24	31
	(21)	(75)	(8)	(104)
Skilled	53	45	32	44
	(24)	(121)	(31)	(177)
Clerical and secretarial	..	32	32	33
		(112)	(290)	(408)
Technical and semi-professional	..	25	27	27
		(11)	(42)	(53)
Managerial and administrative	..	..	41	43
			(60)	(63)
Professional	..	..	27	26
			(42)	(44)
All	59	38	33	37

Table 8.42. *Tanzanian Employees who Believe They Are Over-Qualified by Employment Status: Distribution by Reason for Being in Present Job*

Reason for current employment	Employment status	
	Regular	Casual
To gain experience	41	44
Better job not available	36	44
Other	23	12
	(814)	(107)

Table 8.43. *Tanzanian Employees by Occupation: Percentage Provided with Training Course*

Occupation		
Manual		
Unskilled	4	(285)
Semi-skilled	12	(280)
Skilled	14	(362)
Clerical and secretarial	31	(577)
Managerial and administrative	49	(71)
Technical and semi-professional	53	(88)
Professional	69	(51)
All	23	(1714)

Table 8.44. *Percentage of Total Trained Tanzanian Employees with Percentage of Establishments in which They Are Employed and Percentage of All Employees Employed in Those Establishments*

Percentage of trained employees	Percentage of establishments	Percentage of all employees
53	6	25
76	14	54
100	67	80
(398)	(63)	(1746)

Note: The number of trained employees is summed establishment by establishment, in order of decreasing absolute number of trained employees. When 53% of trained employees has been accumulated, only 6% of all establishments have been counted, and those establishments employ 25% of all employees.

Table 8.45. *Tanzanian Establishments by Ownership and Economic Activity: Percentage of Employees Trained*

Ownership		
Private	9	(672)
Parastatal	29	(664)
Local authority	26	(38)
Government	35	(349)
Economic activity		
Agriculture	30	(20)
Mining	13	(109)
Manufacturing	15	(422)
Public utilities	26	(38)
Construction	0	(221)
Commerce	0	(38)
Transport	34	(489)
Private services	34	(387)

ment and the proportion of the employees who have been provided with a training course.

Private firms on average have less than a tenth of their employees trained, compared with over a third in government establishments and a little less than that in parastatal and local-authority establishments. But as there are correlations between ownership, size, and economic activity of the establishment, it is not at all clear what role is played by ownership itself. There are large differences between economic activities in the proportion of employees who have been given training by the employer. More than a third of the employees in transport and private services have been given a course, whereas none have in construction and commerce. But as there is some correlation between sector of economic activity and the employment of persons in particular occupations, the differences between occupations in the training provided will affect the amount of training provided in different economic sectors (Table 8.45).

The sample is not large enough for a full analysis of the relationship between the employee's level of education and whether he or she has been given a training course. The skilled manual workers who have been given a course have more education than those who have not had a course, but there is no difference with clerical and secretarial employees. For occupations as a whole there is a clear positive relation between the level of education and the proportion provided with a training course (Tables 8.46 and 8.47). There seems to be no attempt to provide training courses as a substitute for education.

Training courses have been given to less than a fifth of all employees.

Table 8.46. *Tanzanian Employees by Occupation and Education: Percentage with Training Course*

Education	Occupation		All
	Skilled manual	Clerical and secretarial	
None	5 (38)	.. (2)	5 (170)
Standards 1–4	8 (65)	0 (8)	5 (238)
Standards 5–6	15 (52)	.. (3)	11 (118)
Standards 7–8	12 (153)	32 (185)	21 (558)
Form I–IV	32 (44)	33 (302)	36 (467)
Post-Form IV	29 (7)	24 (76)	42 (191)

Table 8.47. *Tanzanian Employees by Occupation and Whether Provided with a Training Course: Mean Years of Education*

	Occupation		All
	Skilled manual	Clerical and secretarial	
Course(s)	7.6 (49)	10.0 (179)	10.1 (388)
No course	5.9 (308)	10.0 (397)	7.0 (1320)

There is not much indication that in-service training has been used as a substitute for pre-service education. If anything, those with more education have been given more training and those in 'higher' occupations have the most training. Trained employees are concentrated in a relatively few establishments; a good many establishments have none, as do certain economic activities. Establishments have provided the same amount of training in recent as in earlier periods.

These, in the most summary form, are the conclusions that may be drawn from the tables discussed so far. The tables which follow show data on the relation between training and wages.

Table 8.48 looks at the wage of those at each level of education who have and who have not taken a training course. The wage of those who have taken a course is substantially greater, at some educational levels enormously greater, than that of employees who have not had a course. The same is true for employees in the occupations listed in the table.

At most levels of education, those who have been trade-tested have a higher wage than those who have not (Table 8.49), and the grade of pass

Table 8.48. *Tanzanian Employees by Education, Occupation, and Whether Have Had a Training Course: Mean Wage (Shs per month)*

	Training course	
	Taken	Not taken
Education		
None	1576	665
	(9)	(160)
Standards 1–4	807	677
	(13)	(224)
Standards 5–6	1214	764
	(12)	(103)
Standards 7–8	1017	748
	(117)	(433)
Forms I–IV	1335	1143
	(166)	(298)
Post-Form IV	1915	1637
	(79)	(108)
All	1342	889
	(397)	(1327)
Occupation		
Manual		
Semi-skilled	709	632
	(34)	(245)
Skilled	1226	857
	(49)	(302)
Clerical and secretarial	1088	1008
	(179)	(392)

in the test is positively correlated with the employee's wage (Table 8.50). The evidence suggests that, at least for the employee, training pays, and that it adds to the inequality of pay which is associated with differences in educational attainment.

G. Education and Labour Mobility

The job-mobility rate, that is, the number of employers per year in employment, is low (Table 8.51). Sixty-five per cent of the labour force have had no employer other than the one in their present job. Only 8 per cent have a mobility rate of more than 0.2. There is no particular pattern of mobility by level of education. Even those who have been in employment for 30 years or more have had very few employers. More than half

Table 8.49. *Tanzanian Skilled Manual Employees who Have and who Have Not Taken Trade Test by Education: Mean Wage (Shs per month)*

Education	Taken trade test	Not taken trade test
Standards 1–4	848	829
	(10)	(52)
Standards 5–6	1266	1018
	(19)	(30)
Standards 7–8	910	755
	(57)	(76)
Forms I–IV	1010	1242
	(30)	(13)
All	1009	845
	(122)	(210)

Table 8.50. *Tanzanian Skilled Manual Employees by Grade of Trade-Test Pass: Mean Wage (Shs per month)*

Grade of pass		
Grade 1	1353	(27)
Grade 2	1193	(32)
Grade 3	739	(33)

Table 8.51. *Tanzanian Employees by Education: Distribution by Rate of Job Mobility*

Education	Job-mobility rate[a]			
	0	Greater than 0, not greater than 0.1	Greater than 0.1, not greater than 0.2	Greater than 0.2
None	76	11	7	6 (143)
Standards 1–4	62	18	14	6 (210)
Standards 5–6	50	31	8	11 (106)
Standards 7–8	69	13	10	8 (504)
Forms I–IV	63	16	14	7 (439)
Post-Form IV	68	8	16	8 (158)
All	65	15	12	8 (1561)

[a] Job-mobility rate: Number of previous employers divided by years in wage-employment.

Table 8.52. *Tanzanian Employees by Year Education Completed: Distribution by Number of Previous Employers*

Number of previous employers	Year education completed				All
	1950 and earlier	1951–60	1961–70	1971–9	
0	55	57	57	78	66
1	34	24	30	18	24
2	6	9	9	2	5
3 or more	5	10	4	2	5
	(85)	(202)	(592)	(616)	(1734)

Table 8.53. *Tanzanian Employees by Number of Previous Employers and by Reason for Leaving Last Job: Distribution by Number of Times Out of Wage-Employment*

Reason for leaving job and times out of wage-employment	Number of previous employers			
	1	2	3	4 and more
Lost job				
0	53	60	21	71
1	43	25	23	29
2	2	10	4	0
3 and more	2	5	52	0
	(27)	(8)	(11)	(7)
Chose to leave				
0	78	86	92	79
1	16	6	3	4
2	3	5	0	9
3 and more	3	3	5	8
	(215)	(53)	(15)	(24)

of employees who completed their education in 1950 and earlier have had only the single employer, and only 11 per cent have had more than one previous employer (Table 8.52).

Remarkable, also, is the extent to which employees have moved from one job to another without a break in employment, even when they lost their job rather than chose to leave. More than three-quarters of those with one previous job who chose to leave it moved into their present job without an intervening period of unemployment, but so did more than half of those who did not leave their previous job voluntarily (Table 8.53). Table 8.54 shows that, even for employees who entered the labour

Table 8.54. *Tanzanian Employees by Years Since First Wage-Job: Distribution by Total Months Out of Wage-Employment*

Total months out of wage-employment	Years since first wage-job					All
	0–3	4–7	8–14	15–21	More than 21	
0	98	95	90	86	84	92
1–6	1	1	3	5	5	2
7–12	0	3	4	4	5	3
More than 12	1	1	3	5	6	3
	(424)	(305)	(527)	(160)	(158)	(1573)

Table 8.55. *Tanzanian Employees by Education: Percentage Leaving Previous Job Voluntarily*

Education		
None	55	(33)
Standards 1–4	59	(64)
Standards 5–6	53	(45)
Standards 7–8	82	(120)
Forms I–IV	94	(129)
Post-Form IV	100	(36)
All	78	(429)

force more than 21 years ago, only 6 per cent have had more than a year in total out of wage-employment.

More than three-quarters of the employees who had had a previous employer left their previous job voluntarily. Almost all with secondary education did so, though the proportion was only a little over a half for the uneducated (Table 8.55). More than three-quarters of those who chose to leave their job received a higher wage in their next job, but so did more than half of those who lost their job (Table 8.56). The proportion of employees who are seeking a better job is higher among manual than non-manual workers. Even for manual workers it is less than a third in total, though it is more than a half for those whose education was most recently completed (Table 8.57).

The data show that those who have entered the wage-labour force have stayed there, without long periods either in urban or rural self-employment or in unemployment.

Table 8.58 deals with the relatively few employees who have been out

Table 8.56. *Tanzanian Employees by Reason for Leaving Previous Job: Percentage who Received Pay Rise After Changing Job*

Reason for leaving last job	
Lost job	53
	(92)
Chose to leave	79
	(325)

Table 8.57. *Tanzanian Employees[a] by Year Education Completed and Occupation: Percentage Seeking Better Job*

Occupation	Year education completed				All
	Before 1965	1965–9	1970–4	1975–9	
Manual	24	21	29	55	32
	(21)	(62)	(63)	(44)	(193)
Non-manual	14	20	27	18	18
	(72)	(76)	(83)	(11)	(245)
All	15	20	28	48	25

[a] Employees who completed primary education but have had no further education and who are in their first wage-job.

of employment. More of them spent their time working on their parents' *shamba* as their main activity than in any other activity, particularly of those with only primary education, but it still accounted for less than half the total. Looking for employment was the main activity for nearly half of those with post-primary education. The figures suggest, therefore, that being unemployed, as distinct from not working, is characteristic of the more educated rather than of the less educated, for the latter can neither afford to be unemployed nor have the incentive to wait for a better job.

There is no very clear pattern in the time spent in the last job by level of education: it is longer for those with secondary than for those with primary education, but it is longest for the uneducated. Employees who were in large firms spent longer in their previous job than those who were in small firms. Those who were in government employment spent longer in their previous jobs than those in private employment, with those employed by parastatals in between. Employees who were in construction and in electricity and water stayed for a rather shorter time than those in other sectors (Table 8.59).

Table 8.58. *Tanzanian Employees who Have Been Out of Wage-Employment by Education: Distribution by Main Activity When Out of Employment*

Activity	Education			All
	Below Standard 7	Standards 7–8	Post-primary	
Work on parents' *shamba*	38	48	30	39
Non-agricultural self-employment	26	21	13	22
Looking for employment	20	9	48	22
Other	16	22	9	17
	(61)	(33)	(23)	(117)

Table 8.59a. *Tanzanian Employees with Previous Job by Level of Education: Mean Years in Last Job*

	Education					All
None	Standards 1–4	Standards 5–6	Standards 7–8	Forms I–IV	Post-Form IV	
5.5	3.2	3.9	3.3	4.2	4.3	3.9
(37)	(73)	(56)	(161)	(143)	(54)	(524)

Table 8.59b. *Tanzanian Employees with Previous Job by Size of Firm in Last Job: Mean Years in Last Job*

	Size of firm	
Fewer than 50	50–499	500 and more
3.4	4.0	4.2
(135)	(176)	(164)

Table 8.59c. *Tanzanian Employees with Previous Job by Type of Employer in Last Job: Mean Years in Last Job*

	Type of Employer	
Private	Parastatal	Government
3.4	4.1	4.4
(198)	(143)	(128)

Table 8.59d. *Tanzanian Employees with Previous Job by Sector of Employment in Last Job: Mean Years in Last Job*

				Sector of employment				
1	2	3	4	5	6	7	8	9
3.8	3.7	3.6	2.6	2.6	4.7	4.3	4.4	4.5
(22)	(14)	(106)	(19)	(98)	(44)	(65)	(47)	(113)

Note: 1: Agriculture and forestry; 2: Mining and quarrying; 3: Manufacturing; 4: Electricity and water; 5: Construction; 6: Wholesale and retail trade; 7: Transport and communications; 8: Finance and insurance; 9: Social and personal services

Table 8.60. *Tanzanian Employees with Previous Job by Occupation in Current Job: Distribution by Occupation in Last Job*

Occupation in last job	Occupation in current job				
	Manual, unskilled	Manual, semi-skilled	Manual, skilled	Clerical and secretarial	Other
Manual					
Unskilled	84	12	3	0	0
Semi-skilled	10	77	8	8	6
Skilled	2	4	79	4	7
Clerical and secretarial	4	7	10	80	9
Other	0	0	0	8	78
	(51)	(74)	(117)	(171)	(69)

A high proportion of employees were in the same occupation in their previous job. Not many move up the hierarchy of occupations in changing their job. For instance, only 11 per cent of skilled manual workers were in semi-skilled or unskilled work in the previous job. And some move down the hierarchy: 16 per cent of unskilled manual workers were in higher occupations in their previous job (Table 8.60).

H. Summary

There is a close relationship between the level of education of an employee and his or her wage. A few years of primary education make little difference, but there is a sharp rise between primary and secondary education, and the premium is particularly large for those with education beyond Form IV of secondary school. The inequality of pay for employees with different levels of education is somewhat reduced by overtime and bonus payments, but the incidence of non-monetary benefits enhances the positive relationship between pay and education, as it does between pay and occupation.

There is a clear, positive relationship between the education of employees—whether in terms of the level of education reached or of the years spent in education—and their position in the hierarchy of occupations.

Employees in the occupations requiring greater skill are more highly paid, and the more educated are more highly paid. However, within a given occupation the relationship between wage and education is less clear. It is clearer for cohorts of the same length of employment experience because there is a strong relationship between both length of employment experience and seniority in the firm on the one hand, and pay on the other, which conceals the relationship between education and pay. It is also clear for non-manual workers. But for manual workers, although the relationship exists, it is not a particularly strong one.

Women are paid less than men. The type of primary school attended does not make a consistent difference in pay, though it appears to be an advantage to have attended a private secondary school. There is in general a positive relationship between the amount an employee is paid and his or her examination results, particularly for Form IV-leavers.

Casual employees are paid less than regulars. Supervisors are paid more than those they supervise. These are rather obvious relationships. Of more interest is the extent to which pay depends on the ownership of the establishment. Employees in the higher occupations and with the higher levels of education are paid more in private employment than by government or parastatal bodies. These differences no doubt reflect the operations of incomes policy and manpower planning, which impinge on the better-paid and higher occupations. The government holds down the pay for employees in these categories, which they can directly control, and at the same time restricts the output of them from the educational system in the name of manpower planning. In consequence their pay is bid up in the private sector above what it would be if the supply were less restricted, widening the gap in pay between the private and public sectors.

Firms of every size tend to pay more for more education. Employees with the lower levels of education do better in large firms than small, whereas the relationship is roughly the reverse for employees with secondary education. The provision of benefits in addition to the wage is greater by government and parastatal than by private employers.

The better educated tend to have fewer dependants than the less well educated, so that the wage per dependant for the educated is a bigger multiple of that for the uneducated than is the wage itself.

'Filtering down' has occurred over time. With the increase in the supply of educated employees, persons with a given level of education have entered occupations lower in the hierarchy. Filtering down has lowered the wage for any level of education and compressed the differential for education, reducing over time the premium received by the more educated.

A narrowing of the range of wages by occupation for the most recent cohort entering employment has accompanied the narrowing of the range by education. However, data on the spread at the present time for cohorts with different lengths of employment experience exaggerate the degree of compression. As it is in the better-paid occupations that seniority attracts higher pay, the occupational wage differential within a cohort will tend to widen over time.

It takes longer for an employee to get his first job the less educated he is. Although fewer secondary school-leavers enter employment immediately than in the past, not many of them have a long wait. And a higher proportion of those with education at the level of primary school Standards 5–6 and 7–8 entered employment without a waiting time during the years 1971–9 than in the years before that. The explanation may be a change in school-leavers' expectations, as was discussed in Chapter 5.

Casual labour is quantitatively important, and for manual workers an important prelude to regular employment. its importance in this respect appears, however, to be declining. Casual workers mostly get their jobs by application 'at the gate'. Personal introductions are an important method of recruitment for manual workers. For higher-level jobs recruitment is generally by written application and, particularly for those with the higher levels of education, allocation by government, which is not generally to the job of the employee's first choice.

The relationship between education and occupation is clearly perceived by employees, a high proportion of those with education of Standards 7–8 and above believing that they would not have got their job if they had had less education. But the belief that they are qualified for a better job is widespread. Only a minority believe they are in their present job because no better job is available, and an important reason for their being in their present job is to gain experience.

The provision of training by employers is not widespread, it is not used as a substitute for pre-service education, and the extent of its provision has remained static over time. But those workers who are provided with training receive substantially higher pay. Employees tend to stay in their jobs, and the amount of movement between jobs is small. There is no particular pattern of movement according to the level of education for employees who do change their jobs. A high proportion who change do so without a break in employment, and they generally go into the kind of work they left, there being little upward movement in the occupational hierarchy through changing employers. A high proportion of employees who leave their jobs do so voluntarily.

9

Who Gets Schooling in Tanzania?

The educational attainments of the employees in Dar es Salaam as set out in Chapter 4 are to a large degree the consequence of the expansion of the education system in Tanzania, particularly during the years since Independence. The 1960s were years in which secondary education expanded more rapidly than primary, but this pattern was reversed in the 1970s and, while at the end of that decade universal primary education was in sight, secondary school places remained extremely scarce. The growth of places in government secondary schools was restricted, and private secondary schools were discouraged in the name of manpower planning. The selection of those to be educated is therefore especially concerned with secondary education, and this chapter sets out some of the relationships between the educational attainment of an individual, particularly with regard to secondary education, and his or her various other circumstances. The data enable answers to be provided to 'in what way?' and 'to what extent?', but not to the question 'why?' The data show relationships but not causation, though in places some suggestions about causation are hazarded.

Section A deals with the way the educational level reached by the employees varies with the education of their parents. The way in which the reasons for discontinuing education at a particular point vary with the period of time, the level of education reached, and the education of the employees' parents are set out in section B. The ways in which the size and location of the employees' families vary with the level of education of the employees are dealt with in section C.

Section D repeats the analysis between generations of section A, but for the employees and their children, instead of the employees and their parents. Attitudes to, and expenditures on, the education of children, as they vary with education and income, are examined in sections E and F. Section G investigates the extent to which occupations and wages are affected by family background, independently of education. A summary is provided in section H.

Table 9.1. *Tanzanian Employees by Father's Education: Distribution by Own Education*

Employee's education	Father's education		
	None	Primary	Post-primary
None	20	3	1
Standards 1–6	31	12	1
Standards 7–8	28	39	11
Forms I–IV	14	33	60
Post-Form IV	7	13	27
	(771)	(799)	(140)

A. Education of Employees: Variation with the Education of Their Parents

There is a strong correlation between father's education and the level of education achieved by the employee. Table 9.1 shows that, as the father's level of education increases, the percentage of children attaining high levels of education also increases. Of the employees whose fathers had no education, 21 per cent had at least secondary education themselves, whereas for those whose fathers had primary education the corresponding figure is 46 per cent, and for those whose fathers had secondary or post-secondary education it is more than 85 per cent. These percentages can be seen as roughly indicating the probability, given the education of the father, of getting at least to secondary school, and clearly for children from well-educated family backgrounds the probability is very high. This means that the children of fathers with less than secondary education are competing for the residual secondary school places remaining after the children of fathers with secondary education have in effect claimed their places. The size of the secondary school system, and hence the size of the residual, is therefore a crucial determinant of the probability of children from less-privileged family backgrounds going to secondary school. One consequence of restricting the growth of secondary education for man-power planning reasons is a limitation of the extent of upward mobility from one generation to the next.

Table 9.2 tells the same story as Table 9.1, by showing the different levels of education of the father when employees are grouped by their own educational attainment. The percentage of employees with fathers with no education declines strongly and almost monotonically as the level of education of employees rises and, conversely, the percentage of fathers

Table 9.2. *Tanzanian Employees by Own Education: Distribution by Father's Education*

Employee's education	Father's education		
	None	Primary	Post-primary
None	86	13	1 (174)
Standards 1–4	77	23	0 (227)
Standards 5–6	56	42	2 (114)
Standards 7–8	40	57	3 (545)
Forms I–IV	25	57	18 (457)
Post-Form IV	28	52	20 (193)

Table 9.3. *Tanzanian Employees whose Fathers Had Primary Education by Mother's Education: Distribution by Own Education*

Employee's education	Mother's education	
	None	Primary
None	5	0
Standards 1–6	17	7
Standards 7–8	40	40
Post-primary	38	53
	(438)	(345)

with primary, secondary, or post-secondary education rises almost monotonically with the level of education of employees.

For example, 86 per cent of employees with no education had fathers with no education, while 40 per cent of those with Standards 7–8 and only about 25 per cent of those with Forms I–IV had fathers with no education. A person with a high level of education from a low socio-economic background will therefore be competing for jobs mostly with people who have similar educational qualifications but a higher socio-economic background, with all the advantages this may bring. Hence, upwardly mobile school-leavers may be at a disadvantage in the job-market compared with their educational peers. Evidence about this is presented in a later section.

Table 9.3 shows that, controlling for father's education, mother's education has an independent effect on the probability of going to secondary school. Thus 38 per cent of the children of fathers with primary education whose mothers had no education went on to secondary or

Table 9.4. *Tanzanian Employees by Mother's Education and Father's Education: Mean Years of Education*

Father's education	Mother's education		
	None	Primary	Post-primary
None	5.8	8.1	..
	(736)	(30)	
Primary	8.3	9.5	11.9
	(438)	(345)	(9)
Post-primary	8.9	11.8	11.7
	(31)	(98)	(11)

higher education, while 53 per cent of those whose mothers also had primary education did so.

Table 9.4 shows very clearly the strong positive relation between the education level of one parent (holding the other parent's education constant) and the years of education[1] of the employees. Increasing either the mother's or the father's education from none to primary (holding the other parent constant at none) raises the mean length of education of the child by over two years and, similarly, raising either parent from primary to secondary and over (keeping the other parent with primary) also raises the length of education of the employee by more than two years. Interaction effects are observed along the diagonal, showing the beneficial effect of increasing both parents' education. The difference in years of education of the employee between the socio-economic extremes of both parents with zero education and both with post-secondary education is very high, namely six years. In addition, there may be a difference in the quality of schooling, with the children of more educated parents going to the best schools.

Tables 9.5 and 9.6 show the relationships between the educational levels of the employees' parents. Thus, Table 9.5 shows that 96 per cent of employees whose fathers had no education also had mothers with no education, 55 per cent of those with primary-educated fathers had mothers with no education, and only 22 per cent of those whose fathers had post-primary education had uneducated mothers. No employees whose fathers were uneducated had mothers with post-primary education.

---

[1] Years of education are calculated from level of education attained, hence those who repeated classes would have spent more years in school than the years of education variable indicates.

Table 9.5. *Tanzanian Employees by Father's Education: Distribution by Mother's Education*

Mother's education	Father's education		
	None	Primary	Post-primary
None	96	55	22
Primary	4	44	70
Post-primary	0	1	8
	(771)	(792)	(140)

Table 9.6. *Tanzanian Employees by Mother's Education: Distribution by Father's Education*

Father's education	Mother's education		
	None	Primary	Post-primary
None	61	6	0
Primary	36	73	45
Post-primary	3	21	55
	(1209)	(473)	(20)

Table 9.6 tells the same story from the other side. It shows, for instance, that 61 per cent of employees with uneducated mothers had uneducated fathers, whereas only 6 per cent of those with primary-educated mothers had uneducated fathers, and no employees whose mothers had post-primary education had uneducated fathers. These relationships indicate a high degree of assortative mating, as described in Chapter 6.

Perfectly assortative mating is not possible because there are far fewer educated women than men, but practically all of them are married to educated men, suggesting that, if males and females were similarly distributed across educational groups, mating would be nearly perfectly assortative. Given the advantages of having an educated parent, and particularly two educated parents, the propensity of educated individuals to choose educated spouses will reinforce the unequal distribution of educational opportunities for the next generation. Some evidence on the trend in the pattern of mating is found in section C, where a comparison is made between employees and their parents.

Analysis of the two cohorts of employees, those aged 30 or less and those aged 31 years or more, in Table 9.7 makes it possible to assess the change in intergenerational mobility over time due to the expansion of

Table 9.7. *Tanzanian Employees by Age and Father's Education: Distribution by Own Education*

Employee's age and father's education	Employee's education		
	Standard 6 or less	Standards 7–8	Post-primary
30 years and under			
None	29	48	23 (352)
Primary	10	46	44 (486)
Post-primary	0	12	88 (95)
Over 30 years			
None	68	12	20 (420)
Primary	24	28	48 (312)
Post-primary	8	7	85 (45)
All ages			
None	50	28	21 (772)
Primary	15	39	46 (799)
Post-primary	3	10	87 (140)

education. It was suggested earlier that the probability of children from less-educated families going to secondary school depended on the size of the secondary school system, and hence on the size of the residual once the children from well-educated families had secured places. Because of the restriction on the provision of secondary school places for reasons concerned with manpower planning, the residual of secondary school places has not grown very much, and this is reflected in Table 9.7.

There has been little change over time in the educational achievement of those whose fathers had post-primary education: for both age-cohorts the probability of achieving at least Forms I–IV is very high—over 0.8. Nor has there been any significant change in the much lower chance of employees whose fathers had no more than primary education themselves achieving post-primary education.

Children from well-educated families almost automatically complete primary school, through to Standard 6, while the chance for children from less-educated homes depends on the residual of primary school places. Primary education has expanded very greatly, and Table 9.7 shows the consequence. The percentage of employees with uneducated fathers who themselves completed primary school is four times as high for the younger as for the older cohort (48 per cent as against 12 per cent), and for employees with primary-educated fathers it is more than two-thirds higher (46 per cent as against 28 per cent).

Table 9.8. *Tanzanian Employees by Age and Parents' Education: Mean Years of Education*

Parents' education	Employee's age	
	30 years and under	Over 30 years
Both none	6.9	5.0
	(329)	(407)
One none, one primary	8.0	8.6
	(255)	(213)
Both primary	9.1	10.3
	(242)	(102)
One none, one post-primary	9.4	8.2
	(18)	(13)
One primary, one post-primary	11.6	12.3
	(81)	(26)
Both post-primary	..	..
All	8.3	7.1
	(930)	(767)

This analysis suggests that the expansion of education over the last 20 years or so has not altered the relationship between family background and the chances of getting a secondary education. The chance remains much higher for children from well-educated families. Intergenerational mobility has increased as a result of educational expansion, but in the more limited sense, that the chances of achieving a complete primary education have increased greatly for children from less-fortunate backgrounds and indeed have increased most for children from families with no education.

Table 9.8 shows that the difference in mean years of education between the extremes of parental education has narrowed between the two cohorts from 7.3 to 4.7 years, mainly because of an increase of nearly two years in the mean years of education of those from the least-educated families.

The difference in years of education between employees from homes where both parents have primary and those where one has primary and the other post-primary education has widened over time, from 2 years for the older cohort to 2.5 years for the younger cohort. This widening suggests that for the older cohort education was so scarce that being born to parents with primary education was sufficient to confer a significant advantage. For the younger cohort the numbers of primary school-leavers had increased greatly, while the secondary school-leavers were still very

Table 9.9. *Tanzanian Employees who Desired to Continue Their Education by Period at which Education Ceased: Distribution by Reason for Not Continuing*

Reason for not continuing	Period education completed			
	1931–50	1951–60	1961–70	1971–80
Educational	23	24	42	52
Economic	75	71	49	26
Other	2	5	9	22
	(67)	(186)	(530)	(553)

scarce, and so the advantage conferred on children by having parents with primary education was eroded.

B. Reasons for Discontinuing Education

Around 90 per cent of the employees questioned wanted to continue their formal education at the time they left it. There was no significant variation according to age or level of education. Why had they not continued? There are two main sets of reason. One is educational, particularly examination failure but also the absence of a local school. Other reasons may be classed as economic: inability to pay school fees, the direct cost of education, and inability to do without the income (monetary or non-monetary) which would accrue from working instead of attending school, the indirect cost of education. In addition there is a variety of other reasons. Table 9.9 shows how the relative importance of these different reasons has changed over time. Until the 1960s the reasons were overwhelmingly economic, and predominantly the direct cost of school fees. Since then, educational reasons, particularly examination failures (45 of the 52 per cent in 1971–80 was for that reason), have become of most importance and the undifferentiated 'other' category has also become large. This changing pattern is at any rate in part a reflection of the fact that fees were abolished in secondary schools at the beginning of 1964 and in primary schools in 1973.

The impression given by the data is that access to schooling has become more meritocratic, in the sense that it is less dependent on ability to pay fees and more dependent on passing examinations. Although the General Entrance Examination was renamed the Primary School Leaving Examination in 1967, to emphasize that primary school was intended to provide an education complete in itself, the examination's importance as

Table 9.10. *Tanzanian Employees by Form IV Examination Result: Percentage Reaching Form VI*

Examination result	Percentage reaching Form VI
Division 1	74
	(45)
Division 2	50
	(146)
Division 3	6
	(135)

Table 9.11. *Tanzanian Employees by Father's Education: Distribution by Form IV Examination Result*

Examination result	Father's education		
	None	Primary	Post-primary
Division 1	13	10	11
Division 2	31	41	32
Division 3	32	29	46
Division 4	20	14	11
Fail	2	4	0
Did not sit	2	2	0
	(102)	(225)	(83)

a selection device remained (Morrison 1976: 273–4). Failure to pass the examination is the main reason for those ending their education at primary school, and clearly children from well-educated backgrounds must pass the examinations more often to explain the high correlation reported in section A between father's and own education. Nevertheless, families with higher income have the great advantage that, if their children fail to make the government secondary school, they can pay for private education. Evidence that families (and especially the better off) are willing to pay for private schooling is reviewed in section E.

That lack of success in the national Form IV examination is the major reason for not continuing to Forms V and VI is given direct confirmation in Table 9.10. The percentage going on to Form VI declines monotonically with the results in the examination.

Table 9.11 shows no relationship between success in the examination and the education of the father. Nor is the family background of those

Table 9.12. *Tanzanian Employees with Passes in Form VI Examination by Father's Education: Distribution by Number of Passes*

Number of passes	Father's education		
	None	Primary	Post-primary
1	25	12	16
2 or more	75	88	84
3 or more	35	66	48
4 or more	6	28	35
	(39)	(80)	(30)

who did not continue beyond Form IV different: there is a virtually identical distribution by father's education of those who did not continue after Form IV and of the whole sample. All this suggests that, while it is very hard for children from less-educated backgrounds to get into secondary school, once there they are as likely to go on to the sixth form as children with more-educated parents.

Whereas in the Form IV examination there was no relationship between success and family background, this is not the case with the Form VI examination (Table 9.12). The proportion of candidates with four or more passes increases markedly with the education of the fathers. However, for other levels of achievement the relationship is weak. Certainly, the children of primary-educated fathers do better than those of uneducated fathers, but they also do better than children whose fathers had post-primary education. The weak relationship is consistent with the notion that the Form IV examination selects the most able and determined pupils to continue to Form VI, whatever the family background, and that, whatever the form of influence of family background on Form IV candidates, it no longer operates by the time they take the Form VI examination.

C. Education of Employees and Size and Location of Their Families

Section A recorded the high degree of assortative mating by educational level of employees' parents. Table 9.13 shows that such behaviour is also very strong for the employees themselves. There is a strongly declining monotonic relationship between the level of education of employees and the percentage having spouses with no education, and a strongly increas-

Table 9.13. *Tanzanian Employees by Sex and Education: Distribution by Education of Spouse*

Employee's sex and spouse's education	Employee's education		
	None	Primary	Post-primary
All employees			
None	71	34	22
Primary	28	59	44
Post-primary	1	7	34
	(148)	(685)	(370)
Male employees			
None	71	35	20
Primary	28	63	54
Post-primary	1	2	26
	(142)	(617)	(237)
Female employees			
None	..	25	30
Primary	..	21	5
Post-primary	..	54	65
		(68)	(73)

ing and monotonic relation between the level of education of employees and the percentage having spouses with secondary or more education. For example, 71 per cent of men with no education have wives with no education, while only 35 per cent of those with primary education and 20 per cent of those with secondary education or more have wives with no education, which is strong evidence for assortative mating.

There is a difference in the pattern for men and women. Over 70 per cent of men, but only 35 per cent of women, with secondary and post-secondary education had spouses with no more than primary education. Only 2 per cent of men, but 54 per cent of women with primary education had spouses with secondary or post-secondary education. This difference in the extent of assortative mating is explicable by the scarcity of educated women and relative abundance of educated men. It was suggested in section A that assortative mating may have increased over time as more women were educated. Twenty or so years ago, so few women were educated that many well-educated men would have been unable to find a well-educated wife. Today the number of educated women is much larger relative to the number of educated men, and so there is increased potential for assortative mating. Evidence that this is so comes from a comparison of Tables 9.13 and 9.5. Only 8 per cent of employees whose fathers (first-generation males) had post-primary education had mothers of that educational level, while 26 per cent of male employees (second-generation males) with post-primary education have wives with that education. Similarly, 44 per cent of employees whose fathers had primary education had primary-educated mothers, whereas 63 per cent of primary-educated male employees have wives with the same education. The degree of assortative mating has increased from one generation to the next as the supply of educated women has increased.

The high cost of life in the city, and the limited employment opportunities for women, might have been expected to cause poorer, less well-educated workers to keep their families in the rural areas. But this does not seem to be the case. Over 95 per cent of African male employees have their wives with them in Dar es Salaam, and over 80 per cent have all their children there, regardless of education or income category. On average, employees have 90 per cent of their children in Dar es Salaam— again this is true for each income or education group. It may be because they wish to take advantage of the greater educational opportunities for their children in urban areas. And it is true that around three-quarters of the first children of employees are educated in Dar es Salaam in every income category.

D. Education of Employees' Children: Variation with the Education of Employees

The tables in this section are like those of section A, but they look at the educational attainment of the third generation (children of employees) in relation to that of the second and the first. However, for reasons given in Chapter 6, the third is not strictly comparable with the earlier generations.

Employees have very few eligible children who are totally without schooling. For those with education above Standard 6 the proportion is below 10 per cent, whereas for those with less education it ranges from 13 to 16 per cent. Table 9.14 shows that the education of the parent makes no difference to the years of education acquired by the first child under the age of 15 years, but that there is a strong positive relationship between education of the parent and years of education of the first child aged 15 or over. There is also a marked difference in the proportion of first children age 15 and over who are continuing their education according to the educational level of the parent.[2] For parents with less than

----

[2] The parent is the employee, of course, and is father or mother according to the composition of the sample.

Table 9.14. *Tanzanian Employees by Own Level of Education, Age of First Child, and Whether Education of Child Continuing: Mean Years of Education of First Child*

Whether education continuing and age of first child	Employee's education					
	None	Standards 1–4	Standards 5–6	Standards 7–8	Forms I–IV	Post-Form IV
All						
6–10	2.2	2.1	2.0	2.0	1.6	1.9
	(13)	(26)	(22)	(57)	(43)	(12)
11–14	4.2	3.5	5.0	4.2	5.1	5.0
	(31)	(38)	(16)	(48)	(41)	(6)
15 and over	6.9	6.1	7.9	8.9	11.1	10.7
	(35)	(36)	(22)	(22)	(26)	(10)
Education completed						
15 and over	7.4	6.4	7.3	8.7	⋮	⋮
	(19)	(17)	(9)	(11)		
Education continuing						
15 and over	6.3	5.9	8.4	9.1	11.3	10.4
	(16)	(18)	(13)	(11)	(22)	(8)

Table 9.15. *Tanzanian Employees and Spouses by Education and by Age of First Child: Mean Years of Education of First Child*

Education of both parents	Age of first child		
	6–10	11–14	15 and over
None	2.4	4.0	6.4
	(11)	(23)	(20)
Primary	2.1	4.2	8.1
	(68)	(52)	(36)
Post-primary	1.3	6.0	..
	(17)	(14)	

secondary education, 50 per cent of the first children are continuing their education, whereas for parents with secondary and post-secondary education it is 81 per cent.

Table 9.14 shows that children have a longer education the more educated their parents. This is true for children whose education is complete. For those whose education is continuing, the years of education are very few when their parents are in the lowest education groups. It is probable that these children are still in primary school, and some of them may have entered school at ages well above the normal following the abolition of primary fees in 1973 and the Musoma Resolution of 1974.[3] The large difference between children who are continuing may also be partly due to more repetition by those from less-educated and poorer households, who may also have to take time off school when the family has financial difficulties.[4]

As was remarked in Chapter 6, there is a difficulty about these figures of the education of the employees' children, because only about half of them have completed their education. There is no way of knowing the final educational attainment of the rest, and the figures for average length of education understate what it will be when all have completed.

Table 9.15 shows the effects of the education of both parents on the years of education of the child. There is no beneficial effect on the youngest age, but it is significant for the 11-year-olds and onwards. The difference in the 11–14 years groups is possibly because the children of

[3] As part of the drive to achieve Universal Primary Education, in Nov. 1977 most of the children aged 8–13 who had not previously attended school were swept into Standard 1 along with 7-year-olds, causing a bulge in enrolments.

[4] As years of education are calculated from class level reached in school, the figures would not show years actually spent in school if some classes were repeated.

Table 9.16. *Tanzanian Employees with First Child Aged 15 or More who Has Completed Education by Own Education: Distribution by Education of First Child*

Education of employee	Education of child	
	Below secondary	Secondary
None	84	16 (25)
Primary	87	13 (45)
Post-primary	20	80 (10)

less-educated parents start school later, or have to repeat classes more often, or interrupt their schooling for financial reasons. The figures for children aged 6–10 confirm that, for very young children, parents' background does not affect years of schooling (although it could well affect the quality of school the child is sent to, how much is spent on books and equipment, the amount of out-of-school investment, and so on). It seems that for this group of urban children, who are among the first inputs of the Universal Primary Education system, it is not true that those from the more-educated homes start school earlier than the rest.

Table 9.16 shows the sharp difference between the attainment of secondary school by the children of parents with or without secondary education themselves, and it is this difference which accounts for the difference in length of education shown in earlier tables.

E. Attitudes to the Education of Children: Variation with Employees' Education and Income

In total, 57 per cent of employees say they will pay to send their son to a private secondary school if he fails to gain a place at a government secondary school. Although Table 9.17 shows that the percentage increases with the employee's education and income, it is extremely high for all groups, particularly given that private schools are frowned upon and discouraged. Of course, in practice it may not work out like that, as is suggested by the fact that over 80 per cent of the children of fathers without secondary education who had completed their education did not go to secondary school. It may be that people are unrealistic about how much it will cost to send their children to school. Alternatively, it may be because the supply of private schools has been constrained as a result of strong government discouragement. If so, the scarcity of private schools

Table 9.17. *Tanzanian Employees by Education, by Wage, and by Number of Children: Distribution by Action if Son Could Not Go to Government Secondary School*

	Action by parent			
	Pay fees at private secondary school	Send son to village polytechnic	Make son repeat primary	Other
Education				
None	41	17	4	38 (171)
Primary	46	29	2	23 (864)
Forms I–IV	76	15	1	8 (428)
Post-Form IV	76	14	2	8 (183)
Wage (Shs per month)				
0–1000	49	19	2	30 (1086)
1001–2000	68	20	1	11 (388)
Over 2000	80	12	2	6 (161)
Number of children				
1	62	24	1	13 (187)
3	57	22	0	21 (246)
6 and over	50	22	5	23 (185)

Note: The question put was 'If after leaving primary school your son could not continue to a government secondary school, what would you do?'

may have affected most those of the less advantaged who would have been prepared to pay for their children's education.

More of those with high levels of education (and high wages) say they are prepared to pay fees than of those with less education and lower wages, and the reverse relationships hold with respect to the percentage saying they would send their children out to work (the major element in the 'Other' category in Table 9.17) if they could not get them into a government school. These answers reflect the lack of funds to spend on education for those at the bottom of the income and educational ladder, and the greater importance of foregone earnings when children are at school instead of working.[5] Table 9.17 shows that as the size of the family grows, and hence demands on family resources increase, there is a fall in the percentage saying they would pay for education, which is a further indication of the importance of inability to pay. Nevertheless, although that is almost certainly the major influence, there may also be a difference in perceptions of the returns (pecuniary and non-pecuniary) to education. Families who are low down in the income and educational hierarchy may lack information about job opportunities, or believe that access to well-paying, high-status jobs depends not only on education but also on family background. The proportion of employees with Forms I–IV education who say they would pay for the education of their children increases with the level of education of their fathers. It is 55 per cent for employees with uneducated fathers, 81 per cent for those with primary-educated fathers, and 88 per cent for those whose father had post-primary education. These figures suggest that educational advantages are liable to accumulate from generation to generation. Some evidence on whether returns do differ by family background is presented in section G.

F. Expenditure on Children's Education: Variation with Employees' Education and Income

The total cost of children's education increases strongly and monotonically as the number of children in school increases (Table 9.18). As the level of education of the employee rises total spending on education rises, but the relationship is neither smooth nor monotonic (Table 9.19), though

---

[5] Correspondingly, around 25% of manual workers, but a negligible proportion of those in higher occupations, say they would send their children out to work, and around 40–5% of manual workers say they would pay fees, compared with over 70% of white-collar workers.

Table 9.18. *Tanzanian Employees by Number of Children in School: Mean Expenditure on Education (Shs per annum)*

Number of children in school	Expenditure
1	274
2	752
3	1589
4	1731
5	2039
6 and over	3106

Table 9.19. *Tanzanian Employees by Education and Wage: Mean Expenditure (Shs p.a.) on Education of Children in School, Total, per Child, as Percentage of Income*

	Expenditure		
	Total	Per child	% of income
Education			
None	704	286	6.8 (76)
Standards 1–6	652	269	6.5 (160)
Standards 7–8	959	402	8.1 (115)
Forms I–IV	1631	546	7.9 (125)
Post-Form IV	1159	516	4.5 (30)
Wage (Shs per month)			
0–500	486	243	9.6 (76)
501–750	561	275	7.5 (143)
751–1000	755	341	7.4 (75)
1001–1500	840	366	5.4 (89)
1501–2000	1695	512	8.2 (47)
2001–3000	2004	616	6.9 (65)
Over 3000	3582	1156	7.6 (15)

Note: The percentages are of the incomes of those reporting the data for this table. The incomes are not identical with those of the larger sample reported in Table 8.5.

there is a smooth, positive, monotonic relationship between the employee's wage and spending on education.

An employee's expenditure on education is affected by the number of children paid for within the 'extended family'. Table 9.19 shows that the expenditure per child by level of education changes more or less in step with total expenditure. It rises a good deal less steeply than the em-

Table 9.20. *Tanzanian Employees by Wage and Educational Level of First Child in School: Mean Percentage of Employee's Income Spent on Education of First Child*

Wage (Shs per month)	Educational level of first child	
	Primary	Secondary
0–500	4.9	..
	(55)	
501–750	4.4	..
	(101)	
751–1000	5.2	..
	(48)	
1001–1500	2.7	12.4
	(52)	(7)
1501–2000	2.7	12.3
	(20)	(7)
2001–3000	4.0	4.9
	(22)	(13)
Over 3000	..	8.2
		(8)

Table 9.21. *First Child of Tanzanian Employees in School by Type of School Attended: Mean Expenditure by Employees on Education of First Child (Shs p.a.)*

Type of school	Expenditure	
Government primary	366	(356)
Government secondary	1447	(14)
Private secondary	2597	(28)

ployee's wage, indicating that educational expenditure per child is more equally distributed than total educational expenditure.

There is much less variation in spending as a percentage of income, either by education or by the wage, than in total spending, and in fact the highest percentage of income spent on children's education is for the lowest wage-category. A similar relationship is seen in Table 9.20 for expenditure on the first child. Of course, the wage as the income variable is only a rough indicator of family resources as other members of the family (for example, the spouse) may be working and there may also be non-wage income (for example, from the *shamba*).

Table 9.21 makes plain the big difference in costs between primary and

Table 9.22. *Tanzanian Employees' First Child by Education and Sex: Mean Cost of Education in Year (Shs)*

Education of first child	Male	Female	All
Standard 4 and below	316	308	313
	(151)	(105)	(252)
Standards 5–8	570	368	470
	(66)	(64)	(130)
Forms I–IV	2283	1572	2044
	(27)	(14)	(41)

secondary schooling, even for those in government schools; expenditure on the education of a child at a private secondary school is almost twice what is spent when the child is at a government secondary school, and around eight times what is spent when he or she is at a government primary school. Cost cannot, however, be relied upon as an indicator of quality, for the subsidized government schools tend to be better as well as cheaper.

Despite the apparently non-discriminatory attitude to the education of boys and girls, it seems from Table 9.22 that in fact more is spent on the education of boys than of girls. The survey data do not suggest an explanation.

G. The Independent Effect of Family Background on Occupation and Wages

The possible effects of an employee's family background, independent of his or her educational attainment, which were discussed in Chapter 6, make it necessary to control for educational attainment, and to look at occupation and income by family background.

Table 9.23 shows a fall in the proportion of employees in manual occupations as the educational level of the father rises, both for employees whose own education is at the level of Standards 5–8 and for those with Forms I–IV education. The figures suggest, however, that family background, as indicated by the father's education, has more effect for primary than for secondary school-leavers. The latter are in very scarce supply and face a seller's market for their skills. It is not surprising that employers do not discriminate among them, and that those from

Table 9.23. *Tanzanian Employees by Education, Period when Education Completed, and Father's Education: Distribution by Occupation*

Employee's education and father's education	Employee's occupation		
	Manual	Clerical	Other
Employee's education			
Standards 5–8			
Completed before 1970			
Father's education			
None	78	19	3 (177)
Primary	54	42	4 (202)
Post-primary	50	30	20 (10)
Completed 1970–79			
Father's education			
None	79	18	2 (87)
Primary	74	23	3 (138)
Post-primary	..	..	..
All years			
Father's education			
None	78	19	3 (264)
Primary	62	34	4 (240)
Post-primary	40	47	13 (15)
Forms I–IV			
Completed before 1970			
Father's education			
None	16	53	31 (55)
Primary	13	60	27 (127)
Post-primary	7	37	56 (27)
Completed 1970–79			
Father's education			
None	21	75	4 (48)
Primary	19	70	11 (123)
Post-primary	16	82	2 (55)
All years			
Father's education			
None	19	63	17 (103)
Primary	16	64	20 (250)
Post-primary	14	66	20 (82)

Table 9.24. *Tanzanian Employees by Education, Years of Employment Experience, and Father's Education: Mean Wage (Shs per month)*

Father's education	Employee's education and experience			
	Standards 5–8		Forms I–IV	
	0–7 yrs	More than 7 yrs	0–7 yrs	More than 7 yrs
None	766	1352	596	935
	(44)	(67)	(122)	(150)
Primary	857	1491	591	1007
	(114)	(145)	(170)	(189)
Post-primary	902	1728	550	1323
	(46)	(38)	(7)	(9)

less-educated households do not suffer from having fewer contacts. Primary school-leavers, on the other hand, are in relative abundance, and job applicants from the more-fortunate families are able to use their contacts and superior information in competing for the best jobs. It is also noteworthy that for the earlier cohort the fall in the proportion in manual occupations occurs when the father has some education rather than none, whereas for the later cohort it is the father's having post-primary education that makes the difference.

The wage of an employee tends to be higher the higher the educational attainment of his father (Table 9.24). This is true independently of the employee's own level of education and years of work experience (except for Forms I–IV employees with 7 years or less employment experience).

Other benefits of having a father with secondary education are displayed in Table 9.25. For employees in both educational groups distinguished in the table, a higher proportion obtained employment immediately after leaving school, and a smaller proportion had more than a year to wait, when their fathers had had a secondary education than when their fathers were of a lower educational status. It also appears (Table 9.26) that a higher proportion of employees who had had more than one job changed jobs without an intervening spell of unemployment if their fathers were secondary-educated than if they came from families with a lower level of education.

In summary, the data suggest that family background does have some direct impact on an individual's economic success, independently of his or her educational attainment. A favourable family background may also help an individual get an urban wage-job more quickly, and be less likely to suffer spells of unemployment, because of superior contacts or information.

Table 9.25. *Tanzanian Employees by Education and Father's Education: Distribution by Time between End of Education and Start of Wage-Employment*

Employee's education and time between end of education and start of wage-employment (months)	Father's education		
	None	Primary	Post-primary
Standards 5–8			
Zero	26	27	44
1–12	24	25	41
More than 12	50	48	15
	(197)	(278)	(15)
Forms I–IV			
Zero	51	53	66
1–12	38	30	31
More than 12	11	17	3
	(92)	(211)	(58)

Table 9.26. *Tanzanian Employees with Previous Wage-Employment by Education and Father's Education: Percentage Continuously Employed*

Father's education	Employee's education	
	Standards 5–8	Forms I–IV
None	55	75
	(85)	(37)
Primary	68	82
	(123)	(105)
Post-primary	64	85
	(11)	(27)

H. Summary

Chapter 8 dealt with the relationships between the educational attainment of employees in Dar es Salaam and their occupation, income, and other attributes, that is with the effects of education on the employees themselves. The present chapter has examined the effect of educational attainment on others. Primarily, its concern has been with the relationship between the educational attainment of one generation and that of another. There is evidence on three generations: the parents of the employees, the employees themselves, and the employees' children.

There is a high positive correlation between the economic status of the second generation and the educational attainment of the first. In Tanzania it is likely that the main way in which economic status is passed from generation to generation is through inequality of educational opportunity. Of particular interest and importance is the very high probability of the children of those with secondary school education themselves receiving secondary education, and the counterpart low probability of achieving secondary education if the parent has not been to secondary school.

The education of the employees' mothers has an influence independently from, and additional to, that of the father, and the strength of both influences is compounded by the extent of assortative mating.

The most important conclusion that emerges from the data is that the correlations between the generations substantially limit the degree of intergenerational mobility. Over time, mobility has increased in terms of the ability to obtain a complete primary education, but in terms of access to secondary education there has been no increase in upward mobility.

Although almost all employees, including the youngest, are dissatisfied with the level of education they achieved, the reasons for failing to go further have changed considerably over the last 20 years, mirroring changes in government educational policies. For the most recent cohort, failure in examinations dominates financial difficulties as the main reason for not continuing with education. This change reflects government policies of abolishing fees and selecting entrants to secondary school on the basis of performance in entrance examinations. Though meritocratic, the intensely competitive selection system nevertheless seems to be denying access to a high proportion of the children from poor families as effectively as fees did to earlier cohorts. The children from uneducated households who do go to secondary school seem to do as well as those from well-educated backgrounds.

The size and location of employees' families would affect the intergenerational transmission of inequality. For example, if an educated person always chooses an educated spouse and has a small family which lives in Dar es Salaam, while an uneducated person always marries another uneducated person and has a large family which lives on a *shamba*, this pattern of behaviour will compound the advantages of having an educated parent and the disadvantages of being born to an uneducated parent. In fact, the data suggest that, while assortative mating is strong, there is little difference in the number of dependants per family, or the location of the family, for employees of different educational attainment.

The effect of the drive to Universal Primary Education is apparent in the differences between the second and third generations. Twenty-three per cent of the employees' generation have no education, or no more than Standards 1–4 education, while only 10 per cent of their first children are in that position (and this is an overestimate as some children included in that figure are continuing their education). However, this success story must be tempered by the evidence that the chances of children from less-privileged backgrounds to continue to secondary school and beyond do not appear to have increased from one generation to the next, while the privileged seem to have maintained their extremely high probability of getting their children to secondary school. This relationship between the first and second generations continues to hold between the second and third. It is still true for the second generation, as it was for the first, that almost all the children of parents with post-primary education themselves have that level of education. The picture actually looks rather gloomier for the most recent than for earlier cohorts when considering the chances of children whose parents had no more than primary education achieving post-primary education themselves. (However, as education is still continuing for some, the data are for the lower end of the distribution, so the true picture is somewhat brighter.)

The evidence on employees' attitude to their children's education suggests that the different educational attainment of the children from less-fortunate and more-fortunate families is not because the former do not know or believe in the value of education. The advantage for children from more-educated and affluent families comes from the fact that they tend to be better prepared for the competitive entrance examination to government secondary schools, and that a much higher percentage of the higher-income earners are prepared to pay the fees of private secondary schools. Remarkably, perhaps, employees intend to treat their sons and daughters alike in matters of education, though there may be a divergence between precept and practice.

Spending on education in absolute terms rises strongly as the employee's wage rises, but as a percentage of income there is, if anything, a decline as income rises. Finally, it seems that family background has an independent effect, separately from its effect on the educational attainment of the child, because economic success appears to be correlated with family background even among employees who are themselves of the same educational level.

10

Education and Rural–Urban
Links in Tanzania

This chapter is concerned with how the migration of rural dwellers to the urban labour-market in Dar es Salaam and their integration into it are related to their education. Migrants are defined as those who arrived in the city aged 14 or more. Section A sets out the demographic characteristics of the employees who are migrants and identifies their regions of origin. In section B the educational characteristics of the migrants are analysed in comparison with those of non-migrants and in terms of the differences between migrants of different ages and places of origin. The process of the migrants' integration into the urban labour-market and the role of education in it are examined in section C. The migrants' continuing ties with the rural areas are analysed in relation to education in section D. Section E provides a summary of the conclusions of the chapter. The data refer only to Africans.

A. Demographic Characteristics of Urban Migrant Employees

The high proportion of Dar es Salaam employees who are migrants has already been noted (Chapter 4 and Table 4.5), and in fact only 4 per cent of employees were actually born in the city. Half the migrants arrived during the 1970s and all but 5 per cent since 1950.

Most migrants come to the city young. The great majority (87 per cent) arrived before the age of 27 and 42 per cent before they were 20. Women arrived younger than men, 53 per cent being under 20. On average, women were 2 years younger than the men when they arrived in Dar es Salaam (Table 10.1). In terms of family structure and size, migrants are very similar to non-migrants. In relation to population, migrants come disproportionately from some regions, particularly Coast, Morogoro, and Kilimanjaro (See Map 2, p. xxxiv).

Table 10.1. *Tanzanian African Migrant Employees by Sex: Distribution by Age on Arrival in Dar es Salaam; Mean Age*

	Age on arrival (years)						Mean	
	14–16	17–19	20–2	23–6	27–35	Over 35		
Male	15	25	27	18	11	4	21.8	(1041)
Female	17	36	29	12	5	1	19.8	(1152)
All	16	26	27	18	10	3	21.6	(1193)

There has been a trend over time toward longer-distance migration, perhaps reflecting improvements in transport. The trend may also be associated with the rise in the level of education of migrants, increasing the benefits from migration and hence the feasibility of moving a greater distance to achieve them, as well as with increasing awareness of the benefits of migration and hence a willingness to risk the move. Still another interpretation is based on the fact that, on average, educational levels are higher (or if lower are increasing) in some of the more-distant regions than in those near to Dar es Salaam. Given this fact, if the demand for wage-employees has placed increasing value on education, there could be a shift in the source of employed migrants towards more distant regions. There is a significant difference in the regions of origin of men and women: 36 per cent of male migrants come from the three regions, Coast, Morogoro, and Lindi, compared with only 12 per cent of the women. In contrast, 22 per cent of the women come from Kilimanjaro but only 12 per cent of the men.

B. Educational Characteristics of Migrants

Migrant employees in Dar es Salaam have on average about a year's longer education than non-migrants. While 38 per cent of migrants had some post-primary education, this was the case for only 31 per cent of non-migrants. And only 10 per cent of migrants had no education, compared with 14 per cent of non-migrants. The average time spent in education by migrants increased markedly over time from 2.2 years for those arriving in 1941–50 to 8.7 years for those arriving in the 1970s, most of the increase having occurred by 1966 (Table 10.2). In each period after 1965, the women migrants have significantly more education than the men, which must mean, given the lower education of women in the population as a whole (see Chapter 4), that it is the more-educated women who migrate.

Table 10.2. *Tanzanian African Migrant Employees by Year of Arrival in Dar es Salaam and Sex: Mean Years of Education*

Year of arrival in Dar es Salaam	Males	Females	All
1941–50	2.2	..	2.2
	(37)		(37)
1951–60	5.5	..	5.3
	(66)		(68)
1961–65	7.5	7.0	7.4
	(114)	(12)	(126)
1966–70	8.1	10.0	8.4
	(251)	(48)	(299)
1971–75	8.5	9.1	8.6
	(350)	(58)	(363)
1976–80	8.6	9.9	8.7
	(267)	(31)	(298)
All	7.9	9.2	8.1
	(1042)	(151)	(1193)

Educational attainment increased over time for migrants from all regions, but in proportion it was particularly important for those from regions where the educational attainment was low. Between 1951–60 and 1976–80 the average years of education of migrants to Dar es Salaam from the Coast Region increased by two-thirds (from 3 years to 5 years), and for those from Lindi by 268 per cent (from 1.9 to 7 years); for migrants from Kilimanjaro the increase was of one-quarter (from 8–10.1 years), and for those from West Lake of 13 per cent (from 9.7 to 11 years).

Education and migration are related not only because education increases marketable skills and thus fosters migration, but because migration may be undertaken to further education. A substantial minority of migrants—more than 30 per cent in total—had not completed their education before coming to Dar es Salaam. The percentage was less than 30 only for migrants in the 20–6 age-group, and was generally higher for employees with more education (Table 10.3).

A higher share of migrants with little education (Standard 4 or less) arrive both very young (16 or less) or relatively old (over 26) than of those with more education. Migrants with lower-secondary education in particular are concentrated in the 17–26 age-groups (Table 10.4).

The average time taken to get a job after completion of education was rather longer for persons born in Dar es Salaam (25.9 months) than for those who arrived as children (20.8 months). For migrants the period was

Table 10.3. *Tanzanian Educated African Migrant Employees by Education and Age on Arrival in Dar es Salaam: Percentage who Completed Their Education before Migrating*

Education	Age on arrival				All
	14–19	20–2	23–6	27 and over	
Standards 1–4	74	83.5	73.1	38	68.7
	(61)	(31)	(26)	(29)	(147)
Standards 5–6	67	73.3	81.3	78	73.4
	(39)	(15)	(16)	(9)	(79)
Standards 7–8	65	80.2	74.5	58	69.2
	(229)	(101)	(51)	(31)	(412)
Forms I–IV	56	68.9	91.1	82	69.6
	(118)	(119)	(56)	(39)	(332)
Post-Form IV	37	59.2	56.8	56	54.7
	(19)	(49)	(44)	(36)	(148)
All	63	72.4	76.2	60	67.7
	(505)	(328)	(211)	(168)	(1211)

23.1 months, being longer than that (25 months) for those who had completed their education before migrating, and shorter (19.8 months) for other migrants.

The distribution of activities between completing education and taking up employment is markedly different according to whether the migrants completed their education before or after migrating. For the former group, 73 per cent of the average time of 25 months was spent working on the *shamba* and 4 per cent unemployed, looking for wage-employment. For migrants who completed their education in Dar es Salaam, the corresponding figures are 57 per cent and 9 per cent.

C. Migrants' Process of Adjustment on Arrival: The Role of Education

Migrants who finished their education before they arrived in Dar es Salaam took on average about 6 months before they found an independent income source. Women took markedly longer (8.9 months) than men (5.4 months). Two-thirds found an independent source of income immediately or within a month, while 18 per cent took a year or longer.

The length of this interval is affected by educational attainment. The relationship is not monotonic, for those with a middle-level primary

Table 10.4. *Tanzanian African Migrant Employees by Education: Distribution by Age on Arrival in Dar es Salaam; Mean Age on Arrival*

Age on arrival (years)	Education						All
	None	Standards 1–4	Standards 5–6	Standards 7–8	Forms I–IV	Post-Form IV	
14–16	24	26	10	20	10	3	16
17–19	17	15	39	34	26	10	25
20–22	14	21	19	25	36	33	27
23–26	20	18	20	13	17	30	17
27–35	13	18	11	7	8	16	10
36 and over	12	2	1	1	3	8	3
	(94)	(147)	(79)	(412)	(332)	(148)	(1211)
Mean age on arrival	19.5	19.6	20.0	19.1	20.9	24.7	20.4

Table 10.5. *Tanzanian African Migrant Employees who Completed Their Education before Migrating by Education, Age on Arrival, and Sex: Mean Time (months) to Find an Independent Source of Income after Arrival in Dar es Salaam*

Education	Age on arrival in Dar es Salaam				Sex	
	14–19	20–6	27 and over	All	Male	Female
Standards 1–4	7.8	3.6	1.3	5.6	4.9	..
	(22)	(14)	(6)	(45)	(43)	
Standards 5–6	15.3	22.1	..	15.0	13.6	..
	(10)	(9)		(22)	(20)	
Standards 7–8	8.6	5.6	1.1	7.5	7.4	8.6
	(82)	(75)	(7)	(172)	(154)	(21)
Forms I–IV	5.1	3.2	1.0	3.2	2.5	6.5
	(26)	(74)	(16)	(126)	(104)	(21)
Post-Form IV	1.0	1.9	1.0	1.6	1.6	..
	(7)	(24)	(7)	(37)	(35)	
All	7.9	4.8	1.3	5.8	5.4	8.9
	(147)	(193)	(39)	(402)	(357)	(50)

education have in fact a far longer waiting period than those with either less or more. But those with secondary education have a much shorter wait than those with no more than primary, and a post-Form IV education guarantees a waiting period of less than 2 months (Table 10.5).

The time required to find an independent source of income in Dar es Salaam decreases systematically with age at arrival, from nearly 8 months for those aged 14–19 to 1.3 months for those over 26 (Table 10.5.). The share having an income source immediately rises from under 50 per cent for those arriving at 17–19 years to over 75 per cent for those arriving at 27 years or older. Both education and age at arrival have clear effects independently of each other, as is apparent in Table 10.5. The time taken to find an independent income source has shown no clear trend over time.

Their current employer was the first source of independent income for a little over half of the migrants who finished their education before migrating. Nearly a quarter were self-employed (Table 10.6). The time required to find an independent source of income in Dar es Salaam was short (3.2 months) for migrants whose first source was their current employer. The interval was 14 months for those who entered self-employment or who worked for an artisan. This difference suggests that these latter activities were not the preferred ones, and were taken up only when the attempt to get a more desirable wage-job failed. It is consistent with

Table 10.6. *Tanzanian African Migrant Employees who Completed Their Education before Migrating by Education: Distribution by First Independent Source of Income in Dar es Salaam*

Source of independent income	Education					All
	Standards 1–4	Standards 5–6	Standards 7–8	Forms I–IV	Post-Form IV	
Current employer	23	34	45	68	90	52
Similar job with another employer	12	21	10	18	9	13
Other wage-job	32	15	13	7	0	13
Self-employment	33	30	32	7	1	22
	(54)	(24)	(158)	(118)	(35)	(391)

Table 10.7. *Tanzanian African Employees by Education and Migrant Status: Percentage of Spouses in Dar es Salaam and on the* Shamba

Education	Non-migrant		Migrant		All	
	Dar es Salaam	*Shamba*	Dar es Salaam	*Shamba*	Dar es Salaam	*Shamba*
None	100	0 (42)	89	8 (119)	92	5
Standards 1–4	100	0 (39)	97	3 (149)	97	3
Standards 5–6	100	0 (19)	92	8 (74)	94	6
Standards 7–8	100	0 (48)	94	2 (274)	95	2
Forms I–IV	100	0 (24)	97	2 (206)	97	2
Post-Form IV	100	0 (2)	97	0 (89)	97	0
All	100	0 (174)	95	3 (915)	95	3

this presumption that self-employment was the first source of independent income for nearly a third of those with a primary education, and for a mere 1 per cent of those with post-Form IV education. Migrants from several specific regions had self-employment as their first source of independent income with above-average frequency; whereas the overall average in the sample was 22 per cent, the figure was high for respondents from Kilimanjaro (34 per cent), Tanga (41 per cent), and Lindi (31 per cent).

D. Ties with Rural Areas: Variation by Level of Education

Most employees, whether or not they are migrants, have strong ties with rural areas. Relatively few, however, have their wives (husbands) or children currently living in rural areas, and only a minority possess *shambas*. On the other hand, a large majority send remittances to help support relatives, and an even larger majority plan to live in a rural area at some future date.

Spouses and Children Outside Dar es Salaam

Almost all employees, whether migrants or non-migrants, and regardless of education or income level, have their immediate family in Dar es Salaam. Only 3 per cent of married employees have a spouse on a *shamba*; 95 per cent have one (or more) in Dar es Salaam. Only migrants have spouses outside Dar es Salaam (Table 10.7). The proportion of children in Dar es Salaam is almost as large as that of spouses.

Table 10.8. *Tanzanian African Employees by Age and Education: Percentage of Spouses in Dar es Salaam and on the Shamba*

Age	Education									All	
	None		Primary		Forms I–IV		Post-Form IV				
	Dar es Salaam	Shamba	Dar es Salaam	Shamba	Dar es Salaam	Shamba	Dar es Salaam	Shamba		Dar es Salaam	Shamba
15–30	89	10 (28)	92	5 (262)	97	3 (93)	100	0 (17)		94	4
31–40	90	10 (58)	97	2 (237)	99	0 (108)	95	0 (63)		97	2
41 and over	95	4 (75)	98	2 (108)	92	8 (26)	100	0 (11)		96	3
All	92	6 (161)	95	3 (607)	97	2 (227)	97	0 (91)		95	3

Note: When percentages do not add to 100 it is because spouses are reported as elsewhere, other than Dar es Salaam or *shamba*.

Support for Relatives Outside Dar es Salaam

A high proportion of employees help to support relatives outside Dar es Salaam (Table 10.9), despite the fact that nearly all have their spouses and children in the city. But the employees were almost all (95 per cent) born outside Dar es Salaam and presumably the support is provided for parents or siblings who still live in the countryside. The fact that wage-earners in Dar es Salaam have incomes above the typical rural level would lead one to expect such a flow.

Migrant status affects the likelihood and level of remittances. The share of persons born in Dar es Salaam who support relatives outside the city is only 53 per cent compared with 64 per cent for persons who came to Dar es Salaam as children and 83 per cent for adult migrants (Table 10.9). The share of income so used in about the same (7 per cent) for the first two groups of non-migrants and higher (10 per cent) for migrants, and remittances in absolute terms are much higher for migrants. This difference between migrants and others is more marked for persons with secondary than with primary education (Table 10.9).

The share of an employee's income used to help to support relatives outside Dar es Salaam has a marked positive relationship with his or her level of education, rising from 5 per cent for the uneducated to 11 per cent for those with secondary education (Table 10.9). There is no overall association with the wage; but at each wage level a higher education is associated with a higher share of income used for remittances (Table 10.10). The more educated may spend more on supporting relatives outside Dar es Salaam because they expect higher incomes in the longer run than the less educated, or because they have a greater obligation to relatives arising from their own support while being educated or finding a job in the city.

The tendency to support relatives outside Dar es Salaam is highest for persons aged 21–40, reaching 82 per cent for all respondents (and 89 per cent for migrants) in this age-group, and is somewhat lower for the younger and older cohorts. The decreasing tendency to support relatives among employees over 40 may reflect life-cycle phenomena as well as liability to support, and some selectivity in terms of who has already moved back to rural areas. It is marked for persons with education at Standards 1–4 and 5–6. Average support by men is a little higher (Shs 1047) than by women (Shs 985), but for specific wage-categories up to Shs 1500 per month, women remit more than men. The level of support varies by region of birthplace of the respondents, with those from nearby regions tending to send less: the share of income so used was 7.5 per cent or less for respondents born in the Coast, Morogoro, and Lindi regions,

Table 10.9. *Tanzanian African Employees by Education and Migrant Status: Percentage who Support Relatives Outside Dar es Salaam and Percentage of Income Used in that Way*

Education	Non-Migrant				Migrant		All	
	Born in Dar es Salaam		Born elsewhere					
	% supporting	% of income	% supporting	% of income	% supporting	% of income	% supporting	% of income
None	57 (6)	⋮	55 (35)	5 (33)	73 (128)	5 (105)	69 (170)	5 (142)
Standards 1–4	60 (11)	5 (9)	53 (26)	4 (20)	68 (170)	6 (154)	66 (207)	6 (184)
Standards 5–6	51 (10)	9 (10)	72 (10)	4 (12)	90 (88)	7 (77)	84 (109)	7 (99)
Standards 7–8	65 (19)	10 (16)	67 (75)	8 (66)	84 (430)	9 (389)	81 (524)	9 (471)
Forms I–IV	23 (10)	5 (10)	71 (41)	6 (42)	90 (346)	11 (324)	86 (397)	11 (376)
Post-Form IV	⋮	⋮	64 (19)	9 (14)	90 (152)	11 (137)	87 (171)	11 (153)
All	53 (56)	7 (51)	64 (206)	7 (189)	83 (1316)	10 (1190)	80 (1578)	9 (1430)

Table 10.10. *Tanzanian African Employees by Wage and Education: Percentage of Income Used to Support Relatives Outside Dar es Salaam*

Wage (Shs per month)	Education						
	None	Standards 1–4	Standards 5–6	Standards 7–8	Forms I–IV	Post-Form IV	All
0–500	5 (57)	6 (72)	10 (29)	12 (140)	11 (59)	..	9 (358)
501–750	5 (49)	4 (73)	7 (36)	11 (159)	14 (79)	5 (18)	9 (416)
751–1000	3 (15)	7 (28)	5 (20)	9 (96)	12 (70)	12 (19)	9 (243)
1001–1500	4 (20)	4 (18)	4 (9)	8 (66)	10 (86)	12 (36)	9 (238)
1501–2000	..	9 (9)	..	7 (11)	8 (55)	12 (28)	9 (106)
2001–3000	..	..	..	9 (12)	11 (44)	13 (38)	11 (103)
Over 3000	..	..	..	..	9 (9)	10 (9)	7 (24)
All	5 (147)	5 (202)	7 (100)	9 (486)	10 (406)	11 (155)	9 (1502)

9.5 per cent for those from Dar es Salaam, and 11 per cent or more for those from the rest of the country.

Support for relatives outside Dar es Salaam typically takes the form of money: in 74 per cent of the cases this was the sole form of remittance, in 19 per cent it was employed together with the provision of goods, while provision of goods was the sole form in 6 per cent of cases. The greater the total remittance the smaller the share of respondents who used only money to effect the transfer; goods and money became an increasinly common combination.

Remittances by migrants are used in part for education in about one-quarter of cases and also frequently for food (41 per cent), land acquisition (25 per cent), and farm improvement (20 per cent). Whereas the share of cases in which remittances were used for food and for land acquisition was unrelated to education, the frequency with which funds were used for education, house construction, and farm improvement rose with education.

The first child of 17 per cent of employees is being educated in the rural areas (Table 10.11). One reason is likely to be the lower cost of living and costs of education than in Dar es Salaam. Average educational costs per student were about 20 per cent lower for respondents educating their children in the rural areas (Table 10.12). The frequency of rural education for the first child has no systematic relationship with the earnings of the employees, though it is markedly higher for the children of those with Standards 7–8 (25 per cent) than for employees with less education or with more (Table 10.11).

Possession of a Shamba

Less than a quarter of urban employees possess *shambas*, and this proportion seems small given the fact that the employees make substantial remittances to the rural areas and the great majority intend ultimately to live there (see below). One possible reason for the small proportion is that land is readily available, so that it can be obtained easily enough as retirement approaches. The proportion having a *shamba* does, indeed, increase with age, from 14 per cent for employees aged 15–20 to 32 per cent for those aged over 40 (Table 10.13). Older employees might also more easily afford to acquire a *shamba*, or be more likely to have inherited.

Possession of a *shamba* is not very clearly associated with the employee's level of education, though a smaller proportion of those with the highest than with the lower levels of education do have *shambas*. A

Table 10.11. *Tanzanian African Employees*[a] *by Wage and Education: Percentage of Cases where First Child Educated in the Rural Area*

Wage (Shs per month)	Education						All
	None	Standards 1–4	Standards 5–6	Standards 7–8	Forms I–IV	Post-Form IV	
0–500	13 (20)	7 (23)	29 (7)	14 (17)	..	..	12 (69)
501–750	8 (19)	22 (32)	19 (19)	39 (48)	70 (13)	0 (7)	30 (134)
751–1000	0 (4)	19 (15)	13 (13)	20 (23)	22 (16)	..	17 (75)
1001–1500	12 (14)	0 (10)	0 (8)	12 (13)	3 (28)		5 (80)
1501–2000	..	..	..	..	17 (26)		16 (37)
2001–3000	..	..	33 (5)	16 (10)	3 (22)	11 (15)	10 (57)
Over 3000	..	..	..	..	0 (8)	..	0 (14)
All	9 (67)	16 (85)	16 (55)	25 (117)	16 (114)	7 (25)	17 (467)

[a] Only employees whose first child has been or is being educated.

Table 10.12. *Tanzanian African Employees with Children in School Last Year by Wage and Place of Children's Education: Mean Cost of Education per Child (Shs per year)*[a]

Wage (Shs per month)	Place of education	
	Dar es Salaam	Rural area
0–500	190	160
	(78)	(14)
501–750	281	359
	(141)	(41)
751–1000	415	385
	(96)	(18)
1001–1500	531	198
	(104)	(8)
1501–2000	494	1005
	(63)	(8)
2001–3000	945	428
	(78)	(17)
Over 3000	1309	500
	(18)	(4)
All	480	392
	(576)	(110)

[a] Figures include up to three children for each employee, beginning with the oldest.

higher proportion of migrants than of non-migrants have *shambas*, but the difference is not large (Table 10.13).

The proportion of women with *shambas* is only a little smaller than the proportion of men (21 compared with 23 per cent), and for employees aged 21–40 the figure for women is in fact larger than that for men.

There are marked regional diferences in the proportion of employees who have a *shamba*. For a group of regions on the eastern side of Tanzania (Kilimanjaro, Tanga, Dodoma, Coast, Lindi, Morogoro, Dar es Salaam) the proportion ranges between 24 and 33 per cent. A high proportion of migrants from West Lake also have *shambas* (36 per cent). In contrast, from migrants for another group of regions (Kigoma, Shinyanga, Singida, Tabora), the proportion is below 7 per cent.

A little less than a half of all *shamba* owners acquired the *shamba* by inheritance, a little less than a quarter by purchase, and 17 per cent under a settlement scheme (Table 10.14). Acquisition by purchase increases in importance with the age of the employees. It also increases with income. Nearly three-quarters of the few employees with a wage of more than Shs

Table 10.13. *Tanzanian African Employees by Education, Age, and Migrant Status: Percentage with* Shamba

	Age				All
	15–20	21–30	31–40	41 and over	
Education					
None	..	25	23	28	26
		(40)	(62)	(81)	(187)
Primary	16	23	31	41	27
	(61)	(454)	(264)	(114)	(893)
Forms I–IV	0	10	38	36	20
	(14)	(245)	(125)	(28)	(412)
Post-Form IV	..	11	13	31	13
		(76)	(77)	(13)	(171)
All	14	18	30	32	21
	(84)	(815)	(532)	(236)	(1667)
Migrant status					
Non-migrant	3	13	25	29	18
	(29)	(135)	(87)	(49)	(300)
Migrant	18	20	30	38	26
	(51)	(660)	(442)	(180)	(1333)

3000 acquired their shambas by purchase, compared with 22 per cent of *shamba* owners as a whole. Acquisition through a settlement scheme is important only for the lower paid (Table 10.14). Purchase is a more important method of acquisition for non-migrants (32 per cent) than for migrants (19 per cent), and for those with secondary (40 per cent) than for those with a lower level of education (16 per cent).

The mean *shamba* size, for those with a *shamba*, is only 3.66 acres, with the median a little over 2 acres. Shamba size is not very closely related to either education or earnings, though employees with secondary education have larger *shambas* than others (5.27 compared with 2.91 acres), and employees with a wage of Shs 1000 or more have larger *shambas* than those with a lower wage (4.18 compared with 3.12 acres).

Links with the Shamba

As noted already, rather few employees with a *shamba* have a spouse and/or children living there, though if they had it might be expected to increase the family's income and the productivity of the *shamba*. For the most part, *shambas* are used for subsistence rather than as a source of

Table 10.14. *Tanzanian African Employees with Shamba by Wage and Education: Distribution by Method of Shamba Acquisition*

Method of *shamba* acquisition	Wage (Shs per month)						Education		
	0–750	751–1500	1501–2000	2001–3000	Over 3000	All	None	Primary	Secondary
Inheritance	43	54	55	40	13	46	31	51	44
Settlement scheme	26	10	10	1	0	17	31	16	8
Purchase	9	27	22	55	71	22	13	16	40
Other	22	9	13	4	16	15	25	17	8
	(196)	(105)	(24)	(41)	(13)	(378)	(48)	(231)	(98)

monetary income (only 4 per cent indicated that it was such a source), although the purchase of inputs for the *shamba* is a moderately wide-spread practice (see below). The owner tends to make the cropping decisions even in cases where he or she visits the *shamba* only once or twice during the year.

Most employees who own a *shamba* visit it no more than twice a year. Only a few (5 per cent) had not visted at all in the past year, while over a third (36 per cent) paid one visit. At the other extreme 28 per cent visited at least once a week or lived on the *shamba*. The median number of visits was about 3 and the mean over 12. Frequency is associated with distance, so that persons whose birthplace was in one of the neighbouring regions (and whose *shamba* is presumably there as well) tend with some exceptions, like Morogoro, to make more visits than do those from farther away; respondents from Dar es Salaam, Morogoro, Coast, Lindi and Tanga averaged 15.6 visits, while respondents from other regions averaged only 5.8 visits (Table 10.15).

The presence of a spouse on the *shamba* is associated with fewer rather than more visits. The proportion of respondents who visited no more than twice a year was 47 per cent for those whose spouses were not, but 90 per cent for those whose spouses were on the *shamba*. And whereas 36 per cent of those without a spouse on the *shamba* visited it on average twice a month or more, this number of visits was made by only 7 per cent of those with a spouse on the *shamba*, and by 19 per cent of those who were unmarried.

Most *shambas* (61 per cent) are worked only by family members, but the average number of employed workers is nevertheless nearly one (0.9), with the figure rising from 0.6 workers on *shambas* of one acre or less to 1.2 workers for *shambas* of 5 acres and more. The number of employed workers bears little relation either to earnings or education (Table 10.16). A markedly higher share of *shamba* owners with secondary education hire workers (64 per cent) than of owners with less education (33 per cent), but they hire fewer on average.

Plans to Return to the Rural Area

Though less than 25 per cent of respondents had *shambas*, an impressive 91 per cent of migrant employees planned to live in the countryside at some future time (Table 10.17), as, in fact, did 73 per cent of non-migrants. Such a high share must be a reflection of powerful and pervasive influences, economic and cultural.

Migrant employees with secondary education plan eventually to live in the country in about 86 per cent of cases, compared with over 90 per cent

Table 10.15. *Tanzanian African Employees with Shamba by Region of Birth: Distribution by Number of Visits to the Shamba during the Previous Year; Mean Number of Visits*

Number of visits	Region of birth							All
	Coast and Dar es Salaam	Lindi	Morogoro	Tanga	Kilimanjaro	West Lake	Other[a]	
0	9	0	2	0	0	1	9	5
1	3	49	24	48	58	96	50	37
2	11	0	25	15	24	0	0	10
3–4	13	4	28	9	5	0	3	9
5–23	19	2	5	0	0	0	3	6
24–97	36	22	9	19	8	2	9	21
More than 97[b]	9	23	12	7	5	0	26	11
	(72)	(18)	(38)	(27)	(32)	(28)	(58)	(291)
Mean[c]	21.9	15.7	6.6	11.3	5.1	1.9	8.6	12.3

[a] Excludes Zanzibar and persons born outside Tanzania.
[b] Includes respondents who live on the *shamba*.
[c] Excludes respondents making more than 97 visits.

Table 10.16. *Tanzanian African Employees by Education: Percentage with* Shamba; *Use of Employed Workers*

Education	% with *shamba*	% employing workers
None	28 (190)	28
Standards 1–4	28 (250)	25
Standards 5–6	21 (111)	32
Standards 7–8	27 (546)	38
Forms I–IV	20 (419)	54
Post-Form IV	13 (172)	87
All	23 (1688)	39

Table 10.17. *Tanzanian African Migrant Employees by Education: Percentage who Plan to Return to the Rural Area*

Education	
None	92 (129)
Standards 1–4	95 (173)
Standards 5–6	92 (89)
Standards 7–8	93 (445)
Forms I–IV	86 (349)
Post-Form IV	88 (152)
All	91 (1331)

with less education, so that educational level makes surprisingly little difference.

E. Summary

Nearly all employees in Dar es Salaam arrived there during the rapid migration of the last few decades. Most of them arrived young, and disproportionately from regions nearer to Dar es Salaam, though the trend has been to longer-distance migration.

Migrants have more education than non-migrants, and their educational level rose greatly between the 1940s and 1966. The majority had completed their education before they migrated.

Migrants obtained a job after completing their education with a shorter wait than non-migrants. It took longer for migrants who had completed their education before migrating than for other migrants. Two-thirds of the migrants found an independent source of income immediately or very shortly after they had arrived in the city. In general, the more educated and older the migrant the shorter the wait. A majority had a job with their current employer as their first source of an independent income, but nearly a quarter obtained it from self-employment.

Although almost all migrants have their immediate family with them in Dar es Salaam they retain strong ties with the rural areas. The great majority of employees, migrant and non-migrant, provide support for relatives in rural areas in amounts which are a significant proportion of their income.

A relatively small proportion of employees, even among the lower paid, educate their children in the countryside, although it costs less to do so; the differential between the cost of rural and urban education is not large.

Ownership of a *shamba* varies directly with age and inversely with education. Migrants are more likely to have a *shamba* than non-migrants, but in total only one-fifth of employees have a *shamba*. Less than half of *shamba* owners acquired them by inheritance and nearly a quarter by purchase; well over a half of the better-paid purchased their *shambas*. Shambas are small, though employees with secondary education and a high wage tend to have larger *shambas* than other owners. Owners do not visit their *shambas* very frequently, the majority no more than twice a year, and the average being barely once a month. A majority of *shambas* are worked only by members of the owner's family, but the employment of wage-labour is nevertheless widespread.

Almost all migrants intend to return to the countryside at some time in the future. Even a high proportion of those born in Dar es Salaam say that they intend to move there.

Nairobi and Dar es Salaam: Similarities and Contrasts

In Chapters 5 to 10 the survey results for Nairobi and Dar es Salaam have been shown separately for clarity of presentation and to suit the needs of some readers. This chapter summarizes the results of both surveys, presenting them by topic. It is intended to provide a reader with a rapid review of and a guide to the detailed results, making clear the remarkable similarities and the equally remarkable differences between the wage-employees of the two cities.

The demographic and educational structures of the urban wage-labour force are closely similar in Nairobi and Dar es Salaam. In both cities it is composed overwhelmingly of young, male Africans who are migrants from the countryside and who completed their education before migrating. Very few employees, except in the very youngest age-groups, are unmarried, and most of those who are married, and many who are not, have children. The number of wives and children supported is large, and the number of dependants larger still, and the number varies with the education of the employee, increasing up to a point and then decreasing (Tables 4.1–4.7, 4.13, 4.16). The two cities differ in that in Nairobi migrants are less educated than employees native to the city; in Dar es Salaam it is the other way round (Table 4.12).

In both samples the young are more educated than the old, and the length of education of entrants to the labour-market has been rising; women employees are more educated than men, although in the population as a whole men have more education; Asians are more educated than Africans, and employees than their parents; a much higher proportion of the young than of the old have been educated at government schools, and a much higher proportion of pupils have Form VI education in government schools than in other secondary schools (Tables 4.8–4.11, 4.14, 4.15, 5.24, 8.24). In these respects the two samples are similar. They differ in that in Nairobi employees have had much more education than those in Dar es Salaam, and a substantially higher proportion have post-primary education. The reason for the difference is to be found mainly in the educational policy of the Tanzanian government and the growth of the *harambee* movement in Kenya (Chapter 2). For employees as a whole the proportion with post-primary education is 50 per cent in Nairobi and 38 per cent in Dar es Salaam, for those aged 30 and under the figures are 66 per cent for Nairobi and 41 per cent for Dar es Salaam (Tables 4.9, 4.10). This higher educational level of Nairobi employees is in contrast to that of their parents, who had less education than the parents of Dar es Salaam employees (Table 4.8).

In both samples the wage rises with the level of education. It also rises through the hierarchy of occupations, from unskilled manual through clerical and secretarial to managerial and professional, as does the level of education. The rise in pay with education is particularly large for those who have secondary rather than primary education, and again for those with post-Form IV education. The educational distribution of wages is therefore highly unequal in both countries (Tables 5.1 –5.3, 5.28, 8.1–8.3, 8.28).

The inequality in the educational distribution of pay is considerably greater for Nairobi than for Dar es Salaam employees, particularly in the high premium paid in Nairobi for post-Form IV education. The average wage for employees with that level of education in Nairobi is five times the wage of employees with no education; in Dar es Salaam it is two and a half times. With the wage of the uneducated as 100, that of employees with Standards 5–6 education is 115 in both Nairobi and Dar es Salaam, and that of the lower-secondary educated 219 in Nairobi and 171 in Dar es Salaam; for those with post-Form IV education it leaps to 499 in Nairobi but rises only to 248 in Dar es Salaam (Tables 5.1, 8.1). In Tanzania incomes policy, aided by the high proportion of employment which is in public enterprises, has been successful in restraining the effect of a high demand for educated labour.

In Nairobi, overtime and bonus payments do nothing to narrow the differential; nor do non-monetary benefits. In Dar es Salaam, however, overtime and bonuses narrow somewhat the differential between the primary- and the secondary-educated, though the non-monetary benefits work the other way (Tables 5.5, 5.6, 8.5 and 8.6).

The inequality in the distribution of income from employment is affected by the number of employees' wives, children, and other dependants, but somewhat differently in the two samples. In Dar es Salaam they are an equalizing influence, as the better paid have more than the poorer paid. In Nairobi it is equalizing up to the middle level of wages, but then becomes disequalizing, as the higher paid have fewer dependants than other employees (Tables 5.22, 8.22).

In both samples dependants are a disequalizing influence on the educational distribution of pay. The more educated have fewer dependants than the less educated, even allowing for the fact that the more educated are younger and have had less time to accumulate dependants (Tables 5.23, 8.23).

In neither sample is there a simple relationship between the size of the employing establishment and the wage paid for a given education, though the relationship between education and wage is fairly well maintained for each size group (Table 5.21, 8.21).

An analysis of the Kenya data shows no clear pattern in the educational structure of earnings between the private and the public sectors. The premium for Form IV-leavers over those who completed primary school is roughly the same in private and parastatal (public corporations) employment and lower with government. For employees with post-Form IV education, the premium paid in government employment (243 per cent) approaches that in the private sector (274 per cent), both being much above that paid by the parastatals (133 per cent) (Table 5.20).

The Dar es Salaam data show that there is a much greater equality in the educational structure of earnings in the public sector, where incomes policy can be more easily enforced, than in the private sector. The junior-secondary-educated receive 34 per cent more than those who completed primary school in parastatal and 18 per cent more in government employment. In the private sector the premium is 106 per cent. For those with post-Form IV education, the premium is 61 per cent in parastatal employment, 147 per cent in government, and 260 per cent in the private sector (Table 8.20).

Length of service with an employer and length of time in wage-employment are rewarded with higher pay. This relationship holds in every occupation and for every level of education. Examination success, particularly for Form IV-leavers, is also rewarded. These relationships hold in both countries. There is a difference between them in that it appears to be an advantage in Kenya to have attended a government secondary school, and in Tanzania to have attended a private secondary school (Tables 5.4, 5.7, 5.12–5.18, 5.29, 5.30, 8.4, 8.7, 8.12–8.18, 8.29, 8.30).

Women in the Nairobi sample with higher-primary and lower-secondary education—which includes nearly three-quarters of them—are paid more than men with that education, though in other education groups they are paid less (Table 5.1). Three-quarters of the women with this educational qualification are in the relatively highly paid clerical and secretarial occupations (Table 5.8). But the higher pay for women with this education shown in the sample is not simply a statistical effect, compatible with their being paid less than men in each occupational and educational group, because they are paid more than men in clerical and secretarial employment at every level of experience and education. It appears that for some reason women attract higher wages than men in clerical and secretarial work (Tables 5.7, 5.9). Could it be that female employees of high quality, excluded from managerial jobs by traditional attitudes to women, are confined to secretarial and clerical employment, where their quality finds expression in higher productivity and earnings? But if that is what happens in Nairobi, it does not in Dar es Salaam. In the Dar es Salaam sample, the dominance of men over women is maintained (with a minor exception) in all occupations and at all levels of education and experience (Tables 8.1, 8.7, 8.8, 8.9).

In both samples Asians are paid substantially more than Africans. The differential exists in all occupations and at every level of education (Tables 5.10, 5.11, 8.10, 8.11). Unfortunately, the extent to which this difference is the result of discrimination or productivity cannot be deduced from the sample data.

In both countries there is a clear positive relationship between the educational attainment of employees and their position in the occupational hierarchy. The more educated account for a higher proportion of the labour force the higher the occupation. In Nairobi, employees with postprimary education account for 27 per cent of the total in manual employments and 82 per cent of the total in non-manual employments; in Dar es Salaam the corresponding figures are 9 per cent and 72 per cent. In both cities a higher proportion of workers have post-primary education in non-manual than in manual employments, but the figures at the same time reveal a marked difference between the two cities: the much higher proportion of manual workers who have post-primary education in Nairobi than in Dar es Salaam (Tables 5.2, 8.2). In terms of a particular occupation the difference between the two cities is seen in the proportion of factory machine operators with no more than seven years of experience who have post-primary education. It is 44 per cent in Nairobi and 8 per cent in Dar es Salaam (Tables 5.27, 8.27).

The same phenomenon can be seen from the other side in the occupational distribution of employees of a particular educational level. In the Nairobi sample, 32 per cent of the secondary-educated are manual workers. In Dar es Salaam, with the small output of the secondary-educated in Tanzania, it is no more than 13 per cent, as many more of them have found non-manual jobs.

The other important feature of the relationship between education and occupation is the way it has changed over time. The years of education of recruits to wage-employment have increased. There has been a rise in the level of education of employees in particular occupations, and for every level of education, jobs lower in the hierarchy of occupations have become more important. These changes are found in both samples, but they have gone much further in Nairobi than in Dar es Salaam.

Employees recruited to the labour-market after 1970 have an average of 9.59 years of education in Nairobi, compared with 8.13 in Dar es Salaam, whereas employees recruited before 1961 have 6.63 years in Nairobi and 6.19 years in Dar es Salaam (Tables 5.24, 8.24). In Nairobi, 45 per cent of unskilled manual workers recruited in the period 1977–80 have junior-secondary education compared with 14 per cent in Dar es Salaam, but of those recruited between 1959 and 1965, only 2 per cent in Nairobi and none in Dar es Salaam have that level of education (Tables 5.26, 8.16). To revert to the factory machine operators for whom figures were given in an earlier paragraph, it is notable that no one in either sample in this occupation among those with at least 15 years' experience has post-primary education (Tables 5.27, 8.27).

Employees with full primary education recruited before 1959 are in clerical and secretarial occupations to the extent of 36 per cent in Nairobi and 39 per cent in Dar es Salaam; the corresponding figures for the most recent recruits are down to 12 per cent and 19 per cent. In contrast, the proportion of recruits with that level of education who are in manual occupations has risen, in Nairobi from 56 per cent to 85 per cent and in Dar es Salaam from 38 per cent to 78 per cent (Tables 5.25, 8.25).

Employees with junior-secondary education who started work between 1959 and 1965 are in manual employments to the extent of 15 per cent in Nairobi and 12 per cent in Dar es Salaam. In contrast, employees with that level of education who entered employment between 1977 and 1980 are in manual employments to the extent of 60 per cent in Nairobi and 25 per cent in Dar as Salaam. Between the two periods the percentage of employees with junior-secondary education who are in manual employ-ments doubled in Tanzania but quadrupled in Kenya (Tables 5.25, 8.25).

All these figures show the effect of the increase over a period of some twenty years of the expansion of education in both Kenya and Tanzania, but of the much greater expansion in secondary education in Kenya. They also show, incidentally, the protection given to the position of existing job-holders, who do not appear to be replaced as the younger, more educated enter the labour-market.

There is no clear pattern in the relationship of the wage with education for unskilled and semi-skilled manual workers. For other occupational groups the wage increases with the level of education perhaps because employers recognize that education helps a worker to do a better job (Tables 5.28, 8.28). These relationships are the same for Nairobi and for Dar es Salaam employees, but they hold much more strongly in the Nairobi sample.

The dispersion of the wage by education is narrower for more recent recruits to employment than for employees with longer experience in both Nairobi and Dar es Salaam, but the dispersion is narrower in Dar es

Salaam for all periods of recruitment (Tables 5.29, 8.29). However, there is no clear pattern of change in the dispersion of wages by occupation in either sample (Tables 5.30, 8.30).

It takes longer to get a first job the lower the educational attainment of the job-seeker. This relationship holds in both samples, but in Dar es Salaam a higher percentage of job-seekers have no time to wait and a lower percentage have more than a year to wait than in Nairobi. In both samples a higher percentage of members of the earlier cohort of recruits with post-primary education obtained work without a wait than of the later cohort, though in both cohorts the percentage is higher in Dar es Salaam than in Nairobi. For the primary-educated in Nairobi, a higher percentage of the earlier cohort obtained work without a wait than of the later cohort. In contrast, in Dar es Salaam, a higher percentage of those who completed primary education obtained work without a wait in the later than in the earlier cohort (Tables 5.31, 8.31).

Casual workers in both samples are paid substantially less than regular employees; the differential is partly the result of the 'seniority effect', as employees are paid more the longer they have been in employment (Tables 5.19, 8.19). Although only a small proportion of the work-force is casual labour—only 14 per cent of establishments in Nairobi and 17 per cent in Dar es Salaam have more than a quarter of their workers in casual employment—casual employment is an important prelude to regular employment, and application 'at the gate' is a common method of recruitment for casual workers. Personal introductions are important for manual and clerical workers, and written applications for those with higher educational attainments. These relationships are common to Kenya and Tanzania, but Tanzania is distinctive in that allocation by government is important as a way of getting a first job in the higher-grade occupations and for those with the higher educational qualifications. Thus, 61 per cent of employees in the professions and 34 per cent of those in managerial and administrative occupations obtained their first job in this way, as did 21 per cent of employees with lower-secondary education and 53 per cent of those with post-Form IV education (Tables 5.32–5.36, 8.32–8.36).

In neither Kenya nor Tanzania do many employers provide training, but for workers who do receive training, it is a good thing in terms of higher pay, as is a pass, particularly a good pass, in a trade test (Tables 5.43–5.50, 8.43–8.50).

In both countries employees clearly perceive the connection between education and occupation. They generally believe that they would not have got their present job if they had had less education, and as educational attainment rises so does the proportion of employees who believe they are over-qualified for their present job. In the Kenya sample most employees who believe they are qualified for a better job say they are in their present job because no better job is available; few say that it is to gain experience. In the Tanzania sample, it is the other way round, the majority saying they are in their present job to gain experience (Tables 5.37–5.42, 8.37–8.42).

A surprisingly high proportion of employees have had a substantial number of years in wage-employment. In both Nairobi and Dar es Salaam 55 per cent have been in employment for more than 7 years; in Nairobi more than a quarter, and in Dar es Salaam more than a fifth, have been employed for 15 years or more.

The labour force in both samples seems remarkably settled, in the sense that employees have had few different employers. In the Nairobi sample, 51 per cent of employees have had only their present employer; for Dar es Salaam the figure is 65 per cent (Table 5.51, 5.52, 8.51, 8.52). There is little movement between jobs, and most of those who change their jobs do so voluntarily (Tables 5.55, 8.55). A higher proportion of those who most recently completed their education are looking for a better job than of those with longer experience of employment (Tables 5.57, 8.57). Length of service with a previous employer is not related in a simple way to other variables, and there are some differences between the samples (Tables 5.59, 8.59). Employees experience little unemployment between jobs, whether or not they leave their jobs voluntarily (Tables 5.53, 5.54, 8.53, 8.54). When they are unemployed between jobs, employees spend much of their time working on a *shamba* if they are in the lower educational groups; those with more education spend most of their time looking for employment (Tables 5.58, 8.58).

A high proportion of employees who change their job, whether or not the change is voluntary, receive a higher wage in their new job. (Tables 5.56, 8.56). However, they generally go into the kind of job they left, and there is little upward movement through the employment hierarchy, and some downward movement. In Nairobi, 60 per cent of unskilled manual workers were in the same kind of job previously, for semi-skilled manual workers the figure is 63 per cent, for skilled manual workers it is 71 per cent, and for clerical and secretarial employees 74 per cent; in Dar es Salaam the corresponding percentages are 84, 77, 79 and 80 (Tables 5.60, 8.60). The two samples are strikingly similar in most of these relationships.

In both Kenya and Tanzania, most people who have a secondary-educated parent themselves go to secondary school. The relationship is even stronger when both parents have secondary education (Tables 6.1–6.8, 6.13, 9.1–9.8, 9.13).

Although this relationship between the education of employees and that of their parents is found in both samples, there are marked differences between them. In Nairobi, 36 per cent of employees with uneducated fathers have secondary education compared with 21 per cent in Dar es Salaam. In Nairobi, the proportion has increased from 22 per cent for the older group of employees, little different from the Dar es Salaam figure of 20 per cent, to 54 per cent for the younger group. In contrast, in the Tanzania sample the figure for the younger group is no more than 23 per cent, compared with the older group's 20 per cent (Tables 6.7, 9.7). But those figures are for secondary education as a whole, all six forms, and there is a great difference between the access to lower- and to higher-secondary education. In Kenya, the advantage of an educated father is re-established when it comes to the higher secondary forms. Whereas 33 per cent of employees with uneducated fathers in Nairobi have secondary education of Forms I–IV, compared with 39 per cent of all employees, only 3 per cent of them have post-Form IV education, compared with 11 per cent of all employees. For the older age-group the figure is 2 per cent, and for the younger 5 per cent. In fact, access to post-Form IV education for the children of the uneducated is greater in Tanzania, where the figure is 7 per cent (Tables 6.1, 9.1).

It appears that the relationship between the education achieved by the employees in the samples and that of their parents is being repeated in the relationship between the education of the employees and that of their children. However, too few of the children have completed their education for it to be possible to determine with certainty the final educational levels of the employees' children (Tables 6.14–6.16, 9.14–9.16).

Although many children of employees have not completed their education, so that the level finally to be achieved is not known, there is information on the children who have completed their education, and the similarities and differences in these data between Nairobi and Dar es Salaam are very clear. In both samples the education of the children increases with that of their parents, but the difference between the children of parents with the different levels of education is much smaller in Nairobi than in Dar es Salaam. As the employees' education increases from the uneducated to the primary-educated and to the post-primary-educated, the proportion of their children with post-primary education increases from 57 per cent to 68 per cent and to 88 per cent in Nairobi. In Dar es Salaam the corresponding figures are 16 per cent, 13 per cent, and 80 per cent. Only for employees with post-primary education themselves does the Dar es Salaam percentage approach anywhere near to that in Nairobi (Tables 6.16, 9.16). There are few places in secondary schools in Tanzania and the children of the educated seem to get at least the lion's share. These figures for the education of employees' children compare interestingly with the corresponding figures for the education of employees in relation to that of their parents, where the difference between Nairobi and Dar es Salaam is much smaller. The proportion of employees with post-primary education increases with the education of their fathers from 36 per cent to 66 per cent and to 85 per cent in Nairobi, and from 21 per cent to 46 per cent and to 87 per cent in Dar es Salaam (Tables 6.1, 9.1).

In both countries the importance of examination failure as the reason for discontinuing education has increased over time, and economic reasons—inability to pay fees and meet other costs—have become less important (Tables 6.9, 9.9). For employees with secondary education, in both Nairobi and Dar es Salaam, a failure to perform sufficiently well in the Form IV examination is the main reason for their education having gone no further (Tables 6.10, 9.10).

In the Form IV examination in Kenya, candidates whose fathers had post-primary education achieve much better results than other candidates, but this relationship is not found in the Tanzania sample. (Tables 6.11, 9.11). In contrast, in the Form VI examination there is only a weak relationship between performance and the education of the candidate's father in the Nairobi sample; in the Dar es Salaam sample, there is a strong relationship for the highest level of achievement, but not for others (Tables 6.12, 9.12).

Tanzania and Kenya are similar in that almost all employees want their children to have more education than they had themselves. But the attitudes are different in other ways. In Kenya a high proportion of employees say they would pay private secondary school fees, and the proportion willing to pay is not very strongly correlated with income. In Tanzania willingness is strongly correlated with income, although the proportion willing to pay is almost 50 per cent even for those in the lowest income group (Tables 6.17, 9.17). The other marked difference is in the employees' reason for wanting their children to have more education than they had themselves: in Kenya the great majority want this for economic reasons, and only among employees of high educational and occupational status are non-economic reasons of any importance; in Tanzania, in contrast, roughly two-thirds of all employees claim to want it for non-economic reasons, a figure which rises to nearly three-quarters for employees of high educational and occupational status. Whatever the reason for desiring more education for their children, employees back their wishes with their pocket and make large expenditures on education. Those expenditures are much larger on a child at a secondary than at a primary school. That is so in both countries. However, a Nairobi employee spends more, and a Dar es Salaam employee less, when the child is at a government secondary school than when it is at a private school. But both spend less on a girl than on a boy (Tables 6.18–6.22, 9.18–9.22).

In Kenya a far higher proportion of employees from less-educated home backgrounds have post-primary education than in Tanzania. That does not mean that there is little effect of family background on occupation in Kenya. In both samples the higher the educational level of the father the higher the occupational level of the employee. The figures for employees who left school with complete primary education are illustrative. The proportion in non-manual occupations increases with the educational level of the fathers and the figures differ little between the two samples. In the Kenya sample, 19 per cent of those whose fathers were uneducated are in non-manual employment, compared with 21 per cent in Tanzania. When the fathers had primary education 25 per cent of the employees are in non-manual jobs in Nairobi and 34 per cent in Dar es Salaam. Employees whose fathers had post-primary education are in non-manual employment to the extent of 37 per cent in Nairobi and 46 per cent in Dar es Salaam. These figures suggest the limited number of 'good' jobs that are available in both cities, and the greater ability of those from 'good' backgrounds to obtain them.

Although these figures for primary-educated employees are rather similar in the two samples, there is a marked difference between Nairobi and Dar es Salaam for employees with junior-secondary education. There is still the relation between the education of the father and the occupation of the employee. In Nairobi the proportion in non-manual occupations increases from 59 per cent when the fathers were uneducated, to 63 per cent when they were primary-educated, and to 75 per cent when they had post-primary education.The proportions increase in the same way for Dar es Salaam employees, but are much greater, starting as high as 81 per cent, and rising to 84 per cent and to 86 per cent when the fathers had post-primary education (Tables 6.23, 9.23). The difference between the two samples clearly reflects the greater extent of secondary education in Kenya, resulting in its being much more usual for the secondary-educated to be in manual occupations in Nairobi than in Dar es Salaam.

There is a relationship with family background not only in the kind of work taken up by the employee but also in the level of earnings. In both countries the mean wage rises with the educational level of the employee's father. In both countries, also, the higher the educational level of the parent the shorter the time it takes to get an urban wage-job and the less likely is the employee to suffer spells of unemployment (Tables 6.23–6.26, 9.23–9.26).

It is clearly of benefit for an employee to have had an educated home background as a child. There are several possible reasons for this beneficial effect in employment. Employers may discriminate in favour of recruits from educated homes. The more-educated parent may have been able to afford to keep the child at a better school. But there is also the likelihood that greater 'human capital formation' for the child takes place in an educated family, and that this has a beneficial effect on productivity in future employment.

In both Dar es Salaam and Nairobi the great majority of employees are young and relatively recent migrants from the rural areas. The migrants come disproportionately from particular regions and provinces. The educational level of migrants in both cities has risen rapidly. Most completed their education before migrating. In Nairobi migrants have less education than non-migrants, and in Dar es Salaam more, a fact related to the nature of the non-migrants in Dar es Salaam, who are long-settled and predominantly Moslem (Table 7.1–7.4, 10.1–10.4).

The time it takes a migrant to find a job after arriving in the city, which has been increasing in recent years, is on average much the same in the two cities, but the delay experienced by those with lower-secondary education is twice as long in Nairobi as in Dar es Salaam. Perhaps surprisingly, self-employment is much more common in Dar es Salaam than in Nairobi by those who are waiting for a job (Tables 7.5, 7.6, 10.5, 10.6).

In both cities the migrants retain strong ties with their areas of origin, and the spouses of a majority of Nairobi migrants live there, though the proportion living in Nairobi rises with the employee's income and level of education. In marked contrast, most Dar es Salaam migrants have a spouse with them in the city, even when they have *shambas* (Tables 7.7, 7.8, 10.7, 10.8).

A high proportion of employees in both Nairobi and Dar es Salaam help to support relatives in the countryside, even when their closest relatives are with them in the city, but larger remittances are made from Nairobi than from Dar es Salaam (Tables 7.9, 7.10, 10.9, 10.10).

Remittances from Dar es Salaam are devoted to the acquisition of land to a greater extent than those from Nairobi, but the difference is presumably related to the much smaller proportion of Dar es Salaam than of Nairobi employees who already have *shambas*, and also perhaps to the higher cost of land in Kenya (Tables 7.13, 10.13).

A higher proportion of *shamba* owners acquired them by inheritance, and a lower proportion by purchase, in Kenya than in Tanzania. In Tanzania more use is made of hired labour on the *shamba* than in Kenya, possibly because a spouse is less frequently living there (Tables 7.14, 7.16, 10.14, 10.16).

A high proportion of Nairobi employees, particularly of the lower paid, educate their children in the rural areas. It is a much smaller proportion in Dar es Salaam. This cannot be unrelated to the fact that a much higher proportion of the spouses of Nairobi than of Dar es Salaam employees live in the rural areas and not in the city. It may also be related to the fact that the difference in the cost of education between countryside and city is much smaller in Tanzania than in Kenya (Table 7.11, 7.12, 10.11, 10.12).

Although owners do not visit their *shambas* very frequently (Tables 7.15, 10.15), in both cities almost all employees intend to return to the countryside at some time in the future. Many of those born in the city also say they intend eventually to go to live in the country (Tables 7.17, 10.17).

12

Education, Employment, and Wages: The Major Relationships

Reference was made in Chapter 1 to the range of issues about education, employment, and wages of importance for economic development, development both of the economy and in the economic status of individual employees. It was emphasized in that chapter that the primary purpose of this volume is to present data which throw light on these issues, rather than to draw conclusions from the data. Nevertheless, in earlier chapters suggestions about the implications of the data have been made, and a recapitulation of those suggestions, particularly in terms of comparisons between Kenya and Tanzania, provides a suitable conclusion to the volume.

The expansion of education is a notable feature of the recent development of both countries. It has been accompanied by a concern for the effect on the labour-market of an increase in the number of the educated, and an attempt to counter the expected problems by limiting the rate of expansion, particularly of secondary education, and by 'manpower planning'. It is salutary to remember, however, and it gives some perspective to recent concerns, that such concerns were also being expressed in Tanganyika as long as 60 years ago,[1] when educational development had barely begun.

The major set of issues on which the data from the surveys of the wage-employees in Nairobi and Dar es Salaam throw light concern the effects of a growth in the level of education of the educated labour force, particularly in the extension of post-primary education. The data from the surveys are particularly illuminating on these matters because of the wide difference between Kenya and Tanzania in the development of secondary education. It will be recalled that this difference in the educational level of the labour force in the two cities is the outstanding difference between the two groups of employees which in many ways are closely similar. Fifty

---

[1] See Chapter 2, p. 34.

per cent of the Nairobi labour force, and 66 per cent of those not more than 30 years of age, have post-primary education in Nairobi as compared with 38 per cent and 41 per cent in Dar es Salaam.

There are two main groups of relationships that the data allow to be examined: the relation between education and wage, and that between education and occupation.

Both surveys show that wages rise with education, and the rise is particularly large for employees with secondary over those with primary education, and again for those with post-Form IV education. But despite the abundance of post-primary-educated employees in Nairobi, the premium paid to them is much greater than in Dar es Salaam: the premium paid to employees with post-Form IV education over the uneducated in Nairobi is twice that in Dar es Salaam—500 per cent compared with 250 per cent. This much narrower range of wages by education in Tanzania is noteworthy given its smaller number of secondary-educated employees.

There are a number of possible explanations for the paradoxical result, that a higher relative supply of secondary-educated in the labour force is associated with a higher relative wage. It may be that the growth in the demand for educated labour has been so much faster in Kenya than in Tanzania that, despite the much greater increase in supply, the supply has grown more slowly relatively to demand in Kenya. It is true that economic growth has been a good deal faster in Kenya. However, the data do not indicate that the demand for educated labour in Kenya has been growing at a faster rate than in Tanzania, relatively to the supply. The evidence for filtering down, discussed below, in fact suggests the contrary.

There may be some unidentified characteristics of the economy or of the labour force which differ between the two countries, and which account for the differences in the dispersion of earnings. However, it would be surprising, given the general similarities described in Chapter 4 and summarized in Chapter 11, if the explanation were to be found here. More obvious an explanation is to be found in the institutional differences, specifically, differences in the effectiveness of pay policy.

Both Kenya and Tanzania have pay policies designed to narrow the distribution of earnings, so as to make them more equally distributed than they would otherwise be. In Kenya, the large increase in the supply to the labour-market of the secondary-educated works strongly in the same direction as the pay policy; in Tanzania, because of the much smaller increase in the output from the secondary schools, this effect, if it exists, can only have been small. Yet the educational distribution of incomes is compressed to a greater extent in Dar es Salaam than in Nairobi. The Dar es Salaam data show that there is a much greater equality in the educational structure of earnings in the public than in the private sector. The junior-secondary-educated receive 34 per cent more than those who completed primary school in parastatal, and 18 per cent more in government employment. In the private sector the premium is 106 per cent. For those with post-Form IV education, the premium is 61 per cent in parastatal employment, 147 per cent in government, and 260 per cent in the private sector. This fact suggests that the mechanism for regulating wages has been differentially effective, as might have been expected: in the public sector, pay scales are administratively determined, and policy can be directly implemented; the private sector escapes the effects of pay policy, and wages are in practice largely determined by the market. The market outcome has not occurred in the public sector in Dar es Salaam. Nor has it occurred for the sample as a whole because of the dominance in employment of the public sector, which accounts for 60 per cent of employees in the Dar es Salaam sample. In Nairobi it is only 35 per cent. The absence in Nairobi of any consistent difference between the market and non-market sectors suggests that pay policy has not been effectively implemented, even in the public sector, and that the compression in the structure of earnings has been achieved by the increased supply of educated labour. It seems likely that Kenya's pay policy has been pushing at an open door, the aims of policy having already been achieved by market forces.

The question remains as to whether one or the other of these methods is to be preferred as the economically more efficient method. On this ground, there is evidence in favour of educational expansion and against administrative regulation. As a result of the government's intervention in Tanzania, employees in the private sector who have attained relatively high levels of education earn considerably more than their public-sector counterparts. This segmentation of the labour-market by sector of ownership results not only in new inequities but also in a misallocation of labour.

There is also the question of the mechanism through which educational expansion has compressed the educational structure of earnings. One way could be by the competitive reduction in wages. New entrants to an occupation would posses the same educational qualifications as were required for entry to that occupation before the increase in output from the schools, but at a lower pay. The adjustment might all be borne by the new entrants, accustomed levels of pay being retained by those already in employment, or competition might force wages down all round in the occupation, for new and for existing employees alike. In a freely operating labour-market, though there would be a limit to the adjustment possible by this mechanism, a reduction in the wage of the more educated would be a major response to an increase in their supply. In neither Kenya nor Tanzania does the market seem to have operated freely in this way. However, this does not prevent or even limit an adjustment of the

structure of wages in response to an increase in the supply of the educated.

There is an alternative mechanism: 'filtering down'. Levels of pay
might be maintained and the labour-market might adjust to the increased
supply of the educated by absorbing them into jobs lower in the hierarchy
of occupations than was customary for persons with those particular
educational qualifications to enter in the past. Persons with secondary
education, for instance, might begin to enter manual occupations, whereas in the past, when the secondary-educated were scarcer, they could
always enter clerical or superior occupations. Either of these processes,
reduction in wages or filtering down, or a mixture of them both, would
result in a compression of the educational structure of wages. The second,
filtering-down process could do so even if there were no reduction whatever in wages by occupation. The evidence from the samples indicates
that in East Africa filtering down has been of major importance as a
mechanism by which the labour-market has responded to the increased
supply of the educated, and by which the compression of the educational
distribution of wages has been brought about. The process and extent of
filtering down is indicated by the survey figures. In both samples, though
to a much greater extent in Nairobi than in Dar es Salaam, the educational level of recent recruits to occupations low in the hierarchy is much
above that of earlier recruits, and for example a much higher proportion
of the junior-secondary-educated enter manual occupations among recent
than among earlier recruits.

Filtering down is an important mechanism for the compression of the
educational structure of wages. But there is another question of great
importance raised by the phenomenon of filtering down. When workers
take up work formerly performed, or also performed, by employees with
a lower level of education than themselves, is their additional education
'wasted'? Obviously, it is possible for persons with a particular education
to take up work which could be, and is, performed equally or more
efficiently by others with a much lower level of education. But let not the
extreme case—the Ph. D.-driving-the-bus syndrome—be assumed as representative of all situations. The data on the urban labour force in Kenya
and Tanzania, on the contrary, demonstrate that in every occupational
group the more educated are paid more than the less educated. The fact
that they are paid more in the same occupation suggests that they are
more productive. If that is so, the filtering down of the more educated
raises the productivity of the occupational group they enter. Their additional education is not wasted if they filter down.

On-the-job training cannot, it seems, be relied upon to substitute for
the beneficial effects of education on productivity. Doubtless, to some
extent and in some circumstances, on-the-job training can be a substitute

for education at school; the data show, however, that not only is very little training undertaken but also to an important extent the two are complements, not substitutes, for training is provided mostly for the already more educated. There are likely to be productivity losses, therefore, if the provision of education is held down on the comforting, but erroneous, premise that the resulting loss in the creation of skills will be made up once the school-leaver has taken up employment.

In both Nairobi and Dar es Salaam the hierarchy of occupations runs in step with the hierarchy of educational qualifications, but filtering down has meant that the educational level of employees in an occupation has been rising. In particular, employees with post-primary education are found in manual occupations that would in earlier times have been the monopoly of the less educated, and the proportion of manual workers who have that level of education and the proportion of employees with that level of education who are in manual occupations are much higher in Nairobi than in Dar es Salaam. The difference is especially striking in terms of recruits to the labour-market in different periods, and reflects the different extent of filtering down in the two samples. With the much greater development of secondary education in Kenya, it has gone much further than in Tanzania.

The difference in the development of education is observable in other characterisitics of the labour-market. More school-leavers obtain a job without waiting in Dar es Salaam than in Nairobi, and for those with no more than primary education the proportion is actually higher for the more-recent recruits, suggesting that the shorter waiting times in Tanzania than in Kenya reflect the relatively greater employment opportunities for primary school-leavers resulting from the scarcity of the secondary-educated. For most levels of education and most occupations in which they are engaged, a higher proportion of Tanzanian than of Kenyan employees think they are over-qualified, but many of them are in that job to gain experience. In Nairobi, a higher proportion are in jobs for which they believe they are over-qualified because no better job is available. Both differences could suggest that their taking up employment for which they feel over-qualified is the first stage in an adjustment of their expectations to reality.

The relationship between an employee's level of education and his or her position in the hierarchy of occupations, in other words the fact that education enables an employee to get a better job, is widely recognized. With the extent of filtering down as education develops, it is important that what is unrecognized in the philosophy of the manpower planners should be equally widely recognized, that education enables an employee not only to get a better job but to do a particular job better.

The easiest way, in both Kenya and Tanzania, to ensure a secondary education is to have secondary-educated parents, but if the children of secondary-educated parents have a very high probability of achieving secondary education themselves, the probability for the children of less-educated parents depends on the number of secondary school places available. This is where a striking difference between Kenya and Tanzania becomes apparent. The much greater provision of secondary school places in Kenya than in Tanzania results in a much higher probability of obtaining secondary education for those from the less-educated home backgrounds. The probability of entry to secondary school for the children of the uneducated in Kenya is much lower than for the children of the educated, but even so it is about twice as high as in Tanzania.

However, greater equality of access to Forms I–IV does not mean that the educational influence of family background can necessarily be overcome by expansion. What happens, it seems, is that the inequality is, as it were, pushed up to the next stage of education, to Forms V and VI. The children of the educated maintain the educational advantage of their family background and obtain access to Forms V and VI disproportionately to their place in the lower-secondary enrolment. The children of the uneducated seem to have been unable to compete successfully in sufficient numbers to increase the equality of access rates. The children of the educated carry with them the ability to succeed in academic competition. This ability may be the result of the ability of their parents to pay for the better schools. But it may also be that the out-of-school investment in their human capital made by their parents, wittingly or unwittingly, pays off.

The data imply that the children of the educated carry with them the educational benefits of their background, and that the effect will be felt at some stage on the educational ladder. If the entrance to the lower forms in the secondary schools is widened to let in the children of the uneducated, and access to that level of education becomes more equal, the children of the educated have an advantage in the competition for places in Forms V and VI so that, in proportion to their numbers in the expanded lower forms of the secondary system, access to the higher forms for the children of the uneducated is reduced. Paradoxically, the probability of access might be more equal if the lower-secondary system—Forms I–IV—were smaller. This is the position in Tanzania, where the probability of access to the upper-secondary system is more equal than it is in Kenya. In Tanzania, because of the few places available in Form I, only the extremely able, the cream, of the children of the uneducated move on from primary to secondary school. And as they are the cream they are able to compete on more equal terms with the children of the educated for access to places in Forms V and VI.

It is possible that this effect may be detected in the Form IV and Form

VI examination results. In Kenya, candidates whose fathers had post-primary education achieve much better results than others in the Form IV examination. In Tanzania, the few pupils from the less-educated households who obtain access to secondary school are of a quality that enables them to compete successfully with pupils from more-educated home backgrounds, and little influence of home background can be detected in the Form IV examination results. It is different in the Form VI examinations. In Kenya, home background does not seem to be an influence on the results, the situation corresponding to that in the Form IV examinations in Tanzania. The position is similar in Tanzania, except with respect to the highest level of performance, which is achieved by more candidates from an educated background than by others.

The greater number of secondary school places available to the primary school-leaver in Kenya than in Tanzania means that there is greater upward mobility in Kenya in terms of access to education—but only to a point. And it does not necessarily mean that family background counts for less, and that there is greater upward mobility in other ways. Kenya and Tanzania are much more similar in the relationship between family background and occupation than they are in access to secondary school. The greater access to secondary education in Kenya than in Tanzania does not appear to have led to greater intergenerational job mobility—more chance, that is, of better jobs for the children of the uneducated. In fact, the scarcity of the secondary-educated in Tanzania, and the sellers' market for their skills, has weakened the influence of family background to an extent not achieved in Kenya.

So the effect of family advantages will out, and is not dissipated simply by an expansion of the educational system, so long as there is selection by academic performance at various steps on the educational ladder. The relative advantage of the children of the educated is likely to be maintained, and they will keep one step ahead. These basic relationships are found in both Kenya and Tanzania.

It is evident that the educational advantage of family background does not end with access to education but continues and exerts its effect on the labour-market. It expresses itself not only in the employee's occupation, but also in the wage, the time it takes to get a job, and the chance of periods of unemployment. Over time the importance of examination failure as the reason for education not continuing has become more important, and economic reasons less important, so that the system has become more meritocratic. Nevertheless, the influence of family background remains in both countries.

Education in school is a means of creating human capital for the pupil, but it is not the only means; the home is also an important influence on the accumulation of human capital, in general the more-educated home being a more effective creator of capital than the less educated. Hence, for an employee with a given level of education in school, those from an educated home background are likely to have accumulated more human capital, capital which is of productive value, than those from less-educated homes. These differences are recognized in the labour-market and the observed relationship between earnings and family background is established.

This educational advantage for the children of the educated ensures that they retain an advantage in the labour-market. The process of filtering down ensures that the 'underprivileged' will not rise in the occupational hierarchy simply because more of them move up the educational ladder. They are, in effect, running up the down escalator; more education does little more than keep them in their fathers' jobs. For this reason, the much greater expansion of secondary education, drawing in many more, and a much higher proportion, of the children of the uneducated in Kenya than in Tanzania, has made access to secondary education more equal in Kenya, but it has not had a similarly equalizing effect on the labour-market, on the access to higher-level jobs.

But all this is concerned with relativities: it is concerned with the proportion of the children of the educated relative to the proportion of the children of the uneducated who attain particular levels of education; it is concerned with the changing proportions of each group who attain particular positions in the occupational hierarchy. And relative positions are not all. Although education does not demolish the influence of family background, education has its advantages for the educated, nevertheless. Its benefit is to be measured by the higher wages that more-educated workers can command within any given occupation. The children of the uneducated may be absolutely better off, if more of them have more education, even if their relative position in the occupational hierarchy is unchanged. In any case, where there are so few children of the educated in the labour force, over-emphasis on their relative position has an air of unreality. What real significance can be attached to the more-equal access to upper-secondary places in Tanzania than in Kenya when a mere handful of Tanzanians have the benefit of that level of education? More important is the fact that the earnings of workers from less-educated households are much higher in Kenya than in Tanzania,[2] partly it may be surmised as a result of the productivity gains accruing from their higher education. So it may be concluded that the failure of educational expan-

---

[2] In most years, the Shilling exchange rates were similar enough for the Shilling figures to measure the difference. In 1979, and 1980 the Tanzanian rate was substantially lower than the Kenya rate, so that the Shilling figures understate the Kenyan superiority in earnings, at any rate in terms of foreign exchange.

sion to open the doors to intergenerational job mobility does not remove the important benefits of such expansion.

Employees in both Nairobi and Dar es Salaam retain strong links with the rural areas from which most of them have come to the city. They make transfers of income to the rural areas, some of them possess and operate *shambas*, some have a spouse in the rural areas and educate their children there. These are characteristics common to the two groups, though there are marked differences in the extent of the rural connections. In particular, the majority of Nairobi employees have a spouse in the rural area, whereas most Dar es Salaam employees have a spouse in the city.

It may be presumed that the spouses of Nairobi employees with *shambas* are living and working on the *shamba*. No doubt family income is higher when the wife works the *shamba* and the husband works in town than when they are both in town. Could it be that Kenyans and Tanzanians put different relative valuations on money income and the psychic benefits of family life? Or is the cost of keeping a family so much higher in Nairobi than in Dar es Salaam? Or does the statistical picture fail to reflect the frequent existence of the 'one family, two households' pattern of urbanization that was remarked on in Nairobi (Weisner 1969) in the 1960s? Unfortunately, the surveys provide no data to answer these questions. Of course, the densely farmed and heavily populated Central Province adjacent to Nairobi is readily accessible by bus, taxi, and car, particularly for weekend visits. The nearer districts are in effect an extension of the city.

The expressed intention—even if, in the end, it is no more than that—of almost all employees to retire to the countryside is yet another indication of the ties with the rural areas which are retained by urban employees. Yet these continuing links with their areas of origin are a far cry from the migratory system of earlier days. (See Elkan 1976 for a review of evidence). The urban workers of today are not 'target workers', entering into urban wage-employment to accumulate a sum of money with which to return home. For today's workers the town is where they work, not intermittently, but for their working lives, at any rate if they do not lose their job. And not only do they stay in employment for long periods, they stay for long periods with the same employer. Twenty-five years before these surveys of urban employees in Nairobi and Dar es Salaam were undertaken, the East Africa Royal Commission found a very different state of affairs. They found that 'much of the labour which is employed is migrant labour in the sense that it seeks employment for short periods and returns to the tribal area'. In that system of 'circular migration' the wage was for the unskilled and the inexperienced. The Royal Commission received much evidence which 'emphasized the mutual relationship between low wages and low labour productivity: wages were low because the labour was inefficient and the labour was inefficient because wages were low'. In their turn, low wages made permanent settlement in the towns unattractive and retarded the growth of a stable labour force. A withdrawal from the countryside would substantially have reduced family income.

In 1980, in contrast, the surveys show that the urban labour force—although retaining strong ties with the rural areas, and without a 'withdrawal from the countryside'—was settled, it was experienced in wage-employment, and a high proportion was in occupations requiring skills of one kind or another. Despite the continuing influence of family background, it was paid according to the scarcity of its skills, its education, and its experience, except where intervention decreed otherwise, and the wage structure encouraged stability and the acquisition of skills. A major ingredient in this transformation was the expansion of education.

Appendix

CONFIDENTIAL

Tanzania Survey of Wage Employment and Education

EMPLOYEE QUESTIONNAIRE

Firm Name_____

Firm Number_____

Employee Name_____

Employee Number_____

_____

Employee Questionnaire

		REPLY	CODE
Employee Number	(1-4)		
Card number	(5)		1
Firm number	(6–8)		
Interviewer number	(9–10)		

I. Personal Characteristics

1. Sex: Male (11)

REPLY	CODE
	1
	2

   Female

2. Ethnic group: African (12)

REPLY	CODE
	1
	2
	3
	4
	9

   Asian
   European
   Other
   No reply

3. Are you a citizen?

REPLY	CODE
	1
	2
	9

   Yes (13)
   Wewe ni raia? (13)
   No
   No reply

If no: How long have you lived in Tanzania? (14–15)
   (years)
   Umeishi Tanzanian kwa muda gani?
   (miaka)

(N/A)	00

4. How old are you? (years) (16–17)
   Umri wako ni miaka mingapi?

REPLY	CODE

5. Are you: a. Never married
   Hali ya ndoa   Hujawahi kuoa/kuolewa

   b. Married
      Umeoa/umeolewa

   c. Widowed
      Mjane

REPLY	CODE
	3

   d. Divorced
      Mmeachana

REPLY	CODE
	4

   e. Separated
      Mmetengana

REPLY	CODE
	5

   f. No reply
      Hakuna jibu

REPLY	CODE
	9

REPLY	CODE

6. How many people in addition to yourself do you
help support (regularly in money or kind) with your earnings?
Pamoja na wewe, ni jumla ya watu wangapi
ambao mahitaji yao yanatokana na mapato yako?

		REPLY	CODE
Husbands or wives, fully Waume au wake, yote	(19)		
Husbands or wives, partly Waume au wake, kiasi	(20)		
Children, fully Watoto, yote	(21–22)		
Chila3dren, partly Watoto, kiasi	(23–25)		
Other, fully Wengine, yote	(25–26)		
Other, partly Wengine, kiasi	(27–28)		

II. Family Background

1. What was the highest level of education that your father received?
   Baba yako amesoma mpaka daraja gani?

	REPLY	CODE
None (30)		0
Hakwenda shule		
Primary		1
Shule ya msingi		
Secondary		2
Sekondari		
Other post-primary (e.g. pre-service training)		4
Zaidi ya shule ya msingi (kwa mfano mafunzo ya kikazi)		
Post-secondary		4
Zaidi ya Sekondari		
No reply		9

2. What was his main occupation when you left school?
   Alikuwa anafanya kazi gani wakati ultipoacha shule?

	REPLY	CODE
farmer (31)		1
mukulima		
other self-employed		2
kazi ya binafsi ya aina nyingine		
manual wage-earner		3
kazi ya ufundi wa mikona ya malipo		
non-manual wage earner		4
kazi ya kulipwa ya aina nyingine		
business proprietor		5
biashara yake binafasi		
deceased		6
amefariki		
other (specify)		7
kazi nyingine (eleza)		
don't know		8
no reply		9

   If farmer: When you left school about how much land did he farm?
   Ulipoacha shule alikuwa analima (32–33) shamba kubwa kiasi gani?

	N/A	00

REPLY	CODE

	—

hectares
hekta
or acres
au ektari

If farmer: When you left school did he do *Ki barua* for other?
Ulipoacha shule alikua kibarua   (34)
kwenye mashamba ya watu
wengine?

N/A	0

Yes
No
Don't know
No reply

	1
	2
	3
	9

If farmer: When you left school did others do *ki barua* for him?
Ulipoacha shule alikuwa ameajiri   (35)
vibarua wa kusaidia shambani?

N/A	00

Yes
No
Don't know
No reply

	1
	2
	3
	9

3. What was the highest level of education that
your mother received?
Mama yako amesoma mpaka daraja gani?

none   (36)
hakwenda shule

	0

primary
shule ya msingi

	1

secondary
sekondari

	2

other post-primary (eg. pre-
service training)

	3

zaidi ya shule ya msingi (kwa
mfano mafunzo ya kikazi)
post-secondary
zaidi ya sekondari

	4

don't know
no reply

	5
	9

4. What was her main occupation when you left
school?
Alikuwa anafanya kazi gani wakati ulipoacha
shule?

REPLY	CODE

farmer   (37–38)
mkulima   `01`

other self-employed
kazi yake binafsi ya aina
nyingine   `02`

manual wage-earner
kazi ya ufundi wa mikono ya
kulipwa   `03`

non-manual employee
kazi ya kulipwa ya aina
nyingine   `04`

business proprietor
biashara yake binafasi   `05`

deceased
amefariki   `06`

other (*specify*)
kazi nyingine (*eleza*)   `07`

housewife only
mama wa nyumbani   `10`

don't know   `08`
no reply   `99`

III. Education

	REPLY	CODE

1. What was the highest standard in primary (39)
   school that you completed?
   Darasa la juu kabisa uliofikia kwenye shule ya
   msingi ni lipi?

REPLY	CODE
	0
	1
	2
	3
	4
	5
	6
	7
	8
	9

                    no reply

2. Did you receive a primary leaving certificate?
   Ulipata cheti cha kumalizia shule ya msingi?
              Yes (40)
              No
              No reply

REPLY	CODE
	1
	2
	9

If no primary schooling, proceed to Question 4a.

3. What type of primary school was it? (If more
   than one, last school)
   Shule ya msingi uliyosoma ilikuwa ya aina
   gani? (Kama ni zaidi ya moja, taja
   uliyosoma mwishoni)
         (41)

REPLY	CODE
N/A	0
	1
	2
	3
	9

      a. Government
         Serikali
      b. Private

      c. Mission
         Iliyoendeshwa na
           makanisa
      d. No reply

4. Did you have any education or pre-service
   training after primary school?
   Baada ya kumaliza shule ya msingi uliendelea
   na masomo au ulipata mafunzo ya
   kukuwezesha kupata kazi?
              Yes (42)
              No
              No reply

REPLY	CODE
N/A	
	1
	2
	9

REPLY	CODE

If no: proceed to Question 4a.
If yes: Which of the following types did you
have? (*indicate the order*)
Ulipata elimu ya aina gani kati ya   (43–44),(45–46),
zifuatazo?   (47–48), &
                                                (49–50)

| | N/A | 00 |

a. Government secondary
    Sekondari ya serikali

| | 01 |

b. Self-help secondary
    Shule ya sekondari ya
    kujitegemea

| | 02 |

c. Private secondary
    Sekondari ya "private"

| | 03 |

d. Technical secondary
    Shule ya sekondari ya
    ufundi

| | 04 |

e. Teacher training (non-
    university)
    Shule ya ualimu

| | 05 |

f. University
    Chuo kikuu

| | 06 |

g. Technical College
    Chuo cha ufundi

| | 07 |

h. Trade School
    Shule ya ufundi

| | 08 |

i. Craft School
    Shule ya kazi za mikono

| | 09 |

j. Folk development
    College (*specify length of
    course*)

| | 10 |

k. Government-run pre-service
    training institution (*specify*)
    Shule ya mafunzo (ya
    vijana) kabla ya kuanza
    kazi, inayoendeshwa na
    serikali (taja)

| | 11 |

l. Employer-run preservice
    training school (*specify*)
    Shule ya mafunzo kabla ya
    kuanza kazi inayoendeshwa
    na mwajiri.

| | 12 |

m. Government-run secretarial
    college
    Chuo cha mafunzo ya

| | 13 |

REPLY	CODE

ukarani au biashara
kinachoendeshwa na
serikali.

n. Private secretarial college
chu cha mafunzo ya ukarani
au biashara
kinachoendeshwa na watu
binafsi.

	16

o. Other (*specify*)

	17

p. No reply

	99

If a, b. c or d,—formal secondary school:
Which was the highest form achieved?
Ulimaliza darasa la ngapi?   (51)

N/A	0
	1
	2
	3
	4
	5
	6

        no reply

	9

For those who reached form 4:
What were your results in the National Form 4
Examination
(formerly SC or 'O' levels)?
Matokeo yako ya mtihani wa darasa la 12
yalikuwa-je?   (53)

N/A	0
	1
	2
	3
	4
	5
	6
	9

    a. Division 1
    b. Division 2
    c. Division 3
    d. Division 4
    e. Fail
    f. Did not sit
    g. No reply

What was your grade in the following subjects?
Ulipata nini kwenye masomo
yafuatayo?

N/A	0

    a. Maths   (54)
       Hesabu

    b. English   (55)
       Kiingereza

    c. Your best science subject   (56)
       (*specify*)
       Somo la sayansi ulilofanya

	REPLY	CODE

vizuri
kupita yote (*litaje*)
d. Your practical subject   (57)
(*specify*)
Somo lako la kazi za mikono
(*litaje*)

Which school did you attend? (the last school)   (58)

| | N/A | 000 |
| | — | |
(no reply) | | | 999 |

Were you: a. a border?   (59)

| | N/A | 0 |
ulikowa unakaa bwenini? | | | 1 |
b. a day pupil? | | | 2 |
ulikuwa unakaa nyumbani? | | | 9 |

For those who reached form 6: What were your
results in the National Form 6
Examination (formerly HSC or 'A' level)
(principal passes only)?
Matokeo yako ya mtihani wa darasa la 14
yalikuwa je?   (60)

	N/A	0
a. no passes | | | 8 |
b. 1 pass | | | 1 |
c. 2 passes | | | 2 |
d. 3 passes | | | 3 |
e. 4 or more passes | | | 4 |
f. did no take | | | 5 |
g. no reply | | | 9 |

What were your three best principal
passes and the grade received in each?
Taja masomo kamili matatu uliyoshinda
vizuri kuliko mengine?

1. subject:_____grade:_____   (61–62)
2. subject:_____grade:_____   (63–64)
3. subject:_____grade:_____   (65–66)

Which school did you attend?
(the last school)   (67)
Ulisoma shule gani? (uliyosoma mwishoni)

	N/A	000
	—	
		999

Were you: a. a border?   (68)

| | N/A | 0 |
ulikowa unakaa bwenini? | | | 1 |
b. a day pupil? | | | 2 |
ulikuwa unakaa nyumbani? | | | 9 |

*For those who attended a teacher training college
(College of National Education)*:
How long was the course?_____years.

	REPLY	CODE

Mfunzo yalichukua muda gani?
For what teaching grade did the course qualify you?
Ulihitimu kuwa mwalimu wa ngazi gani? (69)

REPLY	CODE
N/A	0
	1
	2
	3
	4
	5
	9

    a. No qualification
    b. grade A
    c. grade B
    d. grade C
    e. Other (*specify*)
    f. no reply

For those who attended a university:
Did you obtain a degree?
Ulipata shahada (70)

REPLY	CODE
N/A	0
	1
	2
	9

    yes
    no
    no reply

If yes: what was your highest degree?
Ni ipi shahada ya juu kabisa uliyopata? (71)

REPLY	CODE
N/A	0
	1
	2
	3
	9

    a. bachelors
    b. masters
    c. doctorate
    d. no reply

If no: Did you obtain a diploma (*specify*)
Ulipata diploma? (eleza) (72)

REPLY	CODE
N/A	0
	1
	2
	9

    yes
    no
    no reply

What subjects did you study?
Ulichukua masoma gani? (73–74),(75–76)

REPLY	CODE
N/A	00
	01
	02
	03
	04
	05
	06
	07
	08
	10
	11
	12
	13
	14
	99

    general arts
    social sciences
    history
    languages
    geography
    engineering
    sciences
    law
    medicine
    agriculture
    architecture
    commerce
    other (*specify*)

    no reply

REPLY	CODE

Where did you attend university?
Ulisoma chuo kikuu kipi?   (77),(78)

	N/A	0
	Dar	3
	Makerere	2
	Nairobi	1
	elsewhere (*specify*)	4
	No reply	9

4a. What was the highest level of education
    that your spouse received?
    Mke/Mume wako amesoma mpaka daraja gani?

none (79)	0
hakwenda shule	
primary	1
shule ya msingi	
secondary	2
sekondari	
other post-primary (eg. pre-	
service training)	3
zaidi ya shule ya msingi (kama	
mafunzo ya kakazi)	
post-secondary	4
zaidi ya sekondari	
unmarried	5
nakuolewa/hakuoa	
no reply	9

Employee number   (1–4)

Card number   (5) | 2 |

5. Have you attempted a craft trade test?
   Umewahi kujaribu mtihani wa ufundi
   unaotolewa na serikali?

yes	(6)	1
no		2
no reply		9

If yes: What were your results?
Matokeo yake yalikuwa-je?   (7–8)

		N/A	00
Grade I	Pass		00
	Fail		01
	Did not sit		03
Grade II	Pass		04
	Fail		05
	Did not sit		06
Grade III	Pass		07
	Fail		08
	Did not sit		10
No reply			

REPLY	CODE

What subject was the test in?

Mtihani ulikuwa katika somo lipi?   (5),(10)

REPLY	CODE
N/A	0
	1

        a. engineering
           uhandisi

        b. building
           ujenzi

| | 2 |

        c. woodwork
           useremala

| | 3 |

        d. electrical
           umeme (ufundi wa)

| | 4 |

        e. tailoring
           ushonaji

| | 5 |

        f. shoe making
           kutengeneza viatu

| | 6 |

        g. other (*specify*)
           mengine (*yataje*)

| | 8 |

        h. no reply

| | 9 |

6. In what year did you complete your formal
education or preservice training?

Mwaka gani ulimaliza shule au elimu ya
mafunzo ya Kazi?

           19_____   (11–12)

           no reply

REPLY	CODE
N/A	
	99

7. At the time you left formal education did you
want to continue?

Ulikuwa bado unataka kuendelea na masomo
ulipoacha shule?   (13)

           yes

           no

           no reply

REPLY	CODE
N/A	
	1
	2
	9

If yes: why didn't you?

Kwanini hukuendelea?   (14)

REPLY	CODE
N/A	0
	1

        a. grades not high enough
           sikufanya vizuri ya kuteka
           kuhitimu

        b. no school available locally
           ukosefu wa shule nilikoishi

| | 2 |

        c. could not afford school fees
           sikuwa na ada ya shule

| | 3 |

        d. had to work to support
           family
           ilinibidi kufanya kazi kwa
           ajili ya kusaidia familia

| | 4 |

        e. became pregnant
           kwa ajili ya kupata mimba

| | 5 |

REPLY	CODE

    f. other (*specify*)   **6**
        sababu nyingine (*zitaje*)
    g. no reply   **9**

8. Do you want your sons to have more education
    than you had, if they have the opportunity?
    Je, kama itawezekana, unataka watoto wako wa
    kiume wapate elimu zaidi kuliko uliyopata wewe?

             yes   (15)   **1**
             no   **2**
             no reply   **9**

    If yes: Why? (give the main reason)
        Kwa nini?   (16)   N/A   **0**
           a. better job   **1**
               kazi nzuri zaidi
           b. higher pay   **2**
               mshahara mkubwa zaidi
           c. occupation hoped for   **3**
               requires it
               kufuatana na mahitaji ya
               kazi inayonuiwa
           d. position in society   **4**
               kufuatana na mazingara ya
               maisha
           e. service to the community   **5**
               kufuatana na mahitaji ya
               jumuia
           f. cultural enrichment   **6**
               kuendeleza mila na
               utamaduni
           g. no reply   **9**

9. If after leaving primary school your son could
    not continue to a government secondary
    school, what would you do?
    Kama baada ya kumaliza shule ya msingi
    mtoto wako wa kiume hakupata nafasi katika
    sekondari ya serikali utafanya nini?

           a. pay his fees for a private   (17)   **1**
               school
               nitampeleka shule ya
               'private'
           b. send him to a craft school   **2**
               nitampeleka kwenye
               shule ya kazi za mikono
           c. send him out to work   **3**
               nitampeleka kufanya kazi

REPLY	CODE

d. apprentice him (to acquire
   skills)
   nitampeleka mahali
   kujifunza kazi

| | 4 |

e. get him to repeat primary
   leaving
   certificate
   nitamfanya arudie

| | 5 |

f. other (*specify*)
   vingine (*eleza*)

| | 6 |

g. no reply

| | 9 |

9a. Do you want your daughters to have more
    education than you had if they have the opportunity?
    Je, kama ikiwezekana, unataka watoto wako
    wa kike wapate elimu zaidi kuliko uliyopata wewe?

          yes   (18)

	1
	2
	9

          no

          no reply

If yes: Why
    Kwa nini?   (19)

| N/A | 0 |
| | 1 |

a. better job
   kazi nzuri zaidi

b. higher pay
   mshahara mkubwa zaidi

| | 2 |

c. occupation hoped for
   requires it
   kufuatana na mahitaji ya
   kazi inayonuiwa

| | 3 |

d. position in society

| | 4 |
| | 5 |

e. service to the community
   kufuatana no mahitaji ya
   jumuiya

f. cultural enrichment
   kuendeleza mila na
   utamaduni

| | 6 |

g. no reply

| | 9 |

9b. If after leaving primary school your daughter
    could not continue to a government secondary
    school, what would you do?
    Kama baada ya kumaliza shule ya msingi
    mtoto wako wa kikl hakupata nafasi katika
    sekondari ya serikali utafanya nini?

          a. pay her fees for a private   (20)
             school

| | 1 |

REPLY	CODE

nitampeleka shule ya
'private'

b. send her to a craft school | | 2 |
   nitampeleka kwenye
   shule ya kazi za mikono

c. send her to work | | 3 |
   nitampeleka kufanya kazi

d. apprentice her | | 4 |
   nitampeleka mahali
   kujifunza kazi

e. get her to repeat primary | | 5 |
   leaving
   certificate
   nitamfanya arudie

f. keep her at home | | 6 |
   nitamweka nyumbani

g. other (*specify*) | | 7 |
   vingine (*eleza*)

h. no reply | | 9 |

10. *To be asked in English.* How many years did   (21–22)
    you study English?

    Can you speak English?

Not at all (23)		0
A little		1
Fluently		2
No reply		9

    Can you read and write English?

Not at all (24)		0
A little		1
Fluently		2
No reply		9

IV. Earnings

	REPLY	CODE

1. Are you paid by:
   Unalipwa kwa:

		REPLY	CODE
the day	(25)		1
siku			
the week			2
wiki			
the month			3
mwezi			
no reply			9

2. How much did you receive, including housing allowances but excluding annual bonus, from the firm last period (after deductions)? (shillings)
   Malipo kutoka kazini pamoja na marupurupu kwa ajili ya kodi ya nyumba na bila bakshishi ya mwaka yaliluwa kiasi gani mara ya mwisho (baada ya kukatwa kodi ya mapato na mengineyo)?

   Basic wage
   plus housing allowance
   plus overtime payments
   plus other (*specify*)
   less employee NPF contributions
   less tax deducted
   gives   (26–31)

3. How many shillings of this was for overtime? (shillings)
   Kati ya hayo malipo, kiasi gani   (32–35)
   kilitokana na 'overtime'?

4. Did you receive an annual bonus?
   Ulipata bakshishi ya mwaka?

		REPLY	CODE
yes	(36)		1
no			2
no reply			9

		REPLY	CODE
If yes: how much? (shillings)	(37–40)	N/A	0000
kiasi gani?			
no reply			9999

		REPLY	CODE
When do you receive it?	(41–42)	N/A	00
Huwa unaipata lini?			
month			
no reply			99

5. Is housing provided by the firm free or at reduced prices? Je, kampuni inatoa nyumba za kuishi bure au kwa kodi ya chini zaidi kuliko mahali pengine?

	yes	(43)		1
	no			2
	no reply			9

6. Is annual paid leave provided by the firm? Je, unapata likizo ya mwaka (pamoja na malipo)?

		(44)		1
	yes			2
	no			9
	no reply			

7. Are rations provided by the firm free or at reduced prices? Je, kampuni inatoa chakula cha bure au kwa bei nafuu?

	yes	(45)		1
	no			2
	no reply			9

8. Is medical treatment provided by the firm free or at reduced prices? Je, kampuni inatoa matibabu bure au kwa bei nafuu?

	yes	(46)		1
	no			2
	no reply			9

9. Is transport to work provided by the firm free or at reduced prices? Je, kampuni inatoa msaada wa usafiri kwenda na kutoka kazini bure au kwa bei nafuu?

		(47)		1
	yes			2
	no			9
	no reply			

10. Does the employer contribute to the National Provident Fund for you? Je, kampuni inakuchangia kwenye mpango wa National Provident Fund?

	yes	(48)		1
	no			2
	no reply			9

11. Does the employer contribute to any other pension scheme for you?

REPLY	CODE

Je, mwajiri wako anashiriki katika mpango
mwingine wowote wa 'pension' kwa ajili
yako?

yes (49)		1
no		2
no reply		9

12. Will your employer lend you money if
necessary?
Je, mwajiri wako atakukopesha fedha ukiwa
na shida ya lazima? (50)

		1
yes		2
no		9
no reply		

13. Do you have other sources of income from:
Je, una njia nyingine za mapato?

none (51).(52)		0
hapana		
farm		1
shamba		
shop		2
duka		
kiosk		3
kibanda cha barabarani		
taxi		4
houses or rooms you rent		5
out vya kupangisha		
other (*specify*)		6
nyingine (*taja*)		
no reply		9

If yes: Roughly how much (shillings) per month?
Makisio ya haya mapato ni kiasi gani kwa
mwezi?

	N/A	0000
or per day (53–56)		
au kwa siku		
or per year		
au kwa mwaka		9999
no reply		

V. Employment Experience in the Firm

1. In what year did you join the firm?
   19_____
   Ni mwaka gani ulianza kazi hapa?   (57–58)

2. Are you now a regular or casual worker?
   Wewe ni mfanya kazi wa kudumu au kibarua?

	(59)		
Regular			1
Casual			2
no reply			9

3. *If regular*: Did you start in this firm as a
   casual worker?
   Je, ulianza kazi hapa kama
   kibarua?   (60)

	N/A	0
Yes		1
No		2
No reply		9

4. *If no*: Would you have got your job if you had
   received less education?   (61)

N/A	0

   Ungeweza kuipata hii kazi kama ungekuwa na
   kisomo cha chini ya ulichokuwa nacho?

Yes		1
No		2
Don't know		3
No reply		9

If yes to question 3: When you became a   (62)

N/A	0

regular employee,
would you have got
your job if you had
received less
education?
Ulipofanywa mfanya
kazi wa kudumu
ungeipata hiyo kazi
kama ungekuwa na
kisomo chini ya
ulichokuwa nacho?

Yes		1
No		2
Don't know		3
No reply		9

REPLY	CODE

5. *If casual*: Would you have got your job if you
      had received less education?   (63)

N/A	0
No	1
No	2
Don't know	3
No reply	9

6. How did you get your job with this employer?
Ulitumia njia gani kupata kazi hapo
unapofanya sasa?

    a. At the gate   (64–65)(66–57)

	01

       Kuulizia Kwenye 'gate'

    b. By letter, in response to an
       advertisement

	02

       Barua baada ya kuona
       tangazo

    c. By letter, unsolicited

	03

       Barua bila msaada

    d. Through a friend or relative

	04

       Kupitia kwa rafiki au jamaa

    e. Through the Government

	05

       Employment Exchange
       Kupitia Government
       Employment Exchange

    f. Allocation by Government

	06

       Nilipangiwa na serikali

    g. Through a private

	07

       employment agency
       Kupitia kwa kampuni
       inayoshughulika na
       uajiri ya watu binafsi

    h. National Service Scheme

	08

       Mpango wa kujenga Taifa

    i. Other (*specify*)

	10

       Nyingine (*eleza*)

    j. No reply

	99

7. *Fill in details of current occupation on the occupation form.*

8. Is the skill level in your current job higher,
lower, or about the same as in the job you
held when you first joined this employer?
                          (68)

N/A	0

Ujuzi wa kazi yako sasa ni wa juu zaidi, chini
zaidi au ni sawa na wa kazi uliyoanzia kwa
huyu mwajiriwako?

	REPLY	CODE

	REPLY	CODE

Higher

Lower

The same

Don't know

No reply

Higher	1
Lower	2
The same	3
Don't know	4
No reply	9

9. Has the employer given you a training course?

Mwagiri amewahi kukupa mafunzo ya kikazi?   (69)

Yes

No

No reply

	1
Yes	2
No	9

If yes: how many courses?
mara ngapi?   (70)

No reply

(If more than one, the questions relate to the main one.)

N/A	0
No reply	9

Was it: (71)
Ilikuwa:

| N/A | 0 |

pre-service
kabla ya kuanza kazi

in-service
kama mfanya kazi

no reply

pre-service	1
in-service	2
no reply	9

Was it:
Ilikuwa: (72)

| N/A | 0 |

in the firm
kazini

| in the firm | 1 |

in some outside institution
mahali pengine

| in some outside institution | 2 |

no reply

| no reply | 9 |

How long was this course?
(code in months)   (73–74)
Mafunzo yalichukua muda gani?

| N/A | 00 |

weeks
or months
no reply

	99

Was the course: (75)
Mafunzo yalikuwa:

| N/A | 0 |

full-time
kila siku

| full-time | 1 |

part-time
siku moja moja

| part-time | 2 |

no reply

| no reply | 9 |

REPLY	CODE

Did you receive full pay while attending
this course?
Ulikuwa unalipwa mshahara wako wote
ulipokuwa mafunzoni? (76)

REPLY	CODE
N/A	0
	1
	2
	9

yes — 1
no — 2
no reply — 9

Did you receive higher pay after
completing
the course?
Uliongezwa mshahara baada ya kumaliza (77)
mafunzo?

REPLY	CODE
N/A	0
	1
	2
	9

yes — 2
no — 9
no reply

Employee number (1-4)
Card number (5)

CODE
3

10. Do you think your education qualifies you for
a job at a higher level than your present job?
Je, kufuatana na kisoma chako unafikiri
ungeweza kufanya kazi yenye madaraka zaidi
kuliko uliyo nayo sasa? (6)

CODE
1
2
3
9

yes — 1
no — 2
don't know — 3
no reply — 9

If yes: Why are you in your current job? (7)
Kwa nini unafanya hii kazi ya sasa?

REPLY	CODE
N/A	0
	1

a. to gain experience, or skill
kupata mazoezi au uiuzi

b. too junior for higher
job at the moment
umri wangu au muda
niliokaa hapa ni mdogo
kuliko inavyotakiwa

CODE
2

c. no higher level jobs
available
ukosefu wa kazi yenye
madaraka zaidi

CODE
3

d. other (*specify*)
kwa ajili ya sababu
nyingine (*zitaje*).

CODE
4

e. no reply

CODE
9

REPLY	CODE

11. Do you think that you could perform your
present job as well if you had not received
your final stage of education?
Je, unafikiri ungeweza kuifanya kazi yako ya
sasa sawa na kama
vile usingekuwa umefikia daraja la kisomo
ulicho nacho? (8)

N/A	0
	1
	2
	3
	9

        yes

        no

        don't know

        no reply

12. Do you think you could do your present job
better if you had completed the next stage of
education?
Je, unafikiri ungeweza kuifanya kazi yako ya
sasa vizuri zaidi kama ungeendelea na shule
mpaka daraja la juu zaidi kuliko ulilofikia?

        yes (9)

        no

        don't know

        no reply

	1
	2
	3
	9

13. Are you a trade union member?
Umejiunga na chama cha wafanya kazi?

        no (10–11)

        yes

        no reply

	00
	99

14. How much were you paid (after deductions)
when you first joined this firm? (shillings per
month) (12–16)

Ulikuwa unalipwa kiasi gani (baada ya
kukatwa kodi na mengineyo) ulipoanza kazi
kwenye hii kampuni?

        don't know

        no reply

	99999

15. Are you actively looking for a better job in
some other firm?
Je, unajitahidi kutafuta kazi nzuri zaidi
mahali pengine?

        yes (17)

        no

        no reply

	1
	2
	9

VI. Previous Employment Experience

REPLY	CODE

If no formal education proceed to Question 3.

1. Did you interrupt your formal education for a
   year or more?
   Je, ulipokuwa unasoma shule uliwahi kuacha
   masomo kwa mwaka au zaidi halafu ukarudi
   tena kuendelea?

   yes   (18)

   no

   no reply

N/A	0
	1
	2
	9

   If yes: During that time how long did you
   spend doing the following?
   Wakati huo,ulijishughulisha kwa muda
   gani na yafuatayo?

MONTHS	YEARS

   a worked on parent's shamba   (19)
     kusaidia kwenye shamba la
     wazazi

   b worked on own shamba   (20)
     kufanya kazi kwenye shamba lako

   c non-agricultural employment,   (21)
     (eg. street vending, small
     businesses, etc.);
     kazi isiyokuwa ya kilimo (kwa
     mfano ku kutembeza na kuuza
     vitu barabarani)

   d umemployed and looking for   (22)
     wage employment
     kushughulika kutafuta kazi ya
     kulipwa

   e unemployed and not looking for   (23)
     work
     kukaa tu bila kufanya kazi wala
     kutafuta

   f employed in a wage job kufanya   (24)
     kazi ya kulipwa

   g National Service   (25)
     Kujenga Taifa

2. How long was it after you left full time
   education or training before you got wage
   employment? (code in months)
   Baada ya kumaliza shule, ilikuchukua muda
   gani kabla ya kuajiriwa?

	REPLY	CODE

immediately					(26–28)

		000

months

or years

		—

don't know

no reply (*include people*						| | | 999 |

with no formal education)

If not immediately: How long did you spend
				doing the following?

	N/A	000

Ulijishughulisha kwa muda gani na
yafuatayo?

			(code in months)

	MONTHS	YEARS

a worked on parent's shamba		(29–31)
	kusaidia kwenye shamba la
	wazazi

b worked on own shamba			(32–34)
	kufanya kazi kwenye shamba lako

c non-agricultural self-employment,	(35–37)
	(eg. street vending, small
	businesses)
	kazi ya binafsi isiyokuwa ya
	kilimo (kwa mfano kutembeza na
	kuuza vitu barabarani)

d unemployed and looking for		(38–40)
	wage employment
	bila kazi hali unashughulika
	kutafuta kazi ya kulipwa

e unemployed and not looking for	(41–43)
	wage employment
	kukaa tu bila kufanya au kutafuta
	kazi

f Other (*specify*)					(44)

3. Were you in wage employment at any time
before coming to this employer (exclude
employment during school holidays or
university vacation)? Umewahi kuajiriwa
mahali pengine kabla ya hapa ulipo sasa
(kuacha wakati wa likizo ulipokuwa
unasoma)?

			yes				(46)

		1

			no						| | | 2 |

			no reply				| | | 9 |

If no: go to Section VII.

4. In what year did you get your first wage job?
19_____						(47–48)

	N/A	00

Uliajiriwa kwa mara ya kwanza mwaka gani?

			no reply				| | | 99 |

REPLY	CODE

5. Have you been continuously in wage
employment since then (without a break of
more than a month)?
Baada ya hapo, umewahi kukaa bila kuajiriwa
kwa zaidi ya mwezi?

(49)

N/A	0
yes	1
no	2
no reply	9

6. *If no*: How many times have you been out of
wage employment?
Umekaa bila kuajiriwa mara ngapi? (50)
number of times
no reply

N/A	0
	9

How long in total were you out of wage
employment?
Kwa ujumla ni muda gani umekaa bila
kuajiriwa? (51–52)
(months)
no reply

N/A	
	99

What did you do? (main activity) Ulifanya nini? (shughuli muhimu)	First Time MONTHS	Second Time MONTHS	Most Recent Time MONTHS
1 worked on parent's shamba kusaidia kwenye shamba la wazazi			
2 worked on own shamba kufanya kazi katika shamba langu			
3 non-agricultural self-employment (eg. street vending) Kazi binafsi isiyokuwa ya kilimo (kwa mfano kutembeza na kunza vitu barabarani)			
4 unemployed and looking for wage employment Kushughulika kutafuta kazi ya kuajiriwa			
5 Unemployed and not looking for work			

(53–54)
(55–56)
(57–58)

REPLY	CODE

Kukaa bila kufanya au
kutafuta kazi
6 returned to education
Kurudi shuleni
kuendelea na masomo

7. How many *previous* employers have you had?
   Umewahi kuwa na waajiri wangapi kabla
   ya huyu wa sasa?   (59)

REPLY	CODE
N/A	0
1	1
2	2
3	3
4	4
5	5
6	6
7	7
8 or more	8
no reply	9

If none: go to Section VII.

8. (*Exclude wage employment during school or college
   vacations.*)
   What was the name of your employer in?   your last job_____
   Mwajiri wako alikuwa ni nani?   kazi yako ya mwisho
                                             your first job_____
   How many people worked for   kazi yako ya mwanzo
   the establishment?
   Kulikuwa na wafanya kazi
   wangaqpi kwenye hiyo
   karakana?

YOUR LAST JOB			YOUR FIRST JOB		
COL.	REPLY	CODE	COL.	REPLY	CODE
(60)	N/A	0	(61)	N/A	0
		1			1
		2			2
		3			3
		4			4
		9			9

a. less than 50 employees
b. 50–499 employees
c. 500 employees
d. don't know
e. no reply

What goods or service did the
enterprise produce?
Kampuni ilikuwa inatengeneza
vitu au kutoa huduma za aina
gani?

(62–63)	N/A	00	(64–65)	N/A	00
		01			01
		02			02
		03			03
		04			04
		05			05
		06			06

a. agriculture and forestry
b. mining and quarrying
c. manufacturing
d. electricity and water
e. construction
f. wholesale and retail trade,
   restaurants and hotels

	REPLY	CODE

	REPLY		CODE
g. transport and communication	07		07
h. finance, insurance, real estate and business services	08		08
i. community, social and personal services	10		10
j. don't know	11		11
k. no reply	99		99

Was the employer?

Je, mwajiri alikuwa ni?

		REPLY	CODE			REPLY	CODE
	(66)	N/A	0	(67)		N/A	0
a. the government serikali			1				1
b. a parastatal masharika ya uma			2				2
c. in the private sector kampuni ya watu binafsi			3				3
d. a local authority tawala za serikali ya miji au mitaa			4				4
e. no reply			9				9

Fill in details of the occupation on the occupation form.

How long were you in this job?

Ulifanya hii kazi kwa muda gani?

		REPLY	CODE			REPLY	CODE
	(72–73)	N/A	00	(74–75)		N/A	00
months							
years			—				—
(*code in years*) no reply			99				99

Employee number   (1–4)

Card number   (5)   4

	YOUR LAST JOB			YOUR FIRST JOB		
	COL.	REPLY	CODE	COL.	REPLY	CODE
What was your wage at the end of this job? Mshahara wako ulikuwa kiasi gani ulipoiacha hii kazi? (shillings per month)	(6–10)	N/A	00000	(11–15)	N/A	00000
no reply			99999			99999
What was your wage at the beginning of this job? Mshahara wako ulikuwa kiasi gani ulipoianza hii kazi? (shillings per month)	(16–20)	N/A	00000	(21–25)	N/A	00000
no reply			99999			99999

	REPLY	CODE

Why did you leave? (26) | N/A | 0 | (27) | N/A | 0
Kwa nini uliondoka?

    lost job (sacked or made | | 1 | | | 1
    redundant)
    chose to leave (to look | | 2 | | | 2
    for or take up better
    job)
    Other (*specify*) | | 3 | | | 3
    no reply
| | 9 | | | 9

Did you receive higher pay at the (28) | N/A | 0 | (28) | N/A | 0
start of your next job?
Kwenye kazi iliyofuata
ulianzia mshahara mkubwa
zaidi?

    yes | | 1 | | | 1
    no | | 2 | | | 2
    no reply | | 9 | | | 9

VII. Rural–Urban Links

	REPLY	CODE

1. In which district were you born?_____ (30–31) | N/A | 00
   Wewe ni mazaliwa wa wilaya gani?
       no reply | | 99
2. In what district was your father born?__ (32–33) | N/A | 00
   Baba yako alizaliwa kwenye wilaya ipi?
       no reply | | 99
3. How old were you when you
   first came to live in Dar?
   Ulikuwa na umri gani
   ulipoanza kuishi Dar?
     a. born in Dar (34) | NON-MIGRANT | 1
     b. age in years if 1 to 13 | NON-MIGRANT | 1
     c. age in years if 14 or | MIGRANT | 2
       over
     d. don't know | | —
     e. reply | | — | 9

REPLY	CODE

If a non-migrant, proceed to question 6.

4. *If a migrant*: in what year did you come to
live in Dar? (35–36)

Ulianza kuishi Dar mwaka
gani?

N/A	00
	99

5. *If a migrant*: did you complete your formal
education before or after you
came to Dar?

Ulianza kuishi Dar kabla au (37)
baada ya kumaliza shule?

N/A	0

before

	1

after

	2

no reply

	9

If before: how long did it take to find an
independent source of income
when you arrived in Dar?

Baada ya kufika Dar ilikuchukua (38–39)
muda gani mpaka ulipoweza
kujipatia mahitaji yako
mwenyewe?

N/A	00

immediately

	01

months

no reply

	99

How did you earn this?

Mapato yako yalitoka wapi?

a. same employer I have now (40)
mwajiri wa sasa

N/A	0
	1
	2

b. same kind of job with another
employer
kazi kama hii kwa mwajiri mwingine

c. other wage job for a fundi
kazi ya kulipwa ya aina nyingine ya
ufundi

	3

d. other wage job for a firm
Kazi ya kulipwa ya aina nyingine
kwenye kampuni

	4

e. self-employment
kazi ya binafsi

	5

f. no reply

	9

For all respondents:

6. Do you have a shamba (or access to an ujamaa shamba)?

Je, una shamba?

yes, private (41)
ndiyo la binafsi

	1

yes, private and communal

	2

REPLY	CODE

ndiyo, la binafsi na biashara
yes, communal

| | 3 |

ndiyo, la uja maa
no

| | 4 |

no reply

| | 9 |

If no: proceed to question 7.
If yes: How did you acquire it?
    Ulipata je?   (42)

| N/A | 0 |

  a. inheritance

| | 1 |

     uridhi
  b. allocation after land reform

| | 2 |

     kupangiwa ya mpango mpya agawaji
     wa andhi
  c. purchase

| | 3 |

     kununua
  d. land borrowing

| | 4 |

     andhi ya kukopa
  e. marriage

| | 5 |

     ndoa
  f. other (*specify*)

| | 6 |

     vingine (*eleza*)
  g. no reply

| | 9 |

If purchase: Did you take out a loan to help in the purchase?
     Ulichukua mkopo ili kuweza kununua hilo shaba?
                          (43)

| N/A | 0 |

             yes

| | 1 |

             no

| | 2 |

             no reply

| | 9 |

How large is your shamba?
Shamba iako ni kubwa kiasi gani?   (44–46)

| N/A | 000 |

             hectares

| | — |

             or acres

             no reply

| | 999 |

What are the two main cash crops on your   (47–49)
shamba?
Taja mazao makuu mawili yanyokuletea kipato
una fedha?
Indicate crops and also quantities specifying units   (50–52)
of measurement (e.g. coffee and tea; number of
trees)

How many livestock do you have on the shamba?   (53–55)
Una wanyama (mifugo) wangapi shambani
mwako?

	REPLY	CODE

How often do you visit your shamba? (per year) (56–57)

Je, huwa unatembelea shamba lako mara ngapi
(kwa mwaka)?

        no reply

REPLY	CODE
N/A	00
	99

How much did you spend last year on purchased
inputs such as seed and fertilizer for your
shamba? (exclude hired labour)

Mwaka jana ulitumia fedha kiasi gani kununulia
vifaa vya shamba, kama vile mbolea, mbegu na
kadhalika? (58–61)

        shillings

        no reply

REPLY	CODE
N/A	0000
	9999

How many other workers help your family on the
shamba?

Wafanya kazi wangapi wengine wanaisaida
familia yako shambani? (62)

        number

        no reply

REPLY	CODE
N/A	0
	9

Who decides what crops to grow on your
shamba?

Ni nani anayetoa unamuzi kuhusu
mazao yatakayolimwa shambani kwako? (67)

    a. self
       mwenyewe

    b. spouse
       mke/mume

    c. village manager
       mkurugenzi wa kijiji

    d. village committee
       kamati ya kijiji

    e. other (*specify*)
       mtu mwingine (*mtaje*)

    f. no reply

REPLY	CODE
N/A	0
	1
	2
	3
	4
	5
	9

7. Is it your plan at some time to go and live in a
    rural area?

    Je, una mpango wa kwenda kuishi
    mashambani baadaye?

           yes (68)

           no

           no reply

    If yes: when?

        lini? (69)

REPLY	CODE
	1
	2
	9
N/A	0

	REPLY	CODE

a. When my employer retires me
   Nitakapostahafishwa | | 1 |

b. When I have reached a particular age
   (*specify*_____years)
   Nitakapofikia umri fulani (*taja*
   *miaka*_____) | | 2 |

c. When I have saved enough money
   Baada ya kuwa na akiba ya kutosha | | 3 |

d. When I have finished paying for my
   shamba
   Nikimaliza kulipa mkopa wa shamba | | 4 |

e. When I inherit a shamba
   Nitakaporidhi shamba | | 5 |

f. When I have finished building a
   house
   Nikimaliza kujenga nyumba | | 6 |

g. When my children no longer need
   support
   Baada ya watoto kuacha kunitegemea | | 7 |

h. Other (*specify*)
   Wakati mwingine (*eleza*) | | 8 |

                                                    | | 9 |

j. No reply

8. How many wives do you have (or do you
   have a husband)?:
   Je, una wake wangapi (au una mume)?:
   a. In Dar   (70)
      Hapa Dar
   b. On your shamba   (71)
      Shambani kwako

   c. Elsewhere   (72)
      Mahali pengine

9. How many children do you have?
   Je, una watoto wangapi?
   a. In Dar   (73–74)
      Hapa Dar
   b. On your shamba   (75–76)
      Shambani kwako
   c. Elsewhere   (77–78)
      Mahali pengine

10. To what tribe do you belong?   (79–80)
    Wewe ni kabila gani?

| | N/A | 0 |

REPLY	CODE

a. Sukuma — 01

b. Makonde — 02

c. Chagga — 03

d. Haya — 04

e. Nyamwezi — 05

f. Ha — 06

g. Hehe — 07

h. Gogo — 08

i. Nyakyusa — 09

j. Sambao — 10

k. Luguru — 11

l. Bena — 12

m. Turu — 13

n. Other (*specify*) — 14

o. No reply — 99

Employee number

Card number (1–4)

(5) 5

11. Do you use some of your earnings to help
support relatives outside Dar?
Je, unatumia sehemu ya mapato yako kwa
ajili ya kuwasaidia jamaa zako
walio nje ya Dar?

yes (6)	1
no	2
no reply	9

REPLY	CODE

If yes: What forms does this support take?
Hua msaada ni wa aina gani?

    (7)

| N/A | 0 |
| | 1 |

a. remittances of money
    (including school fees)
    Kuwapelekea fedha
    (pampoja na ada ya shule)

b. purchase of goods
    Kuwanunulia vitu

| | 2 |

c. other (*specify*)_____

| | 3 |

    _____

    Nyingine (*eleza*)

d. no reply

| | 9 |

If remittances: (8–9)
how many times a year?
Unapeleka fedha mara
ngapi kwa mwaka?

| N/A | 00 |
| | |

    no reply

| | 99 |

What was the value of your   (10–13)
last remittance (shillings)?
Fedha ulizopeleka mara ya
mwisho zilikwa kiasi gani?

| N/A | 0000 |
| | |

    no reply

| | 9999 |

About how much does the   (14–18)
support you give to relatives
cost you a year? (shillings)
Jumla ya fedha unazotumia
kwa ajili ya kuwasaidia
jamaa zako ni kiasi gani
kwa mwaka?

| N/A | 00000 |
| | |

    no reply

| | 99999 |

What is your help used for?
Msaada wako unatumi wa kwa
manufaa gani?
(*code as follows*:
      yes = 1
      no = 2
      no reply = 9)

| N/A | 0 |

a. education   (19)
    elimu

| | |

b. house construction or   (20)
    improvement
    kujenga au kuimarisha nyumba

	REPLY	CODE

c. farm improvement   (21)
   kuendeleza shamba
d. consumer goods   (22)
   kununulia bidhaa
e. food   (23)
   chakula
f. general purposes   (24)
   matumizi ya kawaida
g. other (*specify*)   (25)
   mengine (*eleza*)

VIII. Education of Children

	REPLY	CODE

1. How many children do you have below primary school age?   (27–28)
   Una watoto wangapi ambao hawajafikia umri wa kwanza shule ya misingi?

   How many children do you have old enough to have gone to school but who never attended?   (29–30)
   Una watoto wangapi ambao wamefikia umri wa kwenda shule lakini hawajawahi kwenda shule?

3. How many children do you have in formal education at present?   (31–32)
   Kwa sasa, ni watoto wangapi wanaosoma shule?

4. How many children do you have who have completed their formal education?   (33–34)
   Una watoto wangapi ambao wameshamaliza shule?

5. Consider your three eldest children aged 6 or over (if any).
   Fikiria watoto wako watatu wakubwa ambao wana umri wa miaka 6 na kuendelea (kama unawo)

Sex: male / female

	CHILD 1			CHILD 2			CHILD 3		
	COL.	REPLY	CODE	COL.	REPLY	CODE	COL.	REPLY	CODE
N/A	(35)	N/A	0	(49)	N/A	0	(63)	N/A	0
			1			1			1
			2			2			2

Age: (years)
don't know or not applicable

	CHILD 1			CHILD 2			CHILD 3		
	COL.	REPLY	CODE	COL.	REPLY	CODE	COL.	REPLY	CODE
	(36–37)		99	(50–51)		99	(64–65)		99

Highest level of education
Elimu ya juu kabisa waliyofikia

	CHILD 1			CHILD 2			CHILD 3		
	COL.	REPLY	CODE	COL.	REPLY	CODE	COL.	REPLY	CODE
no education	(38–39)		00	(52–53)		00	(66–67)		00
Standard 1			01			01			01
Standard 2			02			02			02
Standard 3			03			03			03
Standard 4			04			04			04
Standard 5			05			05			05
Standard 6			06			06			06
Standard 7			07			07			07
Standard 8			08			08			08
Form 1			10			10			10
Form 2			11			11			11
Form 3			12			12			12
Form 4			13			13			13
Form 5			14			14			14
Form 6			15			15			15
University			16			16			16
Other post-secondary (*specify*)			17			17			17
Other (*specify*)			18			18			18
no reply or not applicable			99			99			99

	CHILD 1			CHILD 2			CHILD 3		
	COL.	REPLY	CODE	COL.	REPLY	CODE	COL.	REPLY	CODE
	(40)	N/A	0	(54)	N/A	0	(68)	N/A	0
			1			1			1
			2			2			2
	(41)	N/A	0	(55)	N/A	0	(69)	N/A	0
			1			1			1
			2			2			2
			9			9			9
	(42–43)	N/A	00	(56–57)	N/A	00	(70–71)	N/A	00
			99			99			99

Was/Is the last education institution

  a. Government

  b. Private

Mara ya mwisha alikuwa/yupo kwenye shule ya, au chuo cha:

  a. Serikali

  b. 'Private'

Is the education continuing?

Bado anaendelea na masomo?

  yes

  no

  no reply

If no: when was it completed?

Alimaliza kusoma lini?

19_____ don't know

If yes: How much did the education cost you last year (shillings)?
Mwaka jana ulitumia fedha kiasi gani kwa ajili ya ada na mahitaji ya shule?

(44–47) [   ]　　(58–61) [   ]　　(72–75) [   ]

No reply or not applicable　　9999　　9999　　9999

Is/Was the last education:
Mara ya mwisho alisoma/anasoma:

(48) 　　(62) 　　(76)

a. In Dar
　　Dar　　1　　1　　1

b. in your rural area
　　nyumbani kijijini　　2　　2　　2

c. elsewhere
　　mahali pengine　　3　　3　　3

d. no reply　　9　　9　　9

6. How much did the education of *all* your children cost you last year? (shillings)
Mwaka jana ulitumia fedha kiasi gani kwa ajili ya elimu ya watoto wako wote?

(77–80) N/A [ ] 0000 [ ]

　　no reply　　9999 [ ]

Employee Questionnaire

REPLY	CODE
	6

Employee Number   (1–4)

Card number   (5)

IX. Miscellaneous

1. Occupation
        Current job   (6–11)
        Last job   (12–17)
        First job   (18–23)
2. Wage information obtained from employer
   (shillings per month)
        Basic wage   (24–29)
        Housing allowance   (30–33)
        Overtime payment   (34–37)

      less   Employee contribution to   (38–41)
              NPF   (42–45)
              Tax deducted

For those who reached Form 4 or above:

3. How did you obtain your first wage job (exclude
   National Service or wage employment during
   school or college vacations)?
   Ulipataje kazi yako ya kwanza (kuondoa kazi ya
   kujenga taifa na pia kazi za likizoni
   wakati ukiwa masononi)?

	N/A	0

     1. Government allocation   (46)   [1]
        Kupangiwa na serikali
     2. Application   [2]
        Maombi
     3. Other (*specify*)_____   [3]
        Nyingine (*taja*)
     4. No reply   [9]
        Hakuna jibu

If through Government allocation:
On your list of preferences, was this job:
Kwenye arodha ya mapendekezo, kazi hii
ilikuwa ya

	N/A	0

     1. first   (47)   [1]
        kwanza
     2. second   [2]
        pili
     3. third   [3]
        tatu

	REPLY	CODE

4. lower
   chini zaidi

| | | 4 |

5. not your choice
   haikuwa kwenye chaguo lako

| | | 5 |

6. no reply
   hakuna jibu

| | | 9 |

4. Were you bonded by Government?
   Ulikuwa umelazimika kwa nkataba kuitumikia
   serikali

   Yes   (48)

| | | 1 |

   Ndiyo
   No

| | | 2 |

   Hapana
   No reply

| | | 9 |

   Hakuna jibu
   If yes:
   Kama ndiyo:
   Did you serve out your bond?

| | N/A | 0 |

   Ulitmiza nikataba wako?
   Yes   (49)

| | | 1 |

   Ndiyo
   No

| | | 2 |

   Hapana
   No reply

| | | 9 |

   Hakuna jibu
   If did not serve out bond:
   Kama hukutimiza nikabata:
   Is this because: (50)

| | N/A | 0 |

   Inamaeuisha:
   1. you are still serving
      bado unaendelea

| | | 1 |

   2. transferred by government
      ulihamishwa na serikali

| | | 2 |

   3. managed to move to another job
      uliweza kuhahua kwenye kazi

| | | 3 |

      nyingine

| | | 9 |

   4. no reply
      Hakuna jibu

References

Anderson, J.E. (1975) 'The Organisation of Support and the Management of Self-Help Schools: A Case Study from Kenya', in Godfrey N. Brown and Mervyn Hiskett (eds)., *Conflict and Harmony in Education in Tropical Africa*, George Allen & Unwin Ltd, London, pp. 363–89.

Bowman, Mary Jean (1981) 'Manpower Requirements Forecasting as a Tool of Educational Planning in Tanzania', unpublished, mimeo, report for the World Bank.

Cameron, J. and W.A. Dodd (1970) *Society, Schools and Progress in Tanzania*, Pergamon Press, Oxford.

Elkan, Walter (1976) 'Is a Proletariat Emerging in Nairobi?', *Economic Development and Cultural Change*, 24, 4, July, 695–706.

Hazlewood, Arthur (1979) *The Economy of Kenya: The Kenyatta Era*, Oxford University Press, Oxford.

Huxley, Elspeth (1935) *White Man's Country: Lord Delamere and the Making of Kenya*, Vol. II, Macmillan, London.

International Bank for Reconstruction and Development (1961) *The Economic Development of Tanganyika*, Report of a Mission, Johns Hopkins Press, Baltimore.

International Bank for Reconstruction and Development (1963) *The Economic Development of Kenya*, Report of a Mission, Johns Hopkins Press, Baltimore.

International Labour Office (1967) *Report to the Government of the United Republic of Tanzania on Wages, Incomes and Prices Policy*, Government Printer, Dar es Salaam.

International Labour Office (1978) *Towards Self-Reliance: Development, Employment and Equity Issues in Tanzania*, Report to the Government of Tanzania by a JASPA Employment Advisory Mission, ILO Jobs and Skills Programme for Africa, Addis Ababa.

Jackson, Dudley (1978) *The Disappearance of Strikes in Tanzania: Incomes Policy and Industrial Democracy*, Working Paper Series No. 117, University of Aston Management Centre.

Jackson, Dudley (1979) 'The Disappearance of Strikes in Tanzania: Incomes Policy and Industrial Democracy', *Journal of Modern African Studies*, 17, 2, June, 219–51.

Kenya, Government of (1964) *Kenya Education Commission Report*, Part I, Nairobi.

Kenya, Government of (1965a) *Kenya Education Commission Report*, Part II, Nairobi.

Kenya, Republic of (1965b) *African Socialism and its Application to Planning in Kenya*, Government Printer, Nairobi.

Kenya, Republic of (1965c) *High-Level Manpower Requirements and Resources in Kenya 1964–1970*, Ministry of Economic Planning and Development, Nairobi.

Kenya, Government of (1966) *Development Plan 1966–1970*, Government Printer, Nairobi.

Kenya, Government of (1969) *Development Plan 1970–1974*, Government Printer, Nairobi.

Kenya, Republic of (1973) *Economic Survey*, Central Bureau of Statistics, Ministry of Finance and Planning, Nairobi.

Kenya, Republic of (1974) *Development Plan 1974–1978*, Government Printer, Nairobi.

Kenya, Republic of (1978) *Economic Survey*, Central Bureau of Statistics, Ministry of Finance and Planning, Nairobi.

Kenya, Republic of (1979a) *Educational Trends 1973–1977*, UNICEF for Central Bureau of Statistics, Ministry of Economic Planning and Community Affairs, Nairobi.

Kenya, Republic of (1979b) *Development Plan 1979–1983*, Government Printer, Nairobi.

Mbilinyi, M.J. (1979a) 'Secondary Education', in H. Hinzen and V. H. Hundsdorfer (eds.), *Education for Liberation and Development: The Tanzanian Experience*, Unesco Institute for Education, Hamburg, pp. 97–113.

Mbilinyi, Marjorie (1979b) 'The Arusha Declaration and Education for Self-Reliance', in Andrew Coulson (ed.), *African Socialism in Practice: The Tanzanian Experience*, Spokesman, Nottingham, pp. 217–27.

Morrison, David R. (1976) *Education and Politics in Africa: The Tanzanian Case*, C. Hurst & Co., London.

Muir, J. Douglas and John L. Brown (1978) 'The Changing Role of Government in Collective Bargaining', in Everett M. Kassalow and Ukandi G. Damachi (eds.), *The Role of Trade Unions in Developing Societies*, International Institute for Labour Studies, Geneva, pp. 123–40.

Nyerere, Julius K. (1967a) *Education for Self-Reliance*, Government Printer, Dar es Salaam.

Nyerere, Julius K. (1967b) *Freedom and Unity*, Oxford University Press, London.

Nyerere, Julius K. (1968a) *Freedom and Socialism*, Oxford University Press, Dar es Salaam.

Nyerere, Julius K. (1968b) *Ujamaa: Essays on Socialism*, Oxford University Press, Dar es Salaam.

Nyerere, Julius K. (1979) 'The Arusha Declaration Ten Years After', in Andrew Coulson (ed.), *African Socialism in Practice: The Tanzanian Experience*, Spokesman, Nottingham, pp. 43–71.

Rempel, Henry and William J. House (1978) *The Kenya Employment Problem: An Analysis of the Modern Sector Labour Market*, Oxford University Press, Nairobi.

Ruheni, Mwangi (1972) *What a Life!*, Longman, Nairobi.

Sabot, R. H. (1979) *Economic Development and Urban Migration: Tanzania 1900–1971*, Clarendon Press, Oxford.

Smith, Hadley E. (ed.) (1966) *Readings on Economic Development and Administration in Tanzania*, Oxford University Press, London and Nairobi.

Tanganyika (1961) *Development Plan for Tanganyika 1961/62–1963/64*, Government Printer, Dar es Salaam.

Tanganyika (1963) *High-Level Manpower Requirements and Resources in Tanganyika 1962–1967*, (George Tobias) Government Printer, Dar es Salaam.

Tanganyika and Zanzibar, United Republic of (1964) *Tanganyika Five-Year Plan for Economic and Social Development 1st July, 1964–30th June, 1969*, Government Printer, Dar es Salaam.

Tanganyika, United Republic of (1965) *Survey of the High-Level Manpower Requirements and Resources for the Five-Year Development Plan 1964–65 to 1968–69*, Manpower Planning Unit (R.L. Thomas), Government Printer, Dar es Salaam.

TANU (1967) *The Arusha Declaration and TANU's Policy on Socialism and Self-Reliance*, Government Printer, Dar es Salaam.

Tanzania, United Republic of (1978) *The Economic Survey 1977–78*, Government Printer, Dar es Salaam.

Tanzania, United Republic of (1980) *Basic Facts about Education in Tanzania*, Ministry of National Education, Dar es Salaam.

Tanzania, United Republic of (1981) *Development of Education: Opportunities for External Financing*, unpublished, Unesco, Paris.

Weinstein, Paul A. (1978) Report on Manpower Statistics and Planning in Tanzania, mimeo, University of Maryland, July 1978.

Weisner, Thomas S. (1969) 'One Family, Two Households: A Rural–Urban Network Model of Urbanism', University of East Africa, *Methodological Problems in East Africa: Sociology, Social Psychology, Education*, Proceedings, 5th Annual Conference, 8–12 December, Social Science Council, Vol. III, Nairobi.

World Bank (1975) *Kenya: Into the Second Decade*, Report of a Mission, Johns Hopkins University Press, Baltimore and London.

World Bank (1977a) 'Tanzania: Basic Economic Report, Main Report', unpublished, mimeo, World Bank, Washington DC.

World Bank (1977b) 'Tanzania: Basic Economic Report, Annex III, Labour Market Allocation and Income Distribution', unpublished, mimeo, World Bank, Washington DC.

World Bank (1979) *World Development Report*, World Bank, Washington DC.

World Bank (1981) *Accelerated Development in Sub-Saharan Africa*, World Bank, Washington DC.

World Bank (1982) *World Development Report*, World Bank, Washington DC.

World Bank (1983a) *World Development Report*, World Bank, Washington DC.

World Bank (1983b) *Kenya: Growth and Structural Change*, World Bank, Washington DC.

Index

African Socialism 16
Africanization 1, 17
age of employees and education 52–6
allocation to jobs in Tanzania 198–200, 272
Anderson, J.E. (1975) 29
Arusha Declaration 10, 20, 40
Asians
  education of 54, 267
  pay of 73, 174–5, 270
assortative mating 121–3, 128–9, 225, 230–2

Bowman, Mary Jean (1981) 21

Cameron, J. and W.A. Dodd (1970) 34
casual workers 77, 94–6, 179, 197–8, 272
Central Organization of Trade Unions (COTU) 35, 37
Certificate of Primary Education 117
credentialism 2

Daily Nation (1975) 37
data
  presentation 45
  sources 42–3
Davis manpower survey 18
decolonization 1
Delamere, Lord 26
demographic characteristics of employees 46–8, 142–3, 246–7, 267, 277
dependants of employees 78–80, 182–3, 268–9
development plans 10, 12, 15, 16, 24–5, 36, 37

East African Advanced Certificate of Education 8
East African Certificate of Education (EACE) 8, 28–9, 117
economic and fiscal constraints on education 1
economic growth and education 1–2
economic structure of Kenya and Tanzania 7–8
education
  of employees and their children 130–2, 153–5, 232–5, 258, 274–5
  of employees and their parents 48–52, 118–25, 222–8, 268, 273–4, 283–5
  importance of in Africa 1

as investment in human capital 2, 285
  and occupation 3, 16, 18, 63, 80–7, 92, 164, 183–90, 195, 270–1, 283
  and pay 2–3, 4, 61–3, 67, 89–91, 162–4, 168–9, 192–5, 268–70, 271–2, 280–2
  reasons for discontinuing 125–7, 228–30, 275
  see also 'filtering down'
Education for Self-Reliance 10, 11, 12, 19, 20, 30, 32, 33
educational characteristics
  of employees 48–56, 267–8
  of migrants 54–5, 142–6, 247–9, 277
Elkan, Walter (1976) 287
Employee Questionnaire 42–3, 289–331
employees'
  activities between end of education and start of employment 146, 249
  attitude to their children's education 132–3, 235–7, 275; *see also* expenditure on education
  perceptions of qualifications for jobs 97–8, 198, 200–6, 272–3, 283
  see also length of service; links with rural areas; location of families
examination results of employees
  and their pay 73–7, 177–9, 269
  and their parents' education 127, 228–30, 275
expenditure on education 1, 7, 14–15, 27, 133–7, 237–40, 275

family background and influence on occupation and pay 137–8, 240–2, 276, 284–7
Federation of Kenya Employers 35
'filtering down' 3, 4, 38, 80–7, 97, 183–90, 270–1, 282, 286
  and pay 89–92, 190–5, 281–2
  and productivity 92, 195
  see also education and occupation; occupation and pay

harambee schools 6, 23–6, 27–30, 55, 117 n., 268
Hazlewood, Arthur (1979) 14 n.
Huxley, Elspeth (1935) 26 n.

Industrial Court 36, 37
industrial relations 34, 35–6, 39–41
Industrial Relations Charter 35–6

inequality of pay, *see* education and pay;
   occupation and pay
intergenerational change 4, 123, 225–7, 286
International Bank for Reconstruction and
   Development
   (1961) 15
   (1963) 17
International Labour Office
   (1967) 40
   (1978) 21

Jackson, Dudley
   (1978) 40
   (1979) 40, 41
jobs
   method of application for 96–7, 198, 272
   movement between 4, 107–12, 146, 211–
      18, 273
   protection for incumbents 87, 271
   see also length of service; unemployment

Kenya
   (1964) 16, 28
   (1965a) 16, 18, 28
   (1965b) 16
   (1965c) 18
   (1966) 24
   (1969) 36
   (1973) 13
   (1974) 24, 25
   (1978) 9 n.
   (1979a) 29, 117
   (1979b) 25
Kenya African National Union 12
Kenya Education Commission, *see* Ominde
   Commission

labour force 34–5, 39, 46
   see also industrial relations; jobs
language of instruction in schools 32
length of service 63, 112, 164, 215, 269, 273
links with rural areas 146–59, 253–66, 277–
   8, 287
location of employees' families 128–30,
   147–9, 153–5, 230–2, 253, 258, 277, 287

manpower planning 3, 10, 15–19, 21, 33,
   195, 283
Mbilinyi, M. J. (Marjorie)
   (1979a) 27
   (1979b) 12, 26–7, 31
Morrison, David R. (1976) 12, 16, 26
Muir, J. Douglas and John L. Brown
   (1978) 37
Musoma Resolution 12

National Examinations Council 32

National Union of Tanganyika Workers
   (NUTA) 39, 40
non-wage benefits 67–8, 168–9, 268
Nyerere, Julius K.
   (1967a) 11, 19
   (1967b) 41
   (1968a) 41
   (1968b) 20, 31
   (1979) 31

occupation
   changes of by employees 112, 218, 273
   and pay 63, 67, 89–91, 164, 168, 169,
      192–5, 268
   see also education and occupation;
      'filtering down'
Ominde Commission (Report) 12–13, 14,
   16–18, 24–5, 28–9
ownership of firm and pay 68, 77–8, 169,
   179–82, 269, 281

pay
   and length of employment experience 89,
      192, 269, 273
   policies 34, 36–8, 39–41, 280–1
   and type of school attended 73, 175–7
   see also education and pay; family
      background; 'filtering down'; length
      of service; non-wage benefits;
      occupation and pay; productivity of
      education
Permanent Labour Tribunal (Act) 39–40
population 1, 7
Presidential Decrees 13–14, 37
primary education 2, 7, 8, 10–17, 22, 30–1,
   33
'primary school-leaver crisis' 11–12, 20, 26
private schools 23–4, 26, 28, 55–6, 117 n.
productivity of education 2, 3, 92, 195, 282,
   283, 286

quality of education 27–32

recruitment to jobs and education 93–7,
   196–200, 272–3
relevance of education 30–1
remittances by employees to rural areas
   149–53, 255–8, 277
Rempel, Henry and William J. House
   (1978) 35
retirement plans of employees 159, 263–6,
   278, 287
Ruheni, Mwangi (1972) 33

Sabot, R.H. (1979) 44 n.
school fees and charges 13–15, 23,
   117 n., 133–5, 155, 239–40, 258, 277–8

secondary education 2, 3, 7–8, 15–19, 19–27, 31–2, 117, 267–8, 279–80
shamba ownership by employees 147, 155–9, 253, 258–63, 277–8, 287
Smith, Hadley E. (ed.) (1966) 10
Standard (1966) 20
Standing Committee on Parastatal Organizations (SCOPO) 40, 41

Tanganyika
  (1961) 15
  (1963) 15, 16
  (1965) 16
Tanganyika African National Union (TANU) 11, 12, 39
Tanganyika Federation of Labour 39
Tanganyika and Zanzibar (1964) 15, 16
TANU (1967) 10
Tanzania
  (1978) 9 n., 39
  (1980) 26
  (1981) 32
terminology 6, 23
Thomas manpower survey 18
time to get first job 4, 93, 138, 146, 196, 242, 248–9, 249–51, 272, 277, 283
Tobias report 15–16

Trade Disputes (Settlement) Act, 1962, 40
Trade Disputes Act, 1965, 35
trade tests and pay 107, 210–11, 272
training 4, 98–107, 206–11, 272, 282–3

unemployment 109–12, 138, 213–15, 242, 273
Unesco 10, 21–2, 32
urbanization 5, 7

Weinstein, Paul A. (1978) 39 n.
Weisner, Thomas S. (1969) 287
women
  education of 52–3, 54, 133, 135–7, 143, 240, 247, 267, 269
  occupations of 72, 174, 269–70
  pay of 68–72, 169–74, 269–70
World Bank 11, 15, 17
  (1975) 14
  (1977a) 40
  (1977b) 20–1
  (1979) 9 n.
  (1981) 27
  (1982) 9 n., 27, 39
  (1983a) 9 n.
  (1983b) 38